How Foreign Policy Is Made

OTHER BOOKS BY KURT LONDON

The Seven Soviet Arts

Backgrounds of Conflict:
Ideals and Forms of World Politics

VAN NOSTRAND POLITICAL SCIENCE SERIES

Franklin L. Burdette, *Editor*
UNIVERSITY OF MARYLAND

Godshall, W. L. (EDITOR), *Principles and Functions of Government
in the United States*

London, K., *How Foreign Policy Is Made*

Plischke, Elmer, *Conduct of American Diplomacy*

Dixon, Robert G., Jr., and Plischke, Elmer, *American Government:
Basic Documents and Materials*

KURT LONDON
WITH COLLABORATION OF KENT IVES

HOW
FOREIGN POLICY
IS MADE

SECOND EDITION

D. VAN NOSTRAND COMPANY, INC.
TORONTO   NEW YORK   LONDON

NEW YORK

D. Van Nostrand Company, Inc., 250 Fourth Avenue, New York 3

TORONTO

D. Van Nostrand Company (Canada), Ltd., 228 Bloor Street, Toronto

LONDON

Macmillan & Company, Ltd., St. Martin's Street, London, W.C. 2

PRINTED IN THE UNITED STATES OF AMERICA

To my former colleagues of the
U.S. Department of State
whose intelligence, integrity, and patriotism
I greatly respect and admire

Foreword

THIS book does not propose to offer one more critique of contemporary foreign policies, American or other. Nor does it attempt to sell remedies for the world's political malaises. Its sole purpose is to investigate the machinery by which foreign policies are evolved, formulated, and applied. It deals with problems preceding rather than following the adoption and execution of policies; or, as one may say, it approaches the great issues of world politics from below, not from above. It submits that a correct appraisal of foreign policies is difficult, if not impossible, without an appreciation of the apparatus used by sovereign nations to formulate principles and objectives for living in the world community.

Surprisingly, there does not seem to exist a study covering this aspect of international relations. The appended bibliography reflects the scarcity of literature in this field. Hence this book is, in a sense, a pioneering venture into a branch of foreign affairs that to date has attracted far too little attention. As most first attempts, it may leave some questions unanswered; it may have overlooked facts and alternatives; it may have omitted details. But it will suffice, I trust, as the presentation of a coherent over-all picture. It will show the fundamental elements of the making of foreign policy and outline the issues that move the apparatus of international relations. Particular attention is paid to the contemporary background that gives this picture its character: the contest of political ideologies and the scientific advances in the atomic age.

The very nature of this study necessitated up-to-date postwar documentation. Yet documentary evidence of the many changes in political and social organization, which have occurred as the result of the two world wars and the ideological and technical revolutions, is still scarce. Thus I was fortunate to succeed in securing authentic material from postwar Europe, partly through private channels, partly with the gracious assistance of the Foreign

Office in London and the French Embassy in Washington, D. C. Also, the U.S. Department of State has kindly made available informative documentation.

I should like to acknowledge the faithful co-operation of my able friend, Mr. Kent Ives, whose editorial assistance has contributed much to the preparation of this study. Also, I am greatly indebted to Professor Franklin L. Burdette of the University of Maryland for his constructive and learned advice and to Messrs. Joseph W. Martin and William N. Morell, Jr. for their invaluable suggestions.

K. L.

Washington, D. C.

FOREWORD TO THE SECOND EDITION

Since this book was first prepared, the U.S. Department of State has undergone a major organizational change, the principles of which were recommended in the Report of the Hoover Commission. The British Foreign Office, too, has reorganized itself. No change has been reported from Paris and, of course, no further elucidation has come from the Moscow Ministry of Foreign Affairs.

The revisions which are incorporated in the Second Edition of this book bring it up to date as of March, 1950.

K. L.

Contents

ix

PART THREE: THE EXECUTION OF FOREIGN POLICY

PART FOUR: NATIONAL FOREIGN POLICY AND INTERNATIONAL ORGANIZATION

PART ONE

The Elements of Foreign Policy

CHAPTER ONE

The Meaning of Foreign Policy

INTRODUCTION

THE wars that marred the first half of the twentieth century have
settled only limited areas of dispute. Their outcome has not created, as so many had hoped, a brave new world. On the contrary,
new problems have come to the fore the solutions of which involve such far-reaching decisions that there is reasonable doubt
that a workable and permanent compromise can be reached in the
near future.

Ostensibly, World War I started as a conflict between the economic interests of the great competing European empires. In the
course of its progress, however, the belligerents found that the
traditional issues of markets were superseded by those of freedom
versus domination. During the Great Armistice, 1918-1939, the
effect of the political religions of Sovietism, Fascism, and Nazism
further reduced the one-time importance of economic conflicts as
the causes of war. Competition for foreign markets became a
marginal issue; instead, the far more fundamental problems of the
relationship between state and individual had to be refaced. Even
the Japanese-American war, whose origin was supposedly devoid
of ideological conflicts, soon began to show that more than economics was involved when extreme Japanese nationalism claimed
leadership over all Asia on the grounds of racial and divinely

3

pre-ordained superiority under the principle of *Hakko Ichiu*.[1]

The participation of the Union of Soviet Socialist Republics on the side of the Western Allies in World War II created much confusion in the hearts and minds of many persons and prevented the struggle from becoming a clear-cut issue between liberal democracy and tyrannical statism. The presence of essentially nondemocratic powers such as China—China being neither a democracy nor a capitalist state in the western sense—added to the intellectual and ideological mixup. The apparent toleration by the democracies of such Fascist disciples as Pétain or Franco, a condition that was felt to be a necessary strategic expedient for the hard-pressed Allies during the first years of the war, produced even greater misunderstandings.

All the more astounding, then, was the fact that the people in the western democracies could seriously assume that military victory over the Axis would solve all major problems, and unfinished business could then be negotiated with ease and goodwill. Meanwhile the Soviet leaders, strengthened through victory and the awareness of their vastly increased power, ignored the war weariness of their people and accelerated their plans for ideological conquest.

Thus World War II did not act as a catalyst, unifying the victors, but on the contrary produced an open split between the wartime allies, more or less along ideological lines, which resulted in the formation of two groups of nations. One group, controlled and dominated by the Soviet Union, adheres to the Marxist doctrine in Leninist-Stalinist interpretation, aiming at a "classless society" and trying to achieve a sociopolitical kingdom of heaven on earth through the imposition of a ruthless totalitarian "dictatorship of the proletariat." The other group, led by the United States, is less uniform in its ideological coloration except that all its members are anti-Communist. It consists of nations practicing

---

[1] "A mystical conception, meaning that the peoples of the world should be brought under one 'roof.' The roof was the symbol of imperial rule." (Cf. K. London, *Backgrounds of Conflict*, The Macmillan Company, New York, 1945, p. 91 ff.) Former Foreign Minister Matsuoka once stated: "Japan should take over management of the continent on a large scale, propagate *Hakko Ichiu* . . . and then extend it all over the world." (*Ibid.*)

various shades of capitalist democracy and Fabian socialism; it is not completely free, however, of members with authoritarian tendencies that are at odds with the concept of liberal democracy.

Luckily, the political influence and the potential power of the less democratic followers of the "western" group are of minor significance. Fundamental to the future development of the human race is the ideological struggle between the great leading antagonists of the two groups: the United States, which admits and encourages political and economic liberty, stresses the dignity of the individual, and has limited governmental controls that are invariably intended as a safeguard for rather than a threat to freedom; and the Soviet Union, which sacrifices the individual to the state and unhesitantly utilizes its citizens in any manner to further the political, economic, and social objectives inherent in the Marxist-Leninist doctrine of a collectivist society, where individualism is an arch sin.[2]

As a result, political differences can no longer be ironed out through economic agreements as nineteenth century politicos believed, for economic philosophy is but a manifestation of political creeds. In an age of ideological conflicts, politics and economics are but different sides of the same fabric; a change of economic principles reflects a related change of political principles. Hence moral suasion can no longer be expected to achieve compromise, since it is in the nature of a dogma to remain unalterable whereas democratic rationalism can allow for adjustments and compromise.

In view of these grave conditions, the coresponsibility of democratic citizens for their countries' conduct of foreign affairs has become increasingly crucial. There are, however, some aspects of foreign policy that must be understood if its substance is to be fully appreciated, namely, how it is made and how it is implemented. The apparatus designed to develop policies and the techniques employed to apply or enforce policies are more complex than often supposed. In fact, the task of co-ordinating local-

[2] Speaking before the Air Policy Commission in Washington, D.C., on November 11, 1947, Gen. Dwight D. Eisenhower said: "The problem today is a conflict of ideologies, on the one hand based around the dignity and rights of the individual and on the other the rights and power of the state."

ized policy decisions into a national policy, applicable to global conditions in times of continued and almost unrelieved stress, requires almost superhuman efforts. How simple were the principles that governed international relations even a few decades ago when compared with those of an era that must cope with political religions, atomic energy, and a wide disparity between technological progress and ethical growth.

It is perhaps this very complexity and cross relationship of problems that have prevented peoples all over the world from attaining as much understanding of their governments' conduct of foreign affairs as they might otherwise have done. Although certainly far more alert to matters of international significance than were their fathers, most contemporaries are still surprisingly far from recognizing the full meaning of basic policy decisions and farther from realizing how and why such decisions have been reached. With so much to lose and so much at stake it is surprising that Americans, particularly, have permitted themselves too long to escape the problems of a violently changing world. Only with great reluctance, and as a result of repeated shocks, have a significant number come to realize that indulgence in the great game of domestic politics at the cost of interest in foreign relations is a luxury that can no longer be afforded. Yet one of America's foremost opinion experts, Dr. George H. Gallup, has stated that "On many subjects, particularly those dealing with foreign affairs, the public often reveals an amazing lack of interest and knowledge." [3] As an example he discloses that after four months of discussion of the European Recovery Program, "one-half of the voters say that they have not heard or read about it . . ." and "only one person of six who says he had heard about the Marshall Plan really has a fairly good conception of it." [4] It is a foregone conclusion that many of those who do know something about the European Recovery Program and its administering agency, the Economic Cooperation Administration, have little or no idea how

[3] Conference on The Citizen's Participation in Public Affairs, September 29 and 30, 1947, published by New York University School of Law, January 1948, pp. 19–24.
[4] *Ibid.*

and why such a manifestation of basic United States foreign policy may have developed before being announced and executed.

In a democracy the character of the government is decided by the will of the majority, for a democratic government is bound ultimately to follow the will of the majority if it wishes to remain in power. If this majority is not sufficiently well informed, it can make grave and even disastrous mistakes. It is a popular fallacy to assume that a majority, whatever platform it may adopt, can do no wrong. A multitude of misinformed men and women can as easily commit errors as can an individual.[5]

The possibility of being wrong increases in proportion to the lack of general knowledge and current information. In the history of popular influence on foreign affairs, there has seldom been a surplus of either information or understanding. Democratic governments, as a rule, have had little help from an enlightened public when they have been faced with vital foreign policy decisions. The fact that so little is known about the aspects and techniques of policy formulation and execution is perhaps at the bottom of such failure.[6]

———

There can be no doubt that individual man has succeeded much better in legally institutionalizing relations with his fellow men than have communities with other communities, or in postmedieval times nations with each other. During millenia of slow, painful growth, human life has produced a body of usages, taboos, and laws whose authority man usually has accepted because he has felt that this has been essential for his own protection.

However, he has accepted the law of his own community only. He has refused to be guided by the law of outsiders who did not believe in his own taboos. Nevertheless, his law has not remained eternal: it has changed through evolution or revolution. But so long as it has existed, it has reigned supreme. It has been effective because it has been imposable.

The laws and customs determining the relations between

[5] Cf. Chapter II, "Public Opinion," p. 46 ff.
[6] *Ibid.*

groups or nations, although achieving quite definite shape and substance in the course of the past three centuries, differ precariously from the laws pertaining to individuals in that they are nonenforceable. This does not mean that international law is an illusion. Indeed, there are many instances testifying to the fact that some practices of international law have become firmly entrenched and that the covenants on which it is based or the usages that helped to evolve the covenants have become parts of national laws. Philip C. Jessup takes pains to emphasize that the number of unpublicized cases where international law has been upheld is much higher than the superficial observer may assume. Spectacular breaches of treaties, ever recurring wars, and "The oppression of the weak by the strong are the headlines of the daily press and of the history textbooks," [7] but they present only a part of the picture, if the most spectacular.

Most disputes between nations are of a political rather than a legal nature. The legal ones are, as a rule, justiciable, because they do not necessarily constitute fundamental conflicts between national interests. The political disputes, however, affect such interest and are therefore, in the majority of cases, nonjusticiable for there is no way of enforcing the law except by armed intervention. Naturally, legal rights and political differences frequently overlap, which is the reason why international jurists have felt that, since legal disputes may well be political in nature, the difference between justiciable and nonjusticiable conflicts should be explained by the existence or absence of law.[8] Absence of law, in the international realm, would mean virtual uselessness of treaties or agreements. It is at this juncture that the makers of foreign policy are of necessity affected by the degree to which international law is recognized and applied by the governments, the countries they are concerned with, and by the extent a nation will subordinate its sovereign rights to international law.

International law can be considered an attempt to help adjust

[7] P. C. Jessup, *A Modern Law of Nations*, The Macmillan Company, New York, 1948, p. 6 ff.

[8] L. Oppenheim, *International Law* (H. Lauterpacht, ed.), Longmans, Green and Co., New York, 1944, Vol. II, p. 4 ff.

a nation's interests to those of other nations. In this sense, it is in part the foundation, in part the aim, of foreign policy. To what degree international law may be justiciable, therefore active, will depend on foreign policy decisions. The interpretation of international laws, treaties, and agreements, as much as their creation, is subject to the consent and good faith of the contracting parties. If a nation believes that it must renounce a treaty or disagree with its interpretation, it renders the law nonjusticiable, or passive, for all. The creed of sovereignty is still strong enough to break the law of nations; a "re-examination of international law would involve an alteration of the traditional notion of sovereignty." [9] Under the concept of sovereignty, international law remains subject to the consent of those for whom it was created and to whom it is to be applied. If one of the parties sees fit to break the law, there is little other nations can do, except to apply pressure vis-à-vis weaker nations or go to war.

Most law stands or falls with the character of its interpretation and the effectiveness of its execution. Moreover, every law is interpreted according to prevailing social and political conceptions. Thus governments and people in the orbit of Christian civilization—or a civilization akin to it—understand the principles of international law in similar terms, much as they may have been divided with regard to their national interests. The emergence of political religions, or ideologies, that led to the establishment of totalitarian states has largely eliminated this common ground and therefore caused a considerable setback in the development, recognition, and strengthening of international law. To what extent Nazi-Fascist interpretation of such law has veered away from the norms is a matter of record. So far as the Soviets are concerned, it has been frequently demonstrated that their legal interpretations, based upon Marxism, differ totally from those that grew out of Roman, Canonic, Civil, or Common Law. That is to say, certain over-all provisions may well be adopted by both Western powers and the Union of Soviet Socialist Republics, but when it comes to the practical application of the articles, there

[9] Jessup, *op. cit.*, p. 13.

seems to be little basis for agreement between the representatives of parliamentary democracy and those of the dictatorship of the proletariat, or its satellites.

This means that the ideological cleavage has divided the civilized world into two groups, adhering respectively to pro- and anti-Communist legal philosophies.[10] Each camp will no doubt provide interpretations of international law that can appeal only to adherents of its own school of thought. Since the basic principles of international relations in this time and age are based upon the recognition of the integrity, independence, and equality of each sovereign state, large or small, Soviet ideological policy cannot but be diametrically opposed to such principles and cannot accept the basic maxims of the existing law of nations.

It is especially these aspects of international law and relations that are of outstanding importance to non-Communist makers and executors of foreign policies. They are faced with the dilemma between public and private law, between national interests and international co-operation, between totalitarian and democratic ideologies, between scientific progress and the stagnation of universal ethics, and, particularly, between concise legal requirements and what Mr. Justice Cardozo called a "twilight existence" of international law. On the other hand, the totalitarian administrators of foreign policy, who are but the executive agents of their policy making party leadership, would claim that in a world with different coexisting ideologies traditional international law is merely a temporary expedient of capitalist society, and that the ultimate law of nations should be subordinate to and co-ordinated with the world-conquering political religion: communism.

Briefly, some of the paramount and most urgent objectives of non-Communist statesmen in international law are:

1. The compilation, co-ordination, and organization of existing agreements between nations into one coherent and universally

---

[10] It need hardly be mentioned that the non-Communist group comprises a wide variety of legal views in both the Occident and the Orient. Common to this group is, however, the rejection of a law that is conceived as an instrument of Marxist materialistic dialectics.

applicable body of law, in other words, the codification of this law. (The United Nations has set up a committee to work on this complex problem.)

2. The creation of an international instrument for the enforcement of international law in accordance with Chapter VII, Article 47 of the United Nations Charter. This article provides the legal basis for the establishment of an international police force subject to call by the Security Council. However, although the effort to restrict national sovereignty voluntarily for the sake of peace is highly commendable, it must not be forgotten that a call for action of this police force depends, to date, upon the unanimous consent of the great powers that are permanently represented on the Council. (Three years after the United Nations Charter became international law, such a police force had not been set up.)

3. The application of international law to individuals. While the law of nations is looked upon, as a rule, as applicable to the intercourse of sovereign nations, it also concerns individuals in their relations with states.[11] It is realized that the solution of this vexing problem, which would imply the relinquishment of a nation's rights over its own citizens in favor of an international body, is as far from fulfillment as the relaxation of sovereignty. (However, one may perhaps suggest that the Nuernberg trials in 1946 and 1947 set an important precedent. For the first time, individuals were held responsible for their actions, or toleration of actions, that concerned other nations.)

4. The acceptance of the International Bill of Rights by all member nations of UN as national law. (This Bill of Rights, sponsored by the Economic and Social Council, has been passed by the General Assembly on December 10, 1948. However, its adoption by the member nations is not compulsory since the General Assembly has merely advisory powers. The main obstacle working against a universally valid civil rights legislation is the different conception states have of the value of the individual. Against the democratic state's ideal of the dignity of the individ-

[11] Cf. Jessup, *op. cit.*, p. 17.

ual, to whom the state is servant rather than master, is pitted the totalitarian conception that the state, representing society as a whole, is of overpowering importance and that the individual is but a cog in its wheel.)

The ideological split between the great powers has so confused international relations that the United Nations seems unable to develop into a mature world forum, where disputes can be resolved without resort to violence. Because of this, after a short period of high hopes on the part of the democratic peoples, the organization has lost much influence. This unfortunate development has forced statesmen to adjust their policies only perfunctorily to United Nations provisions, if not to bypass the organization altogether. Consequently, the political strategy of the men who are responsible for their nations' relations with other nations is still concerned with power rather than with reliance on the goodwill of their neighbors. In other words, all the components of power in the possession or control of a nation will be weighed and compared with those of the power of other nations. The result of such considerations will then prompt the policy maker to see whether he can achieve a balance between the power of his own nation and his friends, and that of other nations and their friends. This balance of power has been much maligned but so long as international co-operation has not achieved a status of quasi-world government, it seems to remain the safest means to insure peace, and to secure a nation's minimum aspirations.

DEFINITION

A nation's foreign policy determines its course of action vis-à-vis other nations. It is a program designed to achieve the best possible position for the nation by peaceful means, or by means short of war. In other words, it expresses the sum total of those principles under which a nation's relations with other nations are to be conducted. War is an indication of the failure of a policy or of unsuccessful attempts to execute a policy. In democratic interpretation, war is not considered a policy; however, the threat of war plays as great a role in policy making as a government's concern with the war potentials at home and abroad. Fundamentally, the foreign offices are departments of peace. When they fail to preserve peace, the departments of war take over.

The fundamental policy objectives of every sovereign nation are the preservation of territorial integrity, the maintenance of political independence, and the attainment of a reasonable standard of living for the population. These are, of course, rock-bottom requirements, essential for the continuation of national life. As such they are premises rather than objectives. Over and beyond these requirements, national foreign policy will formulate and try to achieve its aims in accordance with its historic aspirations, its ideological doctrines, and its physical conditions.

A workable foreign policy can never be static. Therefore, to build a policy on a *status quo* is an illusion that can lead only to disappointment, if not disaster. For nations, like human beings, are born, live through periods of adolescence, become mature, and die. Stand-still acts as a cancerous disease on a nation's body.

The birth of a nation is coincidental with the establishment of its territory and the recognition by other powers of its political independence. The process of growth may begin inside the newly drawn boundaries and aims at the consolidation of the nation's political, socioeconomic, and cultural status. But this process need not be completed before the new nation begins to look for objectives beyond its frontiers. Once consolidated, its government may feel that future security will depend on the achievement of objectives such as the possession of military bases or natural resources abroad, and it will then proceed to formulate its policy accordingly. It may also want to export its political ideology.

Such aggressive policies are termed "dynamic." It is easy enough to chart a dynamic course in international relations, but it is quite another matter to apply it. For its execution depends first of all upon internal support and secondly upon the attitudes of other nations, whose policy may well provide for measures to check the advance of would-be usurpers of their national interests.

Every sovereign nation's foreign policy will maintain a minimum but aim at a maximum of security and prosperity. Between these extremes, policy must maneuver. If it is conceived rigidly, excluding compromise, its adjustments to world conditions are only apparent and tactical. If it is flexible and nondogmatic, it has room to develop alternative solutions while still remaining within the framework of the national philosophy.

But every foreign policy that is not running amuck will have to bring "into balance, with a comfortable surplus of power in reserve, the nation's commitments and the nation's power." [12] The estimate of such power cannot be based upon actual (or absolute) values but must take into account relative values. A nation must compare its own resources with those of other nations in order to arrive at a realistic estimate of its strength. If it has the power and resources, it will try to formulate policies designed to neutralize overly powerful states, that is, it will either increase its own strength to match the opponent's or seek to sap the opponent's surplus power. In other words, it will try to *balance the power*.

A hundred years ago such balance could be achieved regionally but this is no longer possible. Foreign policy in the twentieth century will have to work out principles for the balancing of power on a global scale. Thus foreign policy has become world politics.

It is clear, therefore, that a nation's foreign policy embodies its over-all political, economic, and military strategy. It is, in fact, the essence of a nation's political philosophy, economic system, psychological attitudes, scientific status, and cultural traditions. It has of necessity an unalterable core that reflects its national existence and/or ideology, but its superstructure allows for flexibility, adjustments, and alternatives.

Foreign policy "never can, or never should, be divorced from strategy." [13] To a nation's life war is like a threatening disease,

[12] W. Lippmann, *U.S. Foreign Policy: Shield of the Republic*, Little, Brown and Company, Boston, 1943, p. 9.

[13] E. H. Carr, *The Twenty Years' Crisis, 1919-1939*, Macmillan and Co., London, quoted by H. and M. Sprout, *The Foundations of National Power*, Princeton University Press, Princeton, N. J., 1945, p. 32.

and the thought of it is ever present in the minds of responsible statesmen. It is true that war has been condemned as an instrument of foreign policy and that it is genuinely hated by the vast majority of human beings. It is true that, in historical perspective, wars have not always solved long range problems but have often added to their confusion. It therefore remains the most distinguished goal of foreign policy to achieve its objectives without resort to arms. One may perhaps compare national foreign policy with national law. The application of each requires interpretation. Interpretation must be flexible without violating the spirit and substance of the law.

(At this point it seems necessary to emphasize that a clear distinction must be drawn between foreign policy and diplomacy. In contrast to foreign policy, which is the program of outlining a nation's principles and aims in international relations, diplomacy is concerned with the implementation of policies in the policy makers' target area. Diplomats, as a rule, contribute heavily to the political thinking of the responsible statesmen and sometimes considerably aid them in evolving and formulating policies. Yet diplomats cannot be considered policy makers in the proper sense of the term.) [14]

Although the formulation of a foreign policy may be caused by a variety of elements, no policy maker can attempt to proceed without keeping in mind some basic factors that impose limitations upon his planning and, to a considerable extent, predetermine his course of action. These factors are partly measurable in scientific terms, partly imponderables full of uncertainty.

One group of such factors comprises conditions arising out of a nation's physical, economic, and human geography, its commitments to history and tradition, and the status of its technological advance. The appraisal of these factors must, of course, be both absolute and relative.

Another group of factors contributing to policy formulation deals with the internal conditions of a country, public opinion, economic and military policies, and a host of influences from gov-

[14] Cf. Chapter VI.

ernmental agencies and pressure groups that are not themselves in charge of foreign relations. These factors, too, must be appraised from both absolute and relative standpoints.

A third group is concerned with such intangibles as the "national mind"—of which policy makers are part in so far as they represent the character and attitudes of their nation. This group also has to do with the explosive issue of political ideologies and national morale. Again, the policy makers, in order to utilize an appraisal of their own nation fully, must be as familiar as possible with the political or social imponderables of other nations.

To ensure a clear understanding of the complexity of policy making, it will be necessary to examine these factors separately. It should, however, not be inferred that they constitute separate problems. On the contrary, all details are part of an integrated whole, and only for the sake of systematic discussion have they been pigeonholed in the following pages.

BASIC ELEMENTS

Physical Geography. Among the immovable and inescapable bases for the formulation of a national foreign policy are: the size and location of the territory, accessibility and character of the frontiers, climate and population (density and character), natural resources, capacity of industrial production, and transportation facilities. In themselves, these factors are of limited value, and only in comparison with other nations, near and distant, will they become of strategic importance.

Great nations acquired much of their powers because geographic location afforded them a dominant strategic position, access to sea lanes or intracontinental transport routes, and control over vital natural resources. Inevitably, nations with such advantages found themselves endowed with influence of more than local character, provided that their internal conditions permitted an intelligent and orderly organization for the exploitation of such privileges. Hence the chief concern of policy makers for the physical geography of countries extends primarily to large powers rather than to small or middle nations, except where strategic considerations focus special attention on a particular area. For, regrettable as it may be, smaller countries no longer lead an entirely independent political life. They must eventually decide with which group of nations, that is, under what type of leadership, they will wish to combine forces. Such decisions have become imperative in view of the prevalent ideological conflict.

For example, the small and middle states in central, eastern, and southeastern Europe, being close neighbors of the Soviet Union, had little choice but to become Soviet satellites. The small western European states, being in a position to reach their decision freely, and remembering the catastrophic effect of their neutrality prior to World War II, joined forces with the western powers. Their predilection for the West is natural as they belong, by tradition and attitude, to western democracy but they also bank on the West's proclaimed principle of equality of all nations, large and small.

That this ideal could not be fully achieved in practice was due mainly to the position of the chief framers of the UN Charter, who insisted that only the big powers are in a position to either conduct or prevent large scale wars. The organization of the Security Council of the United Nations is a logical result of this reasoning: only the big nations (the United States, Great Britain, the Soviet Union, France, and China) are permanently represented, the six remaining seats of the council being filled by representatives of the small member states of the United Nations through election and for no longer than two years. In other words, world politics has become a monopoly, of sorts, of the most powerful states. Little chance is left to small countries to chart their own course, except in limited fields.

Although it is true that a fairly large territory is a *sine qua non* for any nation aspiring to be a big power and that topographic and climatic conditions are further important factors for the determination of political, economic, and military power, size by itself is not necessarily a symbol of might. A vast land such as China with its hundreds of millions of inhabitants is a great power in name only. So was the Ottoman empire. In both cases, the weaknesses of social and industrial organization prevented the governments of those countries from marshaling their potential strength. On the other hand, European great powers were, or are, much smaller in size than the American or Eurasian territories of the United States or the Soviet Union, yet they were able so to increase their natural resources and to develop such a degree of industrial and military efficiency that they became world powers in fact, and formulated their foreign policy accordingly.

Thus, while a country's physical geography determines its political potentialities, only those large countries with an efficient administration and a popularly accepted or state-enforced national philosophy will be able to organize their potentialities and put them to use. On the other hand, lack of a generally accepted pattern of belief and lack of efficiency will result in ultimate deterioration. Twentieth century Russia is a case in point; the same country that under Czarist rule collapsed on German attack was, under Soviet rule, able to muster strength enough to turn back an even more powerful German onslaught and become the dominant power on the continent.

A country's size and geographic location produce by themselves political problems. A state, we know, is not an inanimate thing but rather like a living being. Thus a group of states form a community of nations as a group of individuals form a community of men. Changes in human relations and concepts produce changes in the character and organization of the communities; exactly the same is true of sovereign nations: their relations are bound to change as the rise or fall of their own and other states creates new conditions in the regional or global "environment." There have been several occasions in modern times when traditions were shattered and old established principles were revolutionized. In particular, such unheavals occurred through the introduction of new techniques of communications and transportation. Once the barriers of oceans, mountains, and deserts could be easily and speedily surmounted, once distance was being conquered, the political position of every country naturally had to be re-evaluated by its leaders.

The technological revolution of the twentieth century has made accessible remote parts of the world and, at the same time, has opened the road for peoples off the beaten track to approach what Simonds and Emeny call "the world that matters." [15] In combination with the ideological revolution, it may well lead to an entirely new formation of geographical power centers. For example, successful Soviet pressure and the civil wars in the Middle East and Asia may conceivably result in a rediscovery of Africa south of the Sahara as a base of political and economic power of some western states. Indeed, air trips from London to Kenya take 14 hours, from Dakar to New York 15 hours. And as western civilization seems to be moving away from its cradle, the Mediterranean, which for thousands of years was the Old World's most important seaway, it may well move westward and establish itself on three main bases facing the Atlantic: western Europe, the Americas, and Africa. Such a development would rearrange the political map of the earth and shift the emphasis of national, colonial, and global politics as radically as did the fall of the Roman Empire or the end of the power of the Medieval Church.

This speculative vista of possible developments, as some policy makers may or may not anticipate it, is only one of the large redeployments of western power and culture that the revolutionary developments of the first half of this century may necessitate: a complete revision of traditional world-political conceptions. This does not preclude some of the time-honored factors of a nation's territory and location from retaining political and strategic significance for quite a while. In contemporary policy making it still matters whether a nation is an inland power or has easy access to the sea; whether boundaries are determined by political dictate or are topographically natural and ethnically justified; whether a country's resources and production centers are conveniently situated or clustered around congested areas; whether a nation's capital is strategically exposed or comparatively well protected; whether unfortified or easily accessible frontiers face friendly, neutral, or hostile neighbors. Although the advanced techniques of locomotion have demonstrated that distance and natural barriers have lost much of their former meaning, they will in all

---

[15] F. H. Simonds and B. Emeny, *The Great Powers in World Politics*, American Book Company, New York, 1935, p. 50 ff.

probability, at least during the last part of this century, retain sufficient importance to affect short-range policy decisions.

Economic Geography. The estimate by policy makers and strategists of not only physical geography but also economic values must be relative rather than absolute. Factors such as the quality and quantity of a nation's natural resources, the degree of its industrial skill ("know-how"), the availability of manpower, and its ability to feed itself become politically significant by contrast with the economic potentials of other nations, whether friends or foes. Having made an estimate of his country's relative strength, and realizing what it means in terms of national defense, the policy maker will then know how far he can go in enforcing his policy, whether he must reduce his aspirations or beat a political retreat until he has regained strength either by marshaling his own forces or by concluding agreements with friendly powers that would improve his bargaining position. Or, on the other hand, if he finds his position strong he may feel that he can be bold and rely on the knowledge that his opponents know his powers and will act accordingly.

The more nearly balanced a country's economy is, the stronger it will find its position. Theoretically, in a balanced economy industrial and agricultural production are about evenly matched, creating a condition in which the state's own natural resources and industrial capacities furnish all the commodities required, and in which the combined agricultural facilities can supply food that may be needed. Surplus production may be exported in peacetimes for the purchase of imported luxuries or stockpiling of scarcer materials; in crises it may serve to obtain foreign currency or be bartered for strategically needed goods.

For a variety of reasons, no country on earth can or will produce all the raw materials and commodities that its economy consumes. As a result, there exist only few relatively balanced economies in the world. The United States and the Soviet Union may be considered as so privileged. Although the level of production in quantity and quality is infinitely higher in the United States, the Soviet Union unquestionably possesses the potentialities of self-sufficiency.

Most other countries, not excluding those of political and strategic importance, do not have a balanced economy. They may have to import vital raw materials to keep their industrial establishments humming. They may be compelled to supplement their basic commodities with imports of "luxuries" which have become necessities (coffee, cocoa).

Examples of overwhelmingly industrial economies are Germany, Japan, and England. Most central, eastern, and southeastern European states within the Soviet orbit [16] and also the countries south of the Rio Grande are predominantly agrarian. France's industrial power is not too strong; its agricultural potential outweighs its production of raw materials and manufactured goods. Italy is still worse off, in that neither its industry nor its agriculture seems able to keep the national economy in healthy balance, for it must import nearly all of its fuel, raw materials and considerable quantities of food. Somewhat surprisingly, there is a possibility that postwar Poland may develop a balanced economy of sorts if the Soviet Union will permit it. Poland lost eastern agricultural areas to the Ukraine but gained in the west by incorporating former German industrial regions.

The preceding are some rather generalized considerations and examples, but it should be understood that a classification into either industrial or agrarian economy is subject to amplification and variation in detail, which may possibly modify the economic significance of a country, particularly in the eyes of the strategist. Moreover, to attempt even a cursory analysis of national economies with respect to strategic considerations would overstep the limits of this brief discussion.

An unbalanced economy can hardly be balanced through the exploitation of territorial possessions overseas. In former times, colonial empires could artificially restore a certain balance in the motherland, if it did not exist there; but in the twentieth century, many dependent territories have fostered nationalism, acquired self-rule, and no longer need tolerate exploitation. Internationally sanctioned trusteeships have done as much to change the

[16] Except areas such as Bohemia and Moravia in Czechoslovakia or the Polish controlled (former German) Silesian industrial region.

status of colonies as have world public opinion and a growing consciousness of international morality on the part of the colonial powers. As a result, many dependent territories have lost their original value and have even become liabilities. Today, colonies or semidependent territories often cost their protectors more money than can be made from them. Thus great empires show a tendency to disintegrate into co-operative groups of territories, with the motherland merely being *primus inter pares.*[17] In wartime, overseas possessions may prove to be of military value (air bases) but the defense of transportation routes is costly and the political reliability of many dependent peoples open to doubt.

Military and political leaders will want to survey the world's natural resources, the deficiencies or surplus of nations in these materials, and the ways and means of transportation to and from these crucial areas. They know that a nation that lacks food or raw materials will want to make certain that it can import them from abroad and that consequently it must try to establish the most economical, most easily protected, and fastest routes of communication for its "life lines." Each nation will plan its foreign policy accordingly. Aside from the consideration of the other countries' efforts, each state will attempt to conclude agreements with key nations so as to be sure of unimpeded continuation of its traffic and provide for the safest possible routes in wartimes. Such agreements cannot easily be enforced, even by powerful nations. Experience shows they are best negotiated on the basis of mutual self-interest and upon a businesslike give and take. They are essentially political measures to strengthen and balance strategic potentials, and their economic aspects are often secondary.

Policy officials are, as a rule, highly sensitive to the extent and nature of economic stability or fluctuation in other important nations. Prosperity and depression are subject to political interpretations and possible policy revisions. Just as in a community of individuals sharp differences between living standards will lead to deterioration of social relations and general unrest, so policy formulation will be influenced by the divergency of the economic

---

[17] This has happened in the British Commonwealth of Nations; it is about to happen in the French empire.

level of the "haves" and the "have-nots." A prosperous country is pretty safe from ideological penetration by rightist or leftist totalitarians, but a people who have to cope with want, unemployment, and hopelessness are especially susceptible to such attacks. It is understandable that Soviet policy makers are following economic conditions in the United States with keen interest because, from their point of view, another American depression would just about put the American people at their mercy—or so they hope.

Within a combination of states, the economic status of each member is pertinent to the maintenance of the balance of power. It has happened that statesmen have had to achieve political objectives through economic action. In such cases, political and economic objectives are merged, as demonstrated by the brilliantly conceived American plan to help European recovery and thereby accomplish an economic stabilization that would in itself serve as the most effective answer to the call of Communism.

To sum up, it may be interesting to quote some of the "fundamental factors that come in operation in modern war . . . ," as outlined by the Preparatory Commission on Disarmament of the League of Nations, the consideration of which will be uppermost in the minds of the statesmen who are charged with policy formulation as well as of the diplomats who are responsible for that policy's execution:

(1) The extent to which it [the state] is self-supporting (for instance as regards fuel, foodstuffs, raw material and manufactured goods), and the extent to which, as a result of its means of transport and the freedom of communications, especially its communications by sea, and of its financial strength, it can obtain the commodities of every kind in which it is deficient from abroad.

(2) The geographical situation, the configuration of its territory, and the development of its system of means of communications of every kind, which might enable or prevent it from rapidly moving and supplying its forces.

(3) The capacity of a country to produce or import war materials in war time . . .[18]

[18] Report of Sub-Committee A of the Preparatory Commission of Disarmament, League of Nations document C 739.M 278, 1926, IX No. 16 CPD 28, p. 12 ff.

Human Geography (Demography). Foreign policy does not only consider facts and figures. It deals primarily with human beings, for countries mean people. Policy is made to act for and upon people and it is therefore understood that the policy makers take into account how many persons live in a given area and under what circumstances, whether they are currently tending to increase or decrease in numbers, and also, what kind of people they are. Human geography, like physical and economic geography, demands comparative study and psychological analysis. Without a reasonably accurate estimate of demographic conditions at home and abroad, policies may be evolved on unsound premises and thus seriously endanger national security.

Modern demography is no mere compilation of population statistics. Figures on the density of population in given areas or on the birth-death ratio in one country as compared with that in another tell only part of the story and are, in themselves, no reliable yardsticks for policy formulation. They must be considered in conjunction with a nation's physical, economic, and political geography, its scientific level and industrial intelligence, its ethnic composition and what is tenuously known as its "national character."

The density of population per square mile may for several reasons turn out to be of political concern. Overpopulated areas of highly industrialized countries have tended to expand, to acquire more "living space." The former Axis powers excused their aggressive policies mainly on the claim that they were "young" nations, growing fast, and must have a chance to grow further—even though on the other hand they were doing everything possible to encourage a population increase. All three powers had definite objectives: Germany sought an outlet toward eastern and southeastern Europe; Italy demanded adjacent territory across the Adriatic and attempted to revive the Roman Empire by controlling the Mediterranean; Japan looked toward control of the Pacific and domination of China.

There can be no doubt that these former aggressor nations were crowded in their national territory and that the slightest economic downward trend could easily be exploited by the governments to stimulate their peoples into a mood of near-frantic national claustrophobia. On the other hand, these governments conveniently overlooked those opportunities that might have helped to solve the problem by diplomatic ways and means, as well as intelligent self-help. After all, during the past three centuries Europe's population has increased at least fivefold, from 100 million to 500 million souls, probably even more, in spite of the war casualties.[19] Yet it is an undeniable fact that during normal, peaceful conditions the living standard of contemporary Europeans is far higher than that with which Europeans had to be content two or three hundred years ago, when population was not very dense. In other words, with intelligent and co-operative action there should be increasing possibility for expansion in nonspatial terms because the advance of science, technology, and social organization has unearthed a multitude of opportunities for more people to live better within the boundaries of a given territory without the need for explosive territorial expansion. A country's national resources are not *per se* fixed and constant. New discoveries may increase their yield or make them altogether dispensable. Population pressure is a relative factor; its validity depends mainly upon the fluctuation of political constellations, technological progress, and psychological conditions.

Overpopulation alone need not necessarily generate dangerous political pressure. Should such pressure be nevertheless exerted, statesmen will have to look beyond the façade of statistics that may confront them. If the theory were correct that the "landman ratio" is a true yardstick of a nation's well-being, "the Argentine ought to have the highest standard of living and the greatest wealth per capita among nations; and, if the land-man ratio referred to minerals as well as land, Mexico would probably have the title to the most luxurious economic status, while Belgium and Switzerland would rank among the poorest countries in the world."[20]

[19] In the *American Sociological Review* of February 1944, Dudley Kirk gives the estimate that "in the past three centuries the population of the European race has increased sevenfold: from 100 million in 1650 to 700 millions at the present time."

[20] K. Brandt, *War in Our Time*, W. W. Norton & Co., New York, 1939; quoted in H. and M. Sprout, *op. cit.*, p. 42.

History has proved that frontiers are not eternal. The constant shifting of national territories and spheres of influence is probably a sign of vigorous demonstration of national life, bad as the consequences of such changes may be for weaker nations and individuals. Neither are the resources of nations immovable or unchangeable factors. Unplanned or excessive exploitation may deplete the resources but scientific or technological progress may increase their output. There is no such thing as the maintaining of a *status quo* in the life of nations nor is such a static society especially to be sought. A nation's life expectancy depends not only on the number but also on the quality of its peoples, as every statesman of experience knows.

Another aspect of population statistics calls for the close attention of long-range policy planners: the curve of proportional increase or decline of the population of the big powers whose political principles determine the state of international relations. Depopulation in particular is a serious problem because in the end it can and will upset the balance of power. French demographic developments, as they compare with Germany's, offer a classic example. About two centuries ago, France was the most populous and most powerful country in Europe, not counting Russia. It was first then, but now it is fifth. On the other hand, the German population increased in inverse proportion to the French decline. Thus in 1939, the Third Reich counted 80 million subjects against continental France's 40 million. There is no indication that this decline has leveled off. Consequently, the elimination of German competition notwithstanding, France can hardly expect to achieve more than the rank of a second class power at best. Moreover this weakening of France also unbalanced the power ratio in Europe, much to the detriment of the balance of world powers and the struggle of western civilization against eastern communism.

In view of this condition, the future of western Europe looks grim, for the nations west of Germany cannot cope with the population increase in eastern Europe, which continues enormous in spite of the alleged loss of 26 million human beings by the Soviet Union in the course of World War II through death and lack of births. Also, it should give men of responsibility cause to consider that the "reported birth rate in the USSR for 1938 was 38.3 per thousand population, or over twice that of the United States in the same year," [21] and that the Soviet average age just before the outbreak of the war was 23 against the West's 32. Population statisticians estimate that in 1970 the Soviet Union will have more men in the age groups between 20 and 34 available for military service than its six biggest European rivals together.[22] This serious outlook is further accentuated by increasingly better exploitation of natural resources by the Soviets and their slow but steady improvement of industrial know-how and their use of scientific methods in agriculture. This not only means that Soviet forces will increase their effective striking power but it also implies that the USSR may be able to maintain the 250 million inhabitants, that it is expected to have by 1970.

Policy makers watching for striking population changes will, in formulating their political course, associate demographic evidence with related problems. If the population increase of a big and dynamic nation goes hand in hand with progress of social organization, political (or ideological) consciousness, and technological advances, other states may devise policies that would attempt either to neutralize such developments, to increase their own defensive strength, or to try to establish friendly relations with the developing power, if this last is historically or ideologically possible. In turn, the decline of a nation's population may call for policy reverses so that the balance of power may be re-established through a new combination of alliances or co-operating nation groups. As a rule it is the population changes of leading powers, not of peripheral nations, that are regarded as pertinent to world politics.

Considerations of these problems do not necessarily affect day-to-day policy making. They are primarily significant for long-view planning. Foreign policy does not always deal with contemporary problems; for the sake of continuity, it must lay the

[21] D. Kirk, "Population Changes and the Post-War World," *American Sociological Review*, February, 1944.
[22] *Ibid.*

groundwork for the nation's future security and prosperity. Fluc-tuation of population and concomitant trends in the country's power potentials are some of the most tangible indicators for future developments to be expected. They are excellent clues for the policy makers when they weigh the prospects of attaining their objectives and what methods they may best employ.

Another problem of demography of prime importance for the development of policies—especially in Europe—requires the appraisal of the character and attitudes of national minorities—the ethnic question. There have always been minorities within the boundaries of a majority's hegemony since well-defined national territories became nation states. For hundreds of years, migration —voluntary or enforced—has obstructed the development of complete homogeneity. Besides, there has been a continuous intermixture of heteronational elements, especially among the many border regions of Europe. Some such groups, once established in national territories, have on occasion grown to be majorities, or even become nations themselves. Other elements, less lucky, were never absorbed and kept their culture identifiable by preserving their language and religion.

Let us insert here that national homogeneity is by no means a premise for the existence or preservation of a modern state. The few relatively homogeneous populations in the world of today have been geographically isolated or inaccessible for a long period, as for instance the Scandinavian countries. But even in these areas blood admixtures from other European nationality groups have continually occurred. That the acquisition of national greatness has nothing to do with homogeneity of population or, as the Nazis called it, "purity of race," is demonstrated by the United States and, to a degree, by the Soviet Union. In both cases there is a preponderant element—Anglo-Saxon in the United States, Slav in the Soviet Union—that furnishes the basis of language and of cultural unity. But both consist of a multitude of national minor-ities, some of which manage to preserve their cultural traditions. While one or another minority may differ with the national majority in a variety of issues, they are on the whole adjusted to their countries' political ideals and social organization. They have consolidated their cultural inheritance but adjusted it to their environment.

Where national minorities exist, they will be the subject of the foreign-policy maker's attention, for their influence upon the majority with whom they live may be considerable—as has often happened in the United States. The understanding of them, their attitude toward the majority, and the majority's attitude toward them, must be the aim of the men whose task it is to evaluate a country's "national mind." There are, on the other hand, groups that have done what they could to remain apart. They have stubbornly isolated themselves and even emphasized their grievances; they are potential sources of trouble and have all too often been the cause of war. As a matter of record, World War II began when Hitler used alleged grievances of German minorities in Czechoslovakia and Poland as a pretext for attack.

Such conflicts are not limited to Europe; for example, ethnic struggles have disturbed the peace in the Middle East and southeast Asia. But they are particularly dangerous in Europe as history has repeatedly demonstrated. A look at an ethnic map shows that there are considerable numbers of national minorities in almost every European country, and the migrations of displaced persons have further added to dissension and confusion. Whether the population exchanges after World War II will reduce minority problems remains to be seen. There is some hope—but not much.

Communist regimes in the eastern part of Europe attempt to eradicate the political significance of national minorities by subordinating nationalism to international communism. Only time will tell whether the Kremlin's orders can enforce ideological unity on a permanent basis in a part of the world that has been torn by strife between national groups since time immemorial.

Even though freedom of worship has become an overwhelmingly accepted postulate throughout the Christian world, and the separation of the state from the church is recognized in many nations, the adherence of ethnic minority groups to religious beliefs that are different from those of the majority has frequently created conflicts. For instance, there is the Transylvanian minority

in Rumania, whose Uniate Church was hotly attacked by the
Greek Orthodox state church and has done much to give the
Transylvanians a character different from the Rumanians and,
for that matter, from the Catholic Hungarians. Among other
religious minorities are the German Lutherans in Catholic, Greek
Orthodox, or Russian Orthodox countries; the Mohammedans
in Yugoslavia; the Christians in Moslem countries. Many of
these groups have remained loyal to the creed of their forefathers,
which has through continuous influence upon many generations
produced quite definite viewpoints and character traits, is accountable for their political orientation, and tends to perpetuate their
distinction from other groups.

Policy makers may have to observe these trends with attention;
many aspects of the minority question might well provide pertinent clues to the understanding of internal conditions of
countries in the troubled zones of Europe and elsewhere.

Technology and Ideology. Technology not only produces
gadgets and devices: it alters social relations, modifies national
attitudes, and changes human character. As new inventions become part of our lives, they create or demand new moral values—
and they may destroy old ones. In this way, technology has continuously influenced the life of individuals and nations. It has
caused revolutions; it has enforced the reversal of policies and
customs. It has raced ahead of human capacity to take stock of
the meaning of new inventions and consistently outdistanced the
progress of ethics, which would interpret the philosophical application of technological triumphs to human living.

A twentieth century statesman searching for solutions of
seemingly endless crises may want to look for historic precedents.
When considering new technological developments that upset his
political calculations, he may think of the far-reaching consequences of England's Industrial Revolution. When trying to find
parallels to the totalitarian upheaval of his times, he may ponder
over the results of the French Revolution, which was an ideological explosion of sorts. He will not find such comparisons as
helpful as he might wish, particularly when he realizes that in his
own era he must cope with the coincidental effect of technology

and ideology—with the fact that at about the same time there occurred the release of atomic energy and the development of the specter of the greatest totalitarian menace of all.

The impact of these events upon foreign relations—and for that matter, upon the life of every human being wherever he may dwell—was bound to stun the policy maker's imagination. Often rooted in an old tradition of conducting foreign affairs, he hesitates to diverge; certainly if he is to counter such unusual problems with unusual solutions, he will find little domestic support. Once again technology has outdistanced ethics and social conceptions, and the triumphs of science, instead of bringing nations closer together, have served to accentuate their dissension.[23]

It is not difficult to recognize why foreign relations in the twentieth century are so much more affected by technology and ideology than they could possibly have been in the past. The advances of science have made it necessary to re-evaluate a nation's geography in the light of shrinking distances and the fact that topographical barriers and even the size of human resources have lost much of their former meaning. As supersonic speed has caught up with time and space, so too atomic energy has given birth to new universes, holding the promise of both better living and swifter disintegration.

With these tremendous developments have come many other new techniques, which promise rapid change in many national economies. Raw materials are being made more useful and productive; substitutes have replaced original matter; new substances have been developed (such as those of the vast plastic world); the quality and quantity of transportation has greatly improved. Since one can hardly say that human ethics has progressed at a similarly startling rate, it is upon technology rather than upon moral considerations that the policy makers and strategists tend to rely. "Today, mere numbers of men, or the possession of raw material, or the holding of strategic positions is not the essential source of power. Only those nations having scientists, engineers and skilled workers who are masters of the knowledge and skills

---

[23] Cf. N. Cousins, *Modern Man Is Obsolete*, The Viking Press, New York, 1945.

required for devising and operating intricate machines and chemical processes can adequately equip armed forces." [24] Consequently, the policy maker who must think in terms of power when formulating his program for action, has no choice but to watch the extent to which science may neutralize, if not devaluate, the geographic advantages his nation may possess. His decision will be all the more difficult to reach since he will find himself in that transitory period where some of the old conceptions of international behavior are still valid in one way or another, while new techniques, making progressively inoperative the old ones, have not yet brought forth a new pattern of thought to control adequately the enlarging technological forces.

To aggravate matters, policy determination has to cope with the problem of ideological disputes, which make the application of policies difficult if not impossible. Statesmen are faced with the enervating element of persistent uncertainty. There is no longer continuity of purpose, for totalitarian governments may change their tactics at any time, necessitating corresponding changes on the part of nontotalitarian states, which can never be entirely sure of the actual relationship of totalitarian tactics to fundamental policies. Between the two nation-groups there is an abyss of suspicion, which has led to many rapid changes of policies and of the men who make them. The resignation of a key figure in a foreign government may compel policy makers in other countries to devise entirely new lines of political speculation or deduction. The change of power from one party to another in a key country may well account for the revision of national policy objectives.

Technology and ideology have upset and confused conventional nationalism. Technology and ideology are by their very nature expansive; since they defy boundaries, their repercussions are global. This means that local disputes affect the whole community of nations and therefore must be met by global policies. The globe, however, is split into two ideological camps. To create policies that meet all these complexities without resorting to arms is indeed a task for supreme ability.

[24] R. Turner, *Technology and Geopolitics*, Military Affairs, American Military Institute, Spring 1943, as quoted by Sprout, *op. cit.*, p. 51.

The "National Mind." A nation's history produces certain stereotypes of behavior and attitudes that common experience sanctifies and that are transmitted from generation to generation. These stereotypes consist of national likes and dislikes, do's and don'ts, *idées fixes,* and what the psychologists call favorable or unfavorable "associations." The result of this heritage has brought about not only national customs but also fairly consistent attitudes toward foreign peoples. Particularly the relationship with neighboring countries quite often implies illogical friendships or enmities and few persons brought up in such an atmosphere of thinking and feeling along established lines can shed such prejudices when they reach maturity. There is little chance of preventing peoples from acquiring such prejudices. Education has not as yet developed to the degree necessary for producing understanding among nations, although efforts in that direction are being made by the United Nations Educational and Scientific Organization (UNESCO). Despite the conquest of space, personal contacts between peoples are slight, misunderstanding of motives is frequent, and freedom of information is profoundly hampered. Many governments, mainly for ideological reasons, obstruct remedial action.

Historic prejudices thus shape a people's national character and also color the views of the men who are in responsible policy making positions. Inheritance of atavistic attitudes, positive and negative, can only with difficulty be neutralized by rational judgment. There are exceedingly few independent thinkers who can free themselves, to a significant degree, from such mental ballast; certainly a whole nation cannot do so unless it submits to revolutionary changes of traditional concepts and persists in pursuing the new ways for generations.

There is danger in generalization. It is risky to judge a whole nation according to one's own preferences. There is no unanimity among experts as to whether or not a nation has a specific character. For the politician, it certainly has. He would reason that people who have lived for centuries in approximately the same territory, under the same climatic conditions, using the same language, growing up in the same culture complex, experiencing the same fortunes in good and bad times, must have developed similar traits, views, preferences, and aversions. Nobody, not even the most independent thinker, can wholly escape such a heritage, and therefore the policy makers themselves cannot help being somewhat subject to bias. They are human, even though their professional experience at home and abroad may have given them exceptional breadth of mind and objectivity. If they recognize these shortcomings in themselves, they may use this insight to good advantage when judging their foreign "opposite numbers." Absurd as it seems, the fate of nations often depends, to no small degree, upon the whims, likes, and dislikes of their leaders.

Lawlessness or ideological rebellion in one country will of necessity affect neighboring states. The type of individual governments, the kind of constitutional law, or the nature of authoritarianism is bound to produce reactions abroad. The peculiar type of (Slav) ideological dictatorship in Moscow is inevitably reflected in the Soviet Union's international relations just as the character of American (Anglo-Saxon) democracy has resulted in a corresponding type of foreign policy and diplomatic behavior. Thus international affairs are conditioned by national beliefs, methods, and practices, and therefore it is essential for the policy maker to explore the national mind of his supporters and opponents.

There is one element in the determination of the national mind that helps to explain the psychology and morale in given areas and that is of equal significance to the strategist and the policy maker: the climate. Whether a climate is temperate or excessively hot or cold accounts for the development of basic traits of the individuals and nations who are subject to it. Under the impact of continuous heat, the body loses alertness and the mind tends to follow suit. Great and long-lasting periods of cold hamper the development of civilization. No great nations ever flourished in the torrid or arctic zones.

It is not surprising that only in temperate zones have powerful modern states developed and persisted. But even within these zones, the differences of temperature, the extent of precipitation, the number of days in which the skies are sunny or overcast, the vehemence of nature's outbursts, and the frequency of such "explosions" (as hurricanes, floods, earthquakes, and so on) create a variety of physical and mental characteristics that is pertinent to the potential of a country and therefore must figure in the calculation of policy making.

One may well go farther and state that the character of a territory in conjunction with its climate, produces distinct emotional and intellectual traits. There are striking differences between people who live in mountainous regions and those who dwell in the plains; there are differences between those who spend most of their days in densely wooded lands and others who are spread along the seacoast. There are certainly definite distinctions between continental and insular populations.

The influence of climate on living conditions contributes heavily to the formation of the national character. For example, it determines a nation's agricultural conditions and nutritional habits. Where the soil is more generous under benevolent skies, the nation, while having its wealth augmented, may be inclined to easier and better living. In territories where the earth must be coaxed or compelled with the help of artificial means to yield enough, the people must work harder and are more inclined to frugality; thus they will be tougher and able to endure what other people who live under more favorable conditions may not be able to "take." People who live under a harsh—though still temperate—climate tend to be mentally and emotionally stable and by nature patient; people under southern skies are more changeable, apt to explode into a straw fire, to be less reliable because of quick variations of temperament.

This appraisal is not quite as generalized as it may appear to be. For example, let us remember the profound effect that natural phenomena like warm highwinds for instance, the sirocco, mistral, monsoon, or samum have upon human beings: nature's outbursts cause emotional outbursts in man, and the law in some countries where these winds happen to blow has recognized that citizens cannot be held entirely responsible for acts they may commit while under the impact of the phenomena. Or, let us think of the differences between the character of people who live in mountainous or isolated regions and others who live in easily accessible, undramatic open country.

The character of many national groups in the Soviet Union was forged by the vastness of endless steppes, violent contrasts of temperature, and, particularly, long hard winters. Those groups consist of hardy, moody but basically stable people of introspective disposition, and their emotions are as full of contrasts as is their climate. But other groups living in the southern regions of the European section of the Soviet Union, for example, Ukrainians and Georgians, show much less of the slow and subdued character than do their northern and eastern fellow citizens. They are less steadfast, less trusty, and have given the Soviet government more internal trouble than all the other groups combined.

Statesmen, more than soldiers, have underestimated climatic influences upon national psychology. The character of a nation cannot be analyzed without consideration of the natural environment; history and politics tell only part of the story. But knowledge of the national mind in foreign countries will permit the policy maker to use psychological methods for his general approach; even more important is such knowledge for the diplomat who is charged with the execution of his government's policies in the field. Again in this field scientific modification of weather may become a potent military and economic force.

Geopolitical Summary. The entire group of geographic, economic, demographic, and psychological factors, as they have been briefly outlined above, is helpful only to the extent to which the leaders of a nation are able and willing to make active use of them. Mere applied political geography, to exemplify the point, would acknowledge past and present forms and frontiers of states without contesting their validity. A more active and dynamic approach would be to study the influence of geography and nature upon the political development and the humanlike development of a growing and changing nation.

This is very much of a geopolitical approach but even though geopolitics was developed by the Haushofer school in Munich, Germany, and sold to Hitler, it is fundamentally nothing else but the synthesis of facts and figures that feed the dynamo of power politics. It will remain a considerable factor so long as power politics remains a factor in world affairs. Moreover, ideological aggression has increased the dynamics of geopolitical policies; the quest for domination is no longer based upon traditional imperialistic motives but primarily serves to speed the establishment of ideological outposts and constitutes what one may call a new ideological imperialism. Geopolitical strategy causes policy makers to strive for the establishment of strongholds in areas whose domination would imply the domination of adjacent areas.[25]

Geopoliticians regard a nation's territory from the point of view of general location, size, and topography. They consider position in respect to access to the sea and relations with other countries. They look to changes of a nation's political status as due to actual or prospective rise or decline of the power of other states in the world. They weigh the past history of such developments and their influence upon the formulation of foreign policies in the past and present.

Whether or not the policy maker formulates his recommendations on the basis of geopolitical or less dynamic principles does not altogether depend·upon his own or his nation's preferences. He will have to keep in mind that geopolitical speculation has not died with Nazism. On the contrary, the shrinkage of the world and the identification of ideological aggression with geopolitical objectives will compel him to devise his formulas accordingly. He also must, more than ever, collaborate with military strategists because the possibility of diplomatic failure will inevitably confront him with the question of whether his nation may be forced to defend itself or its fundamental interests, against geopolitically motivated aggression.

It is from this point of view that a nation's potentials must in the last analysis determine its foreign policy, that strategic considerations covering the possibilities of invasions or aggression will modify the statesmen's political conclusions. While it is true that

[25] Cf. Halford Mackinder's *Democratic Ideals and Reality*, Henry Holt & Co., Inc., New York, 1942, p. 150: "He who rules East Europe, commands the Heartland, who rules the Heartland, commands the World Island, who rules the World Island, commands the World."

the highest purpose of policy makers and diplomats should be the maintenance of peace, the chances of war cannot be ignored. Duty compels every policy maker to consider the possibility of a failure of his peace policies.

There are, however, a number of contributing factors on the formulation and execution of foreign policy that are beyond the power of control by the men who are responsible for their country's conduct of foreign affairs. The most important of these considerations are: the nature of internal and external political conditions, public opinion on foreign affairs, economic questions and conditions, military factors, and the influences exerted on the part of other government agencies that do not themselves handle foreign policy.

CHAPTER TWO

Factors Contributing to Foreign Policy Making

DOMESTIC POLITICS

THE conventional division of politics into foreign and domestic branches may have advantages for the systematic study of political science. But actually it is an illusion and will become increasingly deceptive in the future. In order to understand the deeper meaning of the reasons for this development, it is necessary to digress a little.

Events in the first half of the twentieth century seem to indicate that the age of nation-individualism is passing. At the heyday of the nation-state, that is, during the latter half of the nineteenth century, governments reflected the rugged individualism of their countries. Then the rapid advances of science and the flood of political ideologies created a series of revolutions in the spheres of sociopolitical and economic thought. As a result, far-reaching changes began to take place, dislocating the foundations upon which the nation-states were built.

Outwardly, there were no signs of a disintegration of nation-individualism until after the World War II, when groups of countries were driven into co-operative blocks, either because they felt a union of likeminded countries might be the best way to preserve their respective social and political beliefs or because they were forced by their stronger neighbors to join a "sphere of interest." This step one may perhaps call the beginning of nation collectivism or co-operativism. Not even the United States, greatest nation-individualist of them all, was in a position to stay out and maintain its rugged *status quo*, for it was destined to assume the leadership of the democratic group of nations.

In tracing the phenomena of the deterioration of nation-individualism, it is significant to note that this development is matched by a slow and unrelenting lessening of individualism among the persons who make up the nations. This does not mean that, even in the democracies, the dignity of the individual or the cultural individuality of nations has been sacrificed all along the line. It does mean, however, that neither individuals nor nations could continue to do whatever they desired, lest their activities harm their community or the community of nations. As in the life of individual citizens, so in the life of nations the emphasis of political and economic life is now put upon mutual liability.

In terms of foreign relations this development signifies that in a shrinking world conditions in a country that are likely to endanger the peace can no longer be permitted and that outside intervention is increasingly unavoidable, for the greater good of the greater number of states. In a cautious way, the Charter of the United Nations expresses this thesis, the members realizing that cooperation within the United Nations organization may be the one highway to enduring peace. The charter does not say so, but it surely implies that this co-operation would necessitate a revision of the concept of sovereignty. Through this breach of nationalist philosophy, co-operative action may force the issues for the first time since nation-states came into being.

Inasmuch as a compromise between liberal and totalitarian governments is in practice unattainable, co-operative nation groups will be forced to seek stabilization of power once they are able to balance it. Member nations will therefore no longer be permitted to follow individualistic impulses and shift their position once they have chosen sides. As a consequence, nation cooperatives or collectives are likely to develop a new kind of international self-discipline as it is practiced by members of every every well-functioning co-operative unit. All those who mourn the fading of nation-individualism (of which isolation is an important feature) might take consolation from the hope that international co-operative discipline may perhaps bring about stabilization of power and thereby arrest the disease of war long enough to develop systems and attitudes to cure it. Since apparently war cannot be eliminated altogether until the nation-states have surrendered a part of their sovereignty to a world government, and since it will take a long time for this paradisaic state of affairs to come about, if ever, a stabilized balance of power may turn out to be the relatively safest and simplest way of maintaining a workable truce.

It follows that the security and prosperity of one nation is dependent upon the nature of its relations with other nations and that *the attempt at making domestic aspirations shape foreign policy can succeed under co-operative foreign policies only if a nation's domestic politics will not seriously handicap its foreign relations.*

The change in the character of foreign affairs, however, has not as yet brought about a corresponding revision of views on the relations of domestic politics to international policies. Internal problems still obscure foreign issues. They are likely to confuse the mind of the voter whose education in international relations is, on the average, inadequate, although perhaps a little less so in areas where the ravages of war have compelled people to think more about their position among the world community of nations.

Under a dictatorship the nature and extent of domestic influences upon foreign policy are different from what they are in parliamentary democracies. In countries under authoritarian governments, the indigenous political creed not only permeates national life but also shapes international relations. Ideologies are international as well as national; all the "isms" strive for ultimate global conformity, and it is hard to say where the realm of domestic aspirations ends and that of foreign policy objectives begins.

There can be no such authoritarian regime without a rigidly determined dogma, which preaches a gospel of political, social, economic, and cultural principles and prescribes methods for the achievement of its objectives: the conversion of the unfaithful at home and abroad. Inasmuch as it is claimed that the dogma is untouchable, and the interpretation of its high priests infallible, criticism or doubt is heresy. Heretics and followers of other political religions wherever they live are doomed to ultimate damnation. Offenders at home will be excommunicated.

Hence the political ideology of a totalitarian state not only is a national "religion" but also assumes universal significance as domestic issues are reflected in international affairs, and vice versa. For example, Nazi Germany's doctrine of racial superiority expressed itself in measures against excommunicated minorities at home and in the quest for supremacy of the "German race" abroad. Discriminatory actions inside Germany were transposed into geopolitical designs for world rule. In turn, Soviet communist imperialism, which strives to expand not only for economic and strategic reasons but also in order that advanced ideological outposts may be established, is based upon the application of Marxist-Leninist socialism in the Stalinist version at home. Hence it is evident that the national ideology not only has contributed to but also has shaped foreign policy to the degree where it has become difficult to know whether foreign policy reflects domestic philosophy or whether to a considerable extent global conditions have molded the national creed.

Since totalitarian "dynamics" must have fuel or else burn out, no such regime can help being revolutionary. Therefore its foreign policy is bound to be aggressive and to shunt compromise if by compromise its principles would be affected. The extent to which such a position can be held without causing international conflict will be determined by the relative moral and material strength of the nation. Internal measures to keep the economy solvent, advancing techniques, and high morale are aimed at not so much for the sake of the citizens' prosperity as for the purpose of stockpiling power behind policy planning. The stronger the regime may feel itself to be, the tougher will be its methods in carrying out its foreign policy along the lines of its political creed.

In the pursuit of their tasks, policy makers of dictatorial governments are rarely concerned with domestic politics as democrats know it. Whatever internal cleavages or pressures exist or operate do not come into prominent evidence, as they can be suppressed by both propaganda and the secret police. Disputes that do exist within the rank of an all-powerful party differ radically from the free interplay of factional opinion in democratic countries. There may be contests of power among the leaders of the party but there are no vested interests outside the party that can effectively oppose the party's will.

The one-and-only party dictates its will to the executives of the government, who in the majority of cases are officials of the party. Thus it would be an error to believe, as so many democrats do, that a change of personalities must necessarily imply a change of policy. So long as the political religion persists, its priests are but its instruments. For example, a basic political objective such as the achievement of a Communist world revolution is rigidly fixed and unchangeable. What may appear to be a change of policy is invariably a change of methodology, or of tactics in the application of the policy, because this seems opportune and necessary.

Conditions are quite different in parliamentary democracies. Whatever their system of government or whatever the degree of state control over their economies, the formulation of foreign policy is subject to a variety of pressures brought to bear upon responsible government officials by three powerful forces, namely, the vested interests of socioeconomic groups, the political parties (which do not necessarily reflect the will of these groups articulately), and public opinion.

The degree and nature of these pressures vary according to the degree and kind of social and economic control that the people have imposed upon themselves. Group pressures are stronger and more successful in the United States than in postwar Britain; they were stronger in prewar France than they were in the United States during the Roosevelt administration. All liberal democracies, however, grant to their political and social pressure groups the right to express themselves. They assume that no one group or party except those opposed to the basic principles of democracy would be foolish enough to endanger their country purposely, as this naturally would endanger their own welfare along with that of others.

Now, as a rule, the top policy makers in the democracies are political appointees and therefore duty bound to carry out the voters' will, as must the rest of the administration. They are not free to formulate policies exactly as they see fit. They must somehow co-ordinate their own conclusions with the program of those parties or groups that brought them into power. They can, of course, recommend policies opposing those of their own group, but without the consent of their constituents who voted for their parties' platform they might have to resign if they refused to compromise or undertake the hard task of making the voters accept the new ideas. They may have to modify their policies to appease pressure groups—if they believe in appeasement.

It is true that the crises that followed World War II have produced in parliamentary democracies more bipartisan and coalition policies in the international field than ever before. Yet, up to now no political party has demonstrated that it is ready to relinquish its fundamental position for the sake of international issues. A bipartisan approach to foreign policy in a democracy is the result of national emergency and not of choice. And even in an emergency, fundamental differences of opinion as to policies and methods of their execution cannot help having repercussions upon foreign relations. The conflict created by Henry Wallace with respect to United States policy toward the Soviet Union is just as much a case in point as the eternal struggle for or against high import tariffs or the questions arising out of trading between free enterprises and state monopolies, or large-scale loans, or assistance to foreign countries.

It would be a mistake to assume that any foreign secretary in a parliamentary democracy could recommend basic policies to his head of state or government that clashed with the wishes of the parliamentary majority. Even in a country with a relatively stable foreign policy such as Britain's, a new parliamentary majority will carefully watch its foreign secretary for deviations from its announced principles.

It is unavoidable that in a democracy, where power is granted by the people through the ballot, there will be deals among the parties, the pressure groups, and the government. If the people do not like the result of these deals and compromises, they may vote out the government and change the balance of power among their political parties. Democratic governments rule on the suffrance of the majority's will; if they want to remain in power, they cannot afford to refuse the advice of the majority's spokesmen. Frequently, principles are traded; concessions in domestic matters may lead to similar or related action in foreign affairs. Compromise is in the nature of the democratic process. Its consequences are not always happy, but one may surmise that this is one of the prices that have to be paid for freedom.

The way in which parties or influential groups interpret freedom and democracy will determine the length to which they will go to achieve popularity among their adherents by sacrificing, in the field of foreign affairs, principles that would in the long run benefit the nation. Internal politics in democratic countries is by its very nature short-ranged. It will try to adapt itself to prevailing conditions and accordingly appeals to the voters in terms of immediate objectives. The best foreign policy, however, is one of long-range value. The spoils of politics demand instant collection, and most voters are likely to be interested in the immediate rather than in the more distant future. Unless they are well educated in international affairs, or follow farsighted, unselfish leaders, they may press for concessions on the domestic front as a result of which principles of foreign policy may have to be sacrificed.

✓ The leaders of political parties and socioeconomic groups whose influence upon policy formulation is strong, are, after all, human beings. While elections establish the predominance of specific schools of thought among majorities as well as minorities, the leaders will interpret their groups' attitude much in accordance with their own prejudices. Their ideas about imperialism, isolationism, pacifism, interventionism, or internationalism, just to mention a few, will have repercussions in the foreign offices. Their views on relations with other nations they almost invariably base upon their friendliness to governments that, they presume, may further their own groups' interests, or upon fear or dislike of governments that they regard as a menace to their groups' ideals and objectives. Ideological affinities cannot but affect relations between nations, and it is the influence of the political and group leaders that makes such affinities articulate on the basis of the consensus of their followers.

PUBLIC OPINION

This brings us to the crucial question regarding the opinions of citizens in matters of foreign affairs that in democracies—and in the United States perhaps more than anywhere else—exert considerable influence upon the making of foreign policy. Very rightly, Vera Micheles Dean once wrote that in the United States "no program, however desirable it may seem to any given President or Secretary of State, can be carried out unless it has the support of the voters, as expressed by their elected representatives in Congress, through organs of the press, and other channels." [1] She quoted former Secretary of State Cordell Hull, who in a radio address on United States foreign policy, April 9, 1944 stated:

> It is obvious, of course, that no matter how brilliant and desirable any course may seem it is wholly impracticable and impossible unless it is a course which finds basic acceptance, not only by our Allies but by the people of this country and by the legislative branch of this Government which under our Constitution, shares with the Executive power and responsibility for our final action.[2]

Public opinion, then, is the mighty oracle of democracy and in theory this is as it should be. But how can it be accurately measured? And if it can be determined, on what basis is it formed? Public opinion polls have developed highly scientific methods of sampling views but they have not altogether eliminated the element of imponderables. They have, on the other hand, established the fact that popular views on foreign affairs are based upon scant or biased information, or just prejudices, and that the mass mind reacts emotionally rather than realistically.

In foreign affairs, public opinion cannot be concrete. It can

---

[1] V. M. Dean, "U.S. Foreign Policy and the Voter," *Foreign Policy Reports*, Vol. XX, No. 13, September 15, 1944, p. 150.

[2] *Department of State Bulletin*, April 15, 1944, p. 340.

indicate only general trends. Rarely does it react without prejudice; mostly it is anchored in traditional concepts even though such concepts may be outdated. It is afraid of unconventional approaches; it is quick to reproach policy makers with either being wrong or having no policy at all, but it cannot, by its very nature, suggest anything better. It will easily be influenced by the press, radio, or the movies; in a few cases by books or lectures. But such influence is spotty, in the main. Human nature, being what it is, tends to absorb what it likes and to pass by what it dislikes. Tolerance and objectivity are attributes of individuals; the mass mind that produces public opinion may well be enlightened and its existence in democratic nations is no doubt a blessing, but it lacks the cool, realistic, objective reasoning trained individuals sometimes develop.

There is as yet no way of producing a public opinion on specific issues of foreign relations that could be professionally inspiring to a policy official. Only prevailing currents can be ascertained with reasonable certainty. These currents, however, are emotionally motivated and hardly rational. American public opinion polls, for example, may show that the majority of citizens are suspicious of Soviet manipulations in the Balkans, but public opinion will not be in a position to contribute intelligently to the solution of this complex situation. It may profess to be against war and for the strengthening of the United Nations but it would be at a loss to prove whether the approach of its government toward the achievement of this objective is right or wrong. Its critical faculties are basically negative; it excels in *ex post facto* judgment but its foresight is little developed.[3]

It is all very well to demand that "the State Department itself must be made more promptly responsive to currents of public opinion."[4] Nothing would be more desirable in principle. But the international field requires more background and experience than the average citizen may be expected to possess. In all

[3] Cf. Thomas A. Bailey's excellent study on the impact of American public opinion on foreign policy, *The Man In The Street*, The Macmillan Company, New York, 1948.

[4] V. M. Dean, *op. cit.*, p. 152.

democratic countries the need for more education of the public in international relations has been recognized. There are three ways of pursuing this goal: (1) information by the government; (2) the activities of private associations; (3) systematic education beginning in school.

As democratic governments are duty-bound to inform their citizens on the state of their nations in world affairs, they have established press conferences and information services as a means of planned publicity. It may be noted that the United States, where public opinion is of paramount importance yet where the people during a century and a half of isolation did not develop much interest in foreign affairs, has the smallest domestic information service. As a result of congressional suspicion of everything that may be interpreted as propaganda, the State Department's Office of Public Affairs—established as late as 1944—is a small organization with very little money at its disposal. Its program provides for the publication of a bulletin and a few pamphlets and leaflets; it arranges for occasional lectures, answers "fan" mail, tries its best to fill individual requests for information by American citizens, and measures public opinion and attitudes in a modest way. Budgetary limitations seriously impede this program's effectiveness, as only a small number of groups and individuals can be reached.

In the United States, where the mobilization of public opinion through newspapers and radio is a daily occurrence, private organizations informing the public about the crucial problems of foreign relations have done a splendid job by reaching many citizens on the educated levels. For example, organizations like the American Academy of Political and Social Science, the Brookings Institution, the Carnegie Endowment for International Peace, the Council on Foreign Relations, and the Foreign Policy Association have effectively supplemented the government's efforts for elucidation of foreign policy issues. Less specialized organizations serving adult education, such as the League of Women Voters, the American Association for Adult Education or the International Labor Office, to mention only these few, have made increasing and successful efforts to provide the public with information on world affairs. Extension courses offered by universities and innumerable private lectures are of additional help but on the whole the audiences reached are still comparatively small; they constitute only a fraction of the mass of the voters. Moreover, the circulation of books on the subject leaves much to be desired.

Some progress has been made to familiarize future voters with the fundamentals of foreign relations. Many school curriculums have provided more time for this subject. The effectiveness of this part of the curriculum is, unfortunately, minimized through national bias that will limit critical analysis by one-sided presentation. Although the United Nations Educational and Scientific Organization (UNESCO) is working toward the elimination of such bias on a universal basis, there seems to be little hope, at the present time, of achieving this ideal in the foreseeable future. So long as prejudice has not been purged from the schools of *all* countries, legitimate insistence on self-preservation cannot tolerate the elimination of nationalism, or national ideology, from the text books of one or some countries, while others continue in traditional one-sidedness.

In the British and French foreign offices, there are news and information bureaus of considerable size, as the British and French parliaments have little objection to governmental bureaus being in charge of domestic education in foreign affairs. Consequently, in these countries there are fewer private and semiprivate organizations that would keep people informed on world affairs. Besides, Europeans, for historical reasons, tend to have a fuller background—though possibly more prejudiced—concerning their countries' foreign policy. They have learned by bitter experience that their governments' policies may spell the difference between life and death. They have out of necessity become addicts of political science. But even in Europe, public opinion on foreign affairs has remained vague, unspecific, and emotional. Cordell Hull's ideal that "the people, who are sovereign, must not only educate their servants but must be willing to be educated by them" [5] is as yet unfulfilled.

It need hardly be mentioned that the Soviet government does not hesitate to give its peoples a thorough indoctrination in foreign affairs as it sees them. This education's curriculum is conceived by the Party and carried out by many institutions throughout the USSR, for example, the trade unions' educational departments. The mass media of propaganda, particularly the newspapers and the radio, spread an incessant indoctrination, and since Marxism is an international doctrine, issues of foreign relations must of necessity be part of over-all ideological training. Obviously, such education cannot, and is not designed to, give the people a background in foreign affairs that would enable them by an expression of opinion to exert beneficial influence upon the policy makers.

In totalitarian countries there is public opinion of a kind, else there would not be so much propaganda to influence it. But it can never be as articulate as in the democracies, where it generates real power—no matter whether it is right or wrong. Therefore policy makers under totalitarian ideological compulsion may not consult public opinion. Instead they order their domestic propaganda machine to co-ordinate public opinion with certain policies, that is, prepare for sufficient receptivity and eliminate popular criticism concerning actions that the government has taken in the field of foreign relations as ordered by the party.

In a democracy such an expression of opinion is, theoretically, desirable. Lack of education or disinterest on the part of the people, however, renders public opinion in matters concerning foreign policy vague, if not ineffectual. Indeed, policy makers have found themselves quite often either ahead of it or at odds with it. A classical example of such divergences in United States foreign policy was President Roosevelt's famous "Quarantine" speech [6] wherein he tried to launch new principles of American attitudes toward the German and Italian dangers. At that time, isolationism was still very strong and a large part of the American public refused to accept the President's premises. As a result,

[5] *Department of State Bulletin, op. cit.*
[6] At Chicago, October 5, 1937.

essential measures for American security had to be postponed. A lesser president might have refrained from initiating such preventive laws as the Selective Service Act, Lend-Lease, and the repeal of the Neutrality Act, which were finally passed as the danger signals increased. But in general, the "State Department can not, in fact dares not, fashion a policy that is too far in advance of what public opinion will permit. If it does, the administration will be thrown out of office, and ranking officials with it." [7]

On the other hand, American leaders have demonstrated again and again their readiness and eagerness to have the public collaborate and thereby to learn its views. In 1945, the administration invited about forty private organizations to be present at the San Francisco Conference that created the UN Charter. It wanted to have the benefit of their advice to policy makers and congressional representatives.

However, it must be recalled that despite all the legitimate clamor for popular participation in the making of foreign policy, there is no constitutional provision in any of the democratic charters for giving public opinion a voice in the determination of specific issues. Heads of state or parliamentary bodies have the sole right to ratify treaties with foreign nations, and all public opinion can do is to take a hindsight position or have its opinion registered during parliamentary debates. But neither bad foreign policy nor bad diplomacy can apparently be prevented by popular action, nor can good ones be furthered. Elections remain the only definite way to support or reject ideas for which individual representatives of the people stand: actions by such representatives of the people that do not appeal to the majority of the public cannot expect support at the next elections.

So far as democratic policy makers are concerned, they undoubtedly prefer to share their heavy responsibilities with the majority of their citizens. They appreciate communications by the public to members of the government or parliamentary bodies; they are not unreceptive to such democratic techniques as petitions, letters to the editor, or statements of organizations that are

[7] T. A. Bailey. *op. cit.*, p. 166.

created to make the voice of the people effective. They approve of debates on the radio and in the newspapers. But they also know that at best public opinion can be no more than advisory even though through organizations it may be made articulate. They are aware of the unavoidable fact that such advice cannot be based upon the best and latest information, which is restricted to government officials, who must keep it confidential.

We know that foreign policy can be developed only on the basis of such information and this undeniable fact will of necessity relegate the productivity of public opinion in international relations to very general suggestions. On the other hand, foreign policy is the result not only of scientific investigation, but also of the prevailing political climate. It is this general, rather diffuse, but still significant "feeling" of the masses of voters that sometimes shows the policy makers how far they can go, how quickly they might proceed, and what they could do to explain certain aspects of their policies and motives to an uninformed or biased public.

There is, in a democracy, a great deal of mutual teaching and learning. As Cordell Hull implied, legislators learn from their constituents and vice versa; policy-making officials learn from both and so do the heads of states and governments. This is intellectual cross-fertilization, one of the great achievements of democratic living, under which everybody is entitled to hear and to have his say. Thus domestic politics, following the will of popular majorities, is bound to affect foreign relations; on the other hand, international exigencies will influence the shape of internal conditions. Both domestic and foreign affairs will be affected by popular trends while at the same time having educational effects upon public opinion. So there is a continuous give and take, that contributes to the clarification of the minds of the people and their government—a clarification of trends rather than one of specific issues.

ECONOMIC POLICY

During the nineteenth century the pound sterling was the center of financial gravity, around which the world economy fluctuated. In the twentieth century the dollar has overtaken the pound and has become the universal yardstick for economic values among both the socialist and nonsocialist powers. But the shift of central economic power from London's City to New York's Wall Street was not altogether a source of unmitigated happiness for the United States. In a world of destitution and poverty the responsibilities of a rich nation have proved to be very heavy.

This study is not limited to one particular country but tries to outline the forces, organizations, and sources that make foreign policy in many lands. Yet when it comes to factors of commercial policy, conditions in and decisions of the United States are of such overpowering importance for the world that special emphasis must be given to this country's economic position. The orientation of its foreign policy, which in many instances is based upon economic considerations, cannot help but affect in many ways the future welfare of the whole globe.

Let us recall that the midcentury chasm between the two nation groups led by the United States and the Soviet Union, respectively, is due mainly to ideological cleavage. But political philosophies go hand in hand with economic concepts. The United States has always believed with the framers of its Constitution that economic liberalism guarantees the political freedom of its citizens. It has ever wanted to maintain a state of economic individualism—also called free enterprise—with as few governmental controls as possible. The American people have been suspicious of a planned economy, although co-operatives find much favor in some regions, and federal projects such as the TVA are, on the whole, not regarded as government "interference" in the people's affairs. Capitalism has been restricted, compared with its status a hundred or fifty years ago, but in view of the monopolistic power of some of the great corporations, most restrictions are regarded as safeguards rather than as obstacles to free enterprise, which admittedly can be impeded by monopolistic capitalism as well as by socialism.

The Soviet Union, on the contrary, believes in the Marxian principle of liquidating private enterprise because, in its opinion, capitalism cannot help but exploit those who have no capital. Therefore, the Soviet government, under orders of the Communist Party, has taken over all means of production, all the land and all the natural resources. Without attempting to equalize incomes or needs during the socialistic transition to communism, the "temporary" dictatorship of the proletariat, it has left the incentive of higher earnings untouched but it has totally eliminated profits on capital investments. Soviet "capitalists" may buy government bonds or acquire some extra conveniences, but they cannot own any producing industry, or farm, or real estate, or sizable trade establishments.

Whatever restrictions of United States overseas trade exist are sanctioned by a Congress whose determination to keep free enterprise alive is almost proverbial. They are sanctioned for reasons of economic security. Security may be threatened by inflation, by scarcity of export material inside the United States, or by the probability that exported goods may eventually be used against this country. The restrictions are, however, emergency measures only. Generally, American freedom of trade is matched by the quest of freedom of transportation and the belief that reciprocally granted freedom of the seas and the air is essential for the maintenance of world peace and prosperity.

Contrariwise, the Soviet Union has set up export and import state monopolies that operate in accordance with the rules of the Five Year Plans and are administered by the Ministry of Foreign Trade. Buying in and selling to foreign countries is therefore regulated and strictly subordinated to over-all planning.

No other country has gone quite so far, though the USSR's central and southeastern European satellite neighbors may be expected to adopt similar practices. However, there is a definite tendency, noticeable even in the western European democracies, to establish a considerable degree of state control. Currency and foreign buying, for example, are usually state-regulated and so is transportation. There can be little doubt that such actions are caused by the belief that postwar reconstruction, enormous as it is, can be tackled only by the state, that individuals should not profit from a national emergency and that the political demands of the groups left of center must be met. As a result, the American quest for equal opportunities of free trade will not be subscribed to by any of the war-ravaged nations until their economy has achieved a new stability and a compromise has been reached between the moderates and the radicals at home.

Whether such a compromise can be reached or whether an increasing tendency toward socialism in Europe will create a breach between American economic principles and nontotalitarian regulated (and partially nationalized) economies remains to be seen. Certainly there is an abyss between such mild forms of western socialism and the Marxian economies in the East that is unbridgeable and that may tend to keep the western European versions of socialism rather close to the American free economy.

The two leading, opposing economic philosophies are separated by principles and beliefs that neither group intends basically to compromise. These principles are essentially reflected by the domestic behavior of the two "super powers" that symbolize their respective ideas. Between the comparatively free American private enterprise system and the Marxian socialist planned society, there remain those countries with war-torn economies that cling to political democracy but have introduced socialist measures to meet their emergencies.

Such is the economic order of battle and it matters little that outside it are other "untouched" economies, which proceed with business as usual—for instance, Latin American countries. The decisions that will affect the fate of the world will be made between the two leading economic principles, one liberal, the other totalitarian.

That national conceptions of economy, under such circumstances, must influence the formulation of foreign policy is self-evident. And that everything is being done by the protagonists of the two diametrically opposed concepts of economic policy to defend their ideas and carry them to victory is natural, too. The adherents of free enterprise in the United States proudly point to the achievements of capitalism and stress the low standard of living in the Soviet orbit as being the result of Communist doctrines. The Soviet government, on the other hand, claiming in the words of a Western writer that "depression is a chronic disease of the competitive system" and "twenty times, between 1854 and 1933, had the United States suffered such disasters, of varying severity," [8] can hardly wait to see the day when American free economy will suffer another relapse. It forecasts unemployment and social upheaval, its wish being the father of its thought. Meanwhile, friends and enemies of both systems are watching intently to see which of the "super powers" will be able to meet more successfully the stresses of their time. For "in the future, weaker powers will gravitate toward America or Russia." [9] Eventually, the outcome of the gigantic contest may determine the shape of the world economy for centuries to come.

At this juncture, we need some demonstrations to show how tightly foreign and economic policies dovetail and how much they affect each other.

Equal trade opportunities. One example of politico-economic policies is the American quest for equal trade opportunities, leading eventually to trade expansion. It has always been a fundamental principle of United States policy that abundance of production and consumption rather than scarcity will guarantee the maintenance of peace and many democratic policy makers outside the Western Hemisphere have agreed with their American colleagues that the difficult task of overcoming the impediments of low living standards and fettered economies internally and externally is one of prime importance for the elimination of strife and war.

Trade relations between sovereign states are regulated in treaties the character of which is determined by the commercial policy of the signatories. Among the many devices through which the United States is trying to implement its commercial policies—

[8] H. Finer, *The Road to Reaction*, Little Brown and Co., Boston, 1945, p. 5.
[9] H. D. Lasswell, *World Politics Faces Economics*, McGraw-Hill Book Co., Inc., New York, 1945, p. 20.

and thereby serve the purposes of its foreign policy—is the application of the insertion in trade treaties of the "most-favored-nation" clause. This means that the contracting parties undertake to guarantee their citizens the advantages of a more favorable treaty which their governments may conclude with a third state.[10]

Tariffs. Another crucial problem is that of tariffs. If there are to be equal trade opportunities, import barriers must be progressively removed. However, there are several valid reasons for the maintenance of some tariffs or other trade barriers for the protection of defense industries and against foreign discrimination, subsidy, or dumping. (The principle of reciprocal trade agreements eliminating or decreasing tariffs will be discussed below.)

The role of tariffs in foreign trade has a different—and not so great—importance for the Soviet government. The USSR through VNESHTORG (Ministry of Foreign Trade) controls exports and imports and is in a position to adjust its foreign trade to the fluctuations of a nonsocialist world economy even though this may entail sacrifices for its citizens. Since it controls imports, it needs no tariff protection. It will export only if it needs foreign exchange or can barter its goods for foreign goods it wants. It can fix prices for its exports to cope with any foreign tariffs.

In view of this complete freedom of action on the part of the Soviet government, the Kremlin can use exports or imports as threats against or rewards for political friends or enemies regardless of the consequences to the population. The rouble has no internationally recognized standing, and the Soviets have purposely never attempted to establish it on capitalist stock exchanges; thus the party leaders are free to determine to what length they wish to go in sacrificing their cost accounting books for long-range political objectives. They can always fall back on their large gold reserves and production, which often they use instead of foreign exchange. It is believed that their gold hoard is considerable and that they are able to produce between 200

[10] Cf. Royal Institute of International Affairs, "The Most-Favored-Nation Clause as an Instrument of Commercial Policy," London, 1933.

and 300 million dollars worth of gold yearly. It need hardly be emphasized that such differentiation in economic practices does not make for political understanding or economic tranquility between the Soviet and non-Soviet orbits.

International currency stabilization. Unless this can be achieved, perhaps with the help of the International Monetary Fund of the United Nations, there can be no equality of opportunities for non-Soviet trade, nor can there be an expansion of such trade. The Soviet government, again, is in a different position and does not worry too much about the currency problems of capitalist or semicapitalist states. Their trouble is an internal currency and what they purchase abroad they do not pay for with roubles. The Soviet State Bank is the depository for all foreign exchange; the combines trading with foreign markets deliver their foreign currency to the State Bank, which in turn gives them roubles for their domestic use. When exchange is scarce and credit unavailable, payments will be made in gold, or imports will be reduced.

Foreign relief and rehabilitation. During the war, the United States was the arsenal of democracy. After the war, it became the world's banker and most important granary. As it emerged from the war richer than ever before, less fortunate nations looked to American help as a last hope, but at the same time feared that "dollar imperialism" might attach too many political strings to economic help. As it happened, United States policy largely continued along the lines crystallized during the war, whose essence is the worldwide establishment of the four freedoms. Its political, social, and economic ideals, it believed, could not develop without these freedoms. It had mobilized its armed might and marshaled its economic forces to fight for these ideals and bring about an enduring peace with economic consolidation. In the struggle against Nazi-Fascist aggression the United States had initiated the Lend-Lease program; it then became the principal contributor to UNRRA (United Nations Relief and Rehabilitation Administration); it had granted credits to a number of the members of the United Nations (which it later extended to some ex-enemy countries like Hungary); it loaned huge sums to its western Allies, Britain and France, after the war had been won. It finally devised the European Recovery Program (Marshall Plan) in order to assist those European countries that could promise that they would use American help to overcome the effects of Nazi-Fascist destruction. In this way such political radicalism as thrives on economic deterioration, hunger, cold, want, and hopelessness may be arrested. The Marshall Plan was designed to prevent a new totalitarianism from replacing the old one. Totalitarianism, the United States government felt, grows on despondency and desperation.

The European Recovery Program is one of the best possible practical demonstrations of a foreign policy that is at the same time political and economic. Inasmuch as huge expenditures are involved, the execution of this policy depends upon the explicit consent of Congress. Since money appropriations have to be made, not only the Senate but also the House must pass upon the policy. In this connection it is noteworthy that foreign policies that depend upon economic efforts will involve more parliamentary supervision than will purely political policies; for in the parliamentary democracies, the people's representatives in the "lower" house hold the nation's purse strings. And yet, economic policies will reflect the political principles underlying a nation's over-all way of thinking and acting.

In a world where views on economic theories and practices were about the same, governments could more easily agree on mutual objectives and map out plans for international convalescence. But in a world split along the lines of comparatively or absolutely controlled economies, with some nations trying to combine features of the two economic philosophies, agreements are much more difficult to reach. As a matter of fact, while opportune day-to-day accords are conceivable and feasible, long-range economic policy understandings between the two systems are well nigh impossible. This is re-emphasized by the fact that the Soviet Union did not become a member of any of the international economic organizations that developed as a result of the Bretton Woods Proposals for postwar reconstruction. It attended Bretton Woods as an observer but never took any action in concert with the other United Nations. To be sure, business is still being transacted between the Soviet Union and the United States, or other democracies. But this does not prove the Soviet's willingness to co-operate economically. The Soviet government will buy so long as it is in its interest to do so. Controlled Marxian economy would not strengthen capitalist economy by buying the latter's products unless it needed goods badly.

While the Soviet Union insisted upon a program of economic isolation—which included the small nations along its western borders—and remained reticent about signing treaties with capitalist countries, the United States began to carry out a program of active assistance to war-torn nations immediately after the end of the war. It did not wait until the International Bank for Reconstruction and Development and the International Monetary Fund had been organized. Having already assisted many members of the United Nations under the Lend-Lease legislation and having contributed most of the funds necessary for UNRRA, it started making credits available through the Export-Import Bank (founded in 1934). It later subscribed a major part of the capital for the International Bank and the International Monetary Fund. Also, through special bilateral agreements it granted individual loans to Great Britain, France, Greece, and Turkey; money was earmarked for China to be made available if and when internal conditions would permit better security for the investment.

In December, 1945, the United States government had announced proposals for the expansion of world trade and employment. In accordance with this government's over-all policy, the proposal favored free trade, opposed governmental restrictions anywhere, and denounced restrictive business practices (such as cartels or price fixing) that would impede full employment. The International Trade Organization (ITO), proposed and set up by the Economic and Social Council of the United Nations, has the specific duty of dealing with these problems on an international scale. The council hopes that the member states of the United Nations will be induced to conclude agreements that, if accepted, will reduce tariffs, limit the activities of international cartels, eliminate preferential rates discriminating between the products of different nations, and outlaw export subsidies or dumping.

In recommending similar policies the government of the United States was supported by the majority of the American people. Americans may differ among themselves about the extent of economic aid or the methods of extending such aid but most of them favor international economic co-operation, believing with one of their great spokesmen that "trade is fundamental to the prosperity of the nations, as it is of individuals." The reciprocal trade agreements, introduced by Cordell Hull in 1934, are a case in point. In a message to the Congress, requesting extension of the program, President Roosevelt said:

> We enacted into law a standing offer to reduce our tariff barriers against the goods of any country which would do the same for us . . . This is no longer a question on which Republicans and Democrats should divide . . .[11]

In his message on the Bretton Woods proposals, the President had warned:

> The world will either move toward unity and widely shared prosperity or it will move apart into necessarily competing economic bloc . . . [12]

Such facts and considerations demonstrate that formulation of economic policies is an essential part of the task of foreign policy making. In incorporating economic or commercial objectives in their political aims, policy makers are bound by the nature of their domestic conceptions of political economy. Recommendations for economic policies, views, and measures concerning international commerce, or participation in international economic organizations, will be guided or at least tempered by respective national philosophies. If the people feel that this philosophy should be changed, they will, in democracies, say so at the polls. Great Britain's population, for example, seldom encouraged quick

[11] Message of President Roosevelt to the House of Representatives relative to the extension of the reciprocal trade agreements program, March 26, 1945.

[12] Message on the Bretton Woods proposals of February 12, 1945, quoted in the message of March 26.

and revolutionary changes but when they felt, after the ordeal of World War II, that considerable modifications of their individualistic economy might be the best way of bringing about their country's speedy recovery, they did not hesitate to vote into power a Labor government whose platform called for a partially state-controlled and state-operated economy.

The economic principles of the Soviet Union are, of course, determined by the Marxian doctrine as reinterpreted periodically by the Soviet leaders. The organization of state trading agencies such as the Amtorg in the United States is no political concession but, in the eyes of the Soviet government, a temporary expedient to keep necessary trade going until the USSR has become self-sufficient and does not need to trade with capitalist powers any longer. Thus Marxist economic theory, being a fundamental dogma of the creed, cannot help being reflected in Soviet international commercial relations. It rules Soviet internal affairs and it characterizes the trends of Soviet foreign policy.

Similarly, American ideas about free enterprise have inspired and directed the nature of United States foreign policy. The nature of the domestic economy is, however, subject to heated arguments between conservative and progressive elements. Both sides are represented in the two major parties but it may be said that, rightly or wrongly, conservatism is generally identified with the Republican Party rather than the Democratic Party. As a result, whichever party has been in power in the years since the Civil War has given the national economic policy its own flavor. Differences were comparatively small, however, until the Roosevelt administration, through the New Deal social and economic reforms, created a major chasm between the two parties. (Then, too, it is a long way from Theodore Roosevelt's "big stick" foreign policy to Franklin Roosevelt's "good neighbor policy.")

However, as a result of World War II, legislators of all political shades were compelled to make concessions toward a bipartisan foreign policy, as it became imperative to keep United States foreign relations on a constant level. This should, of course, imply a bipartisan position in matters of economic policy, too, since some of the principal problems of foreign policy hinge on economic matters. These, in turn, concern domestic politics and the vested interests of a free enterprise economy. Thus, serious questions continuously have to be ironed out between the legislative and executive branches of the government with compromises made by both sides. For example, if the price structure in a relatively uncontrolled economy like the United States gets out of hand and becomes inflationary, it threatens the value of the dollar, which is the basis of world trade. What effect will that have upon postwar reconstruction in afflicted democracies—ideologically and economically—and what incentive may it give to the Marxist type of controlled economy? Or, if war-ravaged European countries are not granted loans through such mechanisms as the Export-Import Bank and the International Bank or under the European Recovery Program (Marshall Plan), to what degree may those countries further decline in their standards of living, remodel their former free economies on Soviet principles, and thus become not only economically but also ideologically a grave danger to the Western Hemisphere? Or, if tariffs are kept high or prohibitive, or if other regulations, such as sanitary measures or quotas, prevent imports into the United States, how then can the United States expect to develop its own export trade or how can it expect prompt payment by an economically weakened world? [13] With such trade barriers erected in the United States or any other country, how can political understanding and social pacification be achieved?

Let us recall that the aim of every nation's foreign policy is security and prosperity. There can be no genuine prosperity without security. Security can be achieved in a world where the four freedoms are basic premises of national life and international understanding. Totalitarian ideologies have grown out of the lack of at least one of the freedoms: freedom from want. Want is a great fertilizer of aggression—ideological, political, and

[13] Cf. H. D. Lasswell, *World Politics Faces Economics*, McGraw-Hill Book Co., Inc., New York, 1945. This small book is one of the most concise and pertinent analyses of world political and world economic problems in existence and specifically deals with the clarification and comparison of the American and Soviet points of view.

economic. A foreign policy able to achieve the goal of liberating people from want will have succeeded in eliminating one of the most potential danger sources of unrest, strife, and conflict. Therefore, at least from the point of view of the democracies, a reasonable, broad, and generous economic policy is one of the foremost objectives of the policy makers. Such a policy is possible only if a certain degree of altruism in domestic economic issues may be practiced and if the powerful vested interests recognize that concessions are necessary for their own survival and best interest. For a collapse of democratic free economies abroad will undoubtedly strengthen controlled economies and finally lead to the destruction of economic individualism.

This thesis may be demonstrated by outlining certain over-all policy objectives, economic in type but political in effect, that the United States is considering and, on the other hand, by outlining the methods the Soviet Union is using to further its opposing conceptions.

Realizing that the world economy is interdependent, the United States believes that stability of its own economy is essential not only for the prosperity and security of its own people, but also for the maintenance of liberal democracy at home and abroad and the attainment of world peace. Therefore, the American economy, generally based upon the principle of free and competitive enterprise, will have to try to attain full industrial and agricultural development and full employment while conserving and developing its natural resources and keep its monetary system stable. To what extent the United States should contribute, out of its own resources, to the reconstruction and economic recovery of war-ravaged or underdeveloped countries is a vexing question, and one that has been the subject of heated arguments since the end of World War II. On the premise that destitution in other countries would impede world economy from recovering and that want produces political radicalism, the United States developed a broad program of assistance on a global scale. In addition to the conclusion of reciprocal trade treaties and encouragement of private business abroad, large sums were put at the disposal of the Export-Import Bank and the International Monetary Fund to stimulate the economic recovery of former allied nations. The most important implementation of this policy, however, is the creation of the European Recovery Program, which is set up to help national economies to help themselves. It does not prevent the United States from concluding treaties of commerce and friendship or reciprocal trade agreements with countries that do not participate in the ERP.

While the United States thus is striving for an economy of abundance for itself and both through self-interest and for humanitarian reasons desires to apply this principle to international economy as well, the Soviet Union is opposed to the establishment of prosperity as the United States sees it. The Soviet government knows full well that peace and well-being are disadvantageous for its purposes. Therefore since it is striving to reconstruct its own country as a base for world communism rather than for the good of its citizens, its policies are directed toward universal unrest, lowering of the standard of living, and threatening of security. For there will be no revolution in a country whose citizens are well fed, well housed, and well clad. The Soviet leaders have enough revolutionary experience to realize this. They want eventual prosperity too, but they want it on their own terms. They do not want prosperity produced by capitalistic or semicapitalistic economies. Therefore they declined to participate in the international economic organizations such as the International Trade Organization or the International Bank. Therefore they violently reacted against the Marshall Plan, which, they know, would decrease the chances of leftist rebellion in substandard economies in proportion to the recovery achieved.

Here, then, are examples of two irreconcilable economic points of view, which are implementing each country's conception of foreign relations and over-all policy objectives. Either policy will strive for as strong a national economy as possible and each one knows that failure to succeed means failure to gain support in world politics. This is the reason why the conditions of United States domestic economy are of crucial significance for the future of liberty throughout the world.

MILITARY FACTORS

"If we expect war, we may create an atmosphere favorable to a so-called 'preventive war.' If we do not expect war, we invite aggression." [14] This, in a nutshell, is the dilemma foreign policy makers have had to face since time immemorial. To be sure, war as an instrument of foreign policy has been denounced over and over again by well-meaning statesmen. In the Pact of Paris, or as it is better known, the Kellogg-Briand Pact (of August 27, 1928), fifteen of the world's foremost nations agreed to condemn "recourse to war for the solution of international controversies and renounce it as an instrument of national policy in their relations with one another." The United States Senate, otherwise so disinclined to have the government sign any international political or military agreements, ratified the pact on January 15, 1929. [15]

However, a major violation of the pact began with Japan's attack upon Manchuria in 1931 and, from that time on, aggression followed aggression, and the pact became a fading memory. Its only tangible result was the innovation of undeclared wars, which were called "incidents" by the Japanese war lords and "police actions" by the Nazi and Fascist fuehrers. In this way, aggressor nations could claim they did not violate the letter of the international law even though they clearly negated its spirit and brazenly so boasted. They sought to circumvent the obligations contained in Article II of the pact, which stipulates that settlement of disputes "should never be sought except by pacific means" and thus maintained a legal fiction by avoiding formal declarations of war.

[14] H. D. Lasswell, *op. cit.*, p. 8.

[15] The pact, as signed, was a much watered down version of the original recommendation by the members of the American Committee for the Outlawry of War. It also omitted definitions of permissible and nonpermissible wars, implying that certain types of war were justifiable and thereby reducing the value of the pact. Nor did the pact expressly state how a "pacific settlement" could be arranged. Nevertheless, the pact was a "magnificent gesture toward a new ethical evaluation of war. . . ." (Cf. Sharp and Kirk, *Contemporary International Politics*, Rinehart & Co., New York, 1946, pp. 558-559.)

In a world shaken by ideological contests and ruled by power politics, in an era that has produced the world's two bloodiest wars within the lifetime of one generation, no government can risk relying upon the good intentions of other governments. International bodies have only begun to prepare the way for alleviating mutual suspicions, and the conflict between the totalitarian and democratic nation groups has not helped to make much progress toward a political millenium. Therefore, even governments that traditionally dislike delegating too much power to the military are compelled for security's sake to have their policy makers listen to those who are responsible for national defense. A realistic statesman is bound to recognize that a foreign policy is just as strong as the relative defense potential that can (and will) back it up.

When the meaning of foreign policy was discussed, reference was made to certain principles (such as topographical and demographic conditions) that must determine the limit of a nation's aspirations and thereby establish the fundamentals of national foreign policy.[16] The limitations are created by the relative strength of the armed forces (actual and potential), the capacity of industry and agriculture, the natural resources and stockpiles available, and the quality of the transportation and communications systems, and last but not least the geographical location. These conditions can only mean that the advice of the defense chiefs will confront the makers of foreign policy with definite alternatives, which, in parliamentary democracies, are further narrowed down by the temper of the people, as reflected in the parliamentary bodies. Obviously, the heads of state and their foreign ministers will try their utmost to settle disputes or achieve policy objectives without resorting to destructive means. But at the same time they must be sure that diplomatic actions are coordinated with the development of their defense forces. The extent to which they will push their policy or allow for compromise depends on their own and other countries' actual or potential

[16] Cf. supra, p. 16 ff.

strength—geographically, economically and militarily—and their estimates as to whether or not other governments are bluffing.[17]

One may well believe the spokesmen of governments of all political colors when they assert that the maintenance of peace is their goal. All nations would prefer to gain their objectives with- out war. Wars are expensive, for victors as well as for van- quished. Opinions differ, however, as to how best to maintain the peace without compromising national security. During recent periods of history, the implementation of policies designed to avoid war ranged all the way from disarmament to the highest level of preparedness. Some democratic powers were ready to subscribe to progressive limitations of armament until such time as international agreements would effectively outlaw armaments above the mere policing level, and it is interesting to note that the Soviet Union has given lip service to this policy.

Except in Japan, the influence of the military decreased for various reasons after the end of World War I, at least until Japanese aggression against Manchuria created global uneasiness. In the western democracies, the temper of the people was out- spokenly pacifist; there can be little doubt that this greatly stimulated the Axis powers into underestimating the defense potentials especially of the United States and Great Britain. Un- der the totalitarian regimes, the army became the instrument of the party that determined policy. Neither in the Soviet Union nor in either Italy or Germany did top military leaders retain any appreciable influence upon actual policy formulation. German and Italian documents have shown that the political leaders frequently rejected vital recommendations of their High Com- mands.

However, there were fewer efforts toward universal demili- tarization after World War II than after World War I. The western democracies found it necessary to establish closer rela-

---

[17] There have been exceptions to this rule, however. As Fascist Foreign Minis- ter Ciano's *Diaries* reveal, Mussolini was aware of Italy's low military potential. Yet he entered the war in 1940, believing that the end of the conflict was in sight. He would not leave all the war booty to Hitler, and so he took the oppor- tunity of participating in what he thought was the last phase of the war.

tions between their foreign offices and their defense agencies. They felt that in this way the implementation of democratic foreign policies had a better chance. Also they wanted to avoid having their tendency toward disarmament misunderstood as weakness. Comparatively speaking, the United States, again, made the greatest effort at disarming but it remained aware of the necessity for keeping at least its defense potential strong and alert. Although the Congress of the United States, after the end of World War II, permitted the Selective Service Act to disappear from the statute books, it reversed itself in 1948 by reintroducing a limited military draft law. It has also sought to make the organization of national defense more efficient. It created, by the National Security Act of 1947, a National Security Council with a Central Intelligence Agency to provide it with foreign information, and it arranged for the merger of all the armed forces in a Department of National Defense. The Secretary of State and the secretaries of the defense agencies are the principal members of the National Security Council. Under the chairmanship of the President, a co-ordination of political, economic, and military policies has thereby been achieved. The British Imperial Defense Council works along similar lines.

Conversely, the Soviet leaders ended the power and influence of their military leaders immediately after the end of World War II. The Politbureau did not permit its marshals and generals to become political leaders. Those officers who are now in high government positions are civilians in uniform (like Stalin) or Party men of long standing (like Voroshilov or Bulganin). The Communist Party saw to it that none of its powers was lost to soldiers. In contrast, some military leaders of the United States have become high policy-making officials in nonmilitary agencies of the government.

As a rule, policy-making bureaus in the defense agencies are concerned only with such policies as may affect their own agencies. But they do have offices set up that are designed to secure policy co-ordination between the foreign offices and the defense agencies; they are also charged with the constant survey of foreign political and economic issues and the development of international relations. In the United States, for example, before the consolidation of defense agencies in 1947, the Navy Department had a "Politico-Military Affairs Section in the Office of Naval Operation . . . ," dealing with "high political policy, while other sections are concerned with island governments, U. S. Naval missions, and affairs of navel attaches . . ." In the War Department the "Policy and Strategy Group in the Plans and Operations Division of the General Staff deals with questions of high political policy . . . The War and Navy Departments cooperate in the formulation of political policy in the Joint Chiefs of Staff Committee and in the State-War-Navy Coordinating Committee." [18] The merger of the national defense agencies in 1947 has greatly facilitated the co-ordination of political, economic, and military policies. The events between Pearl Harbor and the crises following the end of the war have made it clear how intimate the connection between foreign policy and national preparedness is.[19] Most European powers learned this principle by bitter experience long ago.

The greater the international tension, the closer will co-ordination between politico-economic and military policy officials have to be. Within the framework of such co-ordination, armed forces agencies are expected to recommend approaches to foreign policy formulation or methods of enforcement. They may have weighty economic or psychological reasons in addition to military and scientific ones, for suggesting policies. But it would be unreasonable to assume that policies originating from military leaders must necessarily be of a belligerent nature. The fervent quest for peace by men like Generals Eisenhower, Bradley, and Marshall is a case in point.

One may state as a general principle that the influence of the armed forces upon foreign policy formulation becomes stronger as foreign relations deteriorate. In such periods, even the most democratic nonmilitarist policy officials are bound to request the advice of the leaders of their national defense agencies.

[18] B. Bolles, "Influence of Armed Forces on U.S. Foreign Policy," *Foreign Policy Reports*, Vol. XXII, No. 14 of Oct. 1, 1946, p. 172.
[19] Cf. Bailey, *op. cit.*, p. 74.

In countries where militarism amounts to a political principle, foreign policy is, of course, inspired—and sometimes ordered—by the chiefs of the armed forces. This, for instance, was the case in prewar Japan whose foreign relations and domestic life were shaped by the leading generals and admirals. Civilian government was more or less powerless and obediently accepted the dictates of the armed forces. Similar conditions have existed, from time to time, in some Central and South American countries where army officers have taken over the reins of government, mostly after a successful revolt, and imposed their will upon whatever civilian policy maker they permitted to remain on duty.

In European countries the influence of the military on foreign policy was stronger before than after the two world wars. The country of militarism *par excellence,* Prussia-Germany, always conceded the last word on international relations to the military leaders, from the time of the creation of Prussia's first powerful army by Frederick William I in the eighteenth century. Under the German Empire, from 1871 to 1918, saber rattling was a familiar accompaniment of German foreign policy and not even the gradual strengthening of the legislature could restrain the generals and admirals. The *Reichstag* could in theory refuse or reduce money appropriations, which it rarely dared to do, but it had no means to control the use of the monies by the War and Navy ministers. As the monarchs were military men by upbringing and tradition, they saw to it—even though they were constitutional rulers—that representatives of their own caste were well and powerfully represented in the government.

On the other hand, neither Nazi Germany nor Fascist Italy permitted their armed forces chiefs to exercise much influence in matters of foreign relations. Hitler and Mussolini were cautious lest their armies and navies move in and take the power out of their hands. Both glorified militarism and fostered military training, behavior, and organization, trying to maintain a warlike spirit among the population. But they were never fully convinced of the political loyalty of their armies and navies.

It was mentioned above that the basic physical and psychological conditions of a nation and its minimum or maximum aspirations in the world must of necessity determine how strongly it can back up its foreign policy. National defense strategy naturally takes its cue from these conditions and thereby may restrain or stimulate, or remain noncommittal, toward policy framers. However, there are a few additional ways in which the armed forces may influence foreign policy or take over the role of the diplomats to lend further emphasis to their government's announced policies.

1. Although, as a rule, the agencies of national defense cannot make foreign policy, it is possible that their actions may force the policy makers to make public statements that amount to either a restatement or a modification of foreign policy. This does not happen often. When it does, it consists of utterances of prominent military leaders or actions by military units that were not previously authorized by the respective chiefs of government. One of the most interesting cases in point was General MacArthur's statement concerning his views on a peace treaty to be concluded between the United States and Japan and the resulting decrease of occupation forces. The Department of State, the sole agency empowered to formulate policy on this matter, presumably did not fully share the general's views and failed to back him up by endorsing what he had said. But there can be no question that his statement precipitated discussions concerning the problem of future relations between the two countries.

2. The armed forces, in order to emphasize their government's determination that certain announced policies will be carried out regardless of opposition, may be called for armed demonstrations. History is full of examples of this "armed" diplomacy. The display of United States navy units in the spring of 1947 near the Greek port of Piraeus was one of the more recent instances of armed forces helping to implement United States policies—in this case, policies concerning Greece and Turkey. Another recent example of United States armed diplomacy was the sending of naval units into the Mediterranean during the negotiations over Trieste in 1947.

3. Conventions concerning armament, too, involve problems of

concern for both political and military experts. For example, the Treaty of Rio de Janeiro, concluded in September 1947 between the United States and all the nations south of the Rio Grande relative to Western Hemisphere defense and exchange of weapons obviously had much military bearing. The United States position on their trusteeship of the Pacific islands, too, is by no means a matter of foreign relations only; it involves important principles of defense strategy, and, therefore, the political negotiators had to consider the views of the defense chiefs on United States territorial security. Following the opinion of the U.S. Navy, President Truman declared that "those Japanese mandated islands captured by United States forces which are needed by America will be kept as long as necessary" but added that they would be kept under "individual United Nations trusteeship." [20]

After most wars, there has been a tendency, in the United States as well as in other countries, to keep the influence of the armed forces at a minimum, although military heroes have occasionally risen to postwar political power. Physical and psychological fatigue, accumulated during the strain of emergency, has tended to express itself in opposition to everything military. But the end of World War II, the establishment of the United Nations notwithstanding, did not produce the traditional swing away from the military. Political tensions had not subsided; on the contrary, they were brought out in the open. Ideological warfare did not cease. The end of shooting did not establish a feeling of security. Therefore the influence of military leaders upon the formulation of foreign policy remained strong and the reorganization of governments all over the world, taking account of existing conditions, provided for continuous and close co-operation between foreign policy and military strategy. The unification of the army, navy, and air forces in the United States and the establishment of the National Security Council proved that the greatest nonmilitarist power of the globe felt that it must support its foreign policy by an efficient organization of national defense. Similar considerations prevented the British government from large-scale demobilization in spite of the grave economic situation it faced.

[20] Cf. B. Bolles, *op. cit.*, p. 176.

Whether or not the influence of military leaders can be kept in bounds by a civilian government will always be a crucial issue for a nation's position in international affairs. "A strong statesman . . . can probably control a General Staff and keep its offensive spirit within what he decides to be its due bounds. Even the strongest statesman, however, may be overborne by the arguments of the military experts, which naturally he cannot refute on technical grounds. Less strong witted and less assured statesmen . . . are always liable, in times of crisis, to yield, against their better judgement, before the arguments of the General Staff, and to subordinate political to military aims." [21]

OTHER GOVERNMENT AGENCIES

We have so far listed among factors contributing to foreign policy domestic conditions, public opinion, economic issues, and problems of national defense. It is necessary to add a few words about the contributions by government agencies other than those directly connected with the conduct of foreign affairs. These agencies are concerned with finance, trade and commerce, labor, internal affairs, agriculture, law, transportation, and communications.

In the United States, the Treasury Department plays a very important role by actively participating in international commercial relations. As far back as 1942-43 it authored the program of an international bank and monetary fund which was later accepted as a basis for the establishment of these agencies. The Treasury may be ordered by the President to control foreign funds; for example, it seized Axis assets during World War II. It has initiated financial policies that have been accepted by American occupation authorities in Germany and finally incorporated in the State Department's over-all policy planning. It was responsible for financing the war, thereby giving the political and military leaders the means to carry out their policies and strategy. It is the administrating agency for the collection of tariffs and, as such, is

[21] R. B. Mowat, *Diplomacy and Peace*, Williams & Norgate Ltd., London, 1935, p. 125.

in control of the Coast Guard in peacetimes. It has officials sitting in a number of specialized agencies of the United States government wherever financial questions are involved.

In Great Britain, the Treasury plays an even greater role in the country's over-all policies. Whereas in the United States approval for funds to be allocated comes from the Congress, with the United States Treasury being a mere executive agency, the British Treasury must approve every penny to be spent—a condition that makes this ministry one of the most important in the Commonwealth. Also, top-level Treasury officials exercise control over government business that is not strictly financial, such as the civil service. The nominal head of the Treasury, the "First Lord," is the prime minister himself; the actual head, the "Second Lord," mostly called the chancellor of the exchequer, is the finance minister of the nation. The exchequer, under parliamentary orders, has an imposing list of duties and it has, because of its semi-independence and because its chancellor is the ranking cabinet member of the United Kingdom, often influenced foreign policies pertaining to financial, political, and defense matters. It may be assumed that Treasury opinion, concerned about Britain's postwar economic crisis, was an important factor in the cabinet decision that British occupation forces in Europe and the Middle East were to be reduced or withdrawn.

Such extraordinary influence on the part of the Treasury in national and international affairs is unusual. A similiar influence will not be found, for instance, in the Ministry of Finance or Ministry of Budget of the French Republic, whose position may be likened to that of the United States Treasury Department.[22] There as here the personality and initiative of the leading officials rather than the constitutional position granted to them made them as influential as they are. In prewar Germany, departments concerned with finance were strictly subordinated to political agencies, and this is even more the case in the Soviet Union, where the role of money is quite different from that in non-Marxist economies.

---

[22] Except that in the United States the Bureau of the Budget is a separate agency.

Soviet domestic currency is not on the international market, and if the Soviet government wants to purchase abroad, it pays in foreign exchange (mostly dollars) or in gold. Although the scarcity of machinery and goods necessitates a certain degree of Soviet foreign trade, which the government controls just as it controls foreign currencies, money inside the USSR may not be regarded as influential in international relations. Certainly, Soviet foreign policy is not affected by monetary considerations.

The commerce departments play a different, though important, role in the formulation of foreign policy. Some of their functions have, in fact, been taken over by the foreign offices. In the United States, commercial policy is developed in the State Department, which, as was described above, has also organized a number of influential economic offices. The role of the Department of Commerce is mainly advisory. Its commercial agents in foreign countries are under the wing of the State Department, and its Office of International Trade is a research and analysis agency rather than one that determines policy.

Conditions are somewhat different in Britain, where there exists a Department of Overseas Trade. Since 1917 it has had the task of administering foreign economic relations and of recommending commercial policies. It is not an entirely independent agency, as it is subject to supervision by both the Foreign Office and the Board of Trade (the equivalent of the U.S. Department of Commerce). Its existence is the reason that there are few economic bureaus in the Foreign Office.

The position of the Ministry of Commerce in France or prewar Germany resembles that of the U.S. Department of Commerce. In the Soviet Union, however, the situation is quite different. The Soviet Foreign Office is less concerned with foreign economic relations than is any other such agency. The Ministry of Foreign Trade is in charge. The latter supervises the state trading monopolies and otherwise is an executive organ of the policies laid down by the party. The principles of Soviet government prevent the ministry from formulating commercial policy; what it may do is to recommend methods. But in Soviet eyes, the existence of the Ministry of Foreign Trade is not one of choice but of temporary necessity. For trade between state monopolies and private enterprise is awkward for both parties, to put it mildly; the Soviets would prefer to be able to deal with other state monopolies only and then develop barter trade, which they are now pursuing with neighboring countries in central and southeastern Europe.

The contributions of the ministries of the interior differ with the respective governmental organizations. In the United States, the Department of the Interior happens to be in the business of oil administration. Oil, as is universally recognized, is an explosive issue in international politics.[23] The State Department, trying to cope with the thorny problems of oil, has set up a specialized bureau dealing with this matter, but oil, wherever it is found, has universal implications and thus the Secretary of the Interior, who controls the Petroleum Administrator's Office, cannot help invading the scene of foreign affairs. Apart from this, the particular tasks of the U.S. Department of the Interior pertain to the improvement of internal productivity rather than to political matters, and by this token contribute at least indirectly to this country's position in the world. For example, its reclamation projects may considerably affect the thinking of both policy makers and strategists.

In contrast, the British Home Office's duties are much narrower. It is exclusively concerned with domestic administrative matters such as internal safety, supervision of elections, or filing petitions to the Crown by British subjects. It naturalizes aliens, whereas in the United States most of these tasks are fulfilled by the Department of Justice. It has little if anything to contribute to foreign relations. The French Ministry of the Interior, too, supervises the police (as do most European ministries of the Interior) and is mainly occupied with domestic political and social conditions. The same was true in prewar Germany and Italy. European ministries of the interior have often been identified with the seat of the police power of the state. They were, however, unconcerned with the

---

[23] This department's Division of Territories is responsible for internal affairs of such United States territories as Alaska or Puerto Rico but it does not handle aspects of foreign policy that may concern any of these regions.

problems of health and welfare, which in many countries are handled by specialized ministries. As international agreements on health and welfare are on the statute books of almost every nation, the respective ministries have developed a considerable degree of interest in foreign affairs.

There is no all-Union ministry of the interior in the Soviet Union; there are, however, ministries of home affairs established in the constituent union republics, which, as we recall, have their own "state" governments. Needless to say, these agencies have no connection whatsoever with foreign policy making.

The labor departments of the democratic states contribute considerably to foreign policy. Being concerned with labor's position in a changing world, their representatives participate in international attempts at improving labor's conditions all over the world. The U.S. Department of Labor selects the United States delegates to the International Labor Organization (ILO) and presumably most other non-Soviet labor ministries select their own delegates. There is no labor department in the Soviet Union, since there is no problem of labor-management relations in that country. The trade union organizations take care of questions that may arise regarding working and living conditions.

The political and economic conditions of any country depend a great deal upon the position and behavior of labor and so it is to labor that the Soviet Union tries to direct its political campaign. Labor can, of course, make or wreck a country's economy, and thereby strengthen or jeopardize its defenses. Therefore, in the matter of foreign relations, specifically with countries in the Soviet orbit, the problems of labor are seriously considered by policy makers.

The ministries of agriculture, too, play their part in foreign policy. Being responsible for their respective countries' food situation, their counsel is indispensable for policy and strategy. In the aftermath of World War II, food is an essential for peace and order. The United Nations Food and Agriculture Organization is one indication of world concern for food production and distribution. The U.S. Department of Agriculture maintains agents in many countries. Agricultural attachés, who work under the supervision of the State Department and who collect information about the world's agriculture, exchange new inventions and see to it that United States agriculture is protected from the influx of animal or plant diseases. The British Ministry of Agriculture and Fisheries and the French Ministry of Agriculture perform about the same duties for their respective countries and so do the corresponding agencies of the world's other civilized countries. In the Soviet Union, there is no all-Union ministry of agriculture yet each constituent republic has not only such an agency but, in addition, a Ministry of Food Industry and a Ministry of State Grain and Livestock Farms.[24]

The justice departments contribute their part if they are empowered, as the one in the United States is, to fight international cartels or to work on such cases of international law as the legal advisors of the foreign offices might not handle. Again, the Soviet Union has no all-Union justice department, leaving it to the republics to supervise their respective legal organizations. Questions of international law are handled by the Minindel, its advisory bodies, and, in cases of particular importance, decided upon by the Politbureau.

Mention may finally be made of the departments dealing with transportation, communications, and the mails. These functional agencies naturally contribute, at least technically, to their countries' foreign relations. Their technical advice is necessary for policy makers and foreign affairs researchers. Among such agencies are the post offices, maritime and aeronautics administrations, bank, and tariff commissions.

This is but a very brief survey of factors contributing to foreign policy formulation, as they come to the policy makers' attention from other agencies of their own government. Many other instances of indirect contributions could be mentioned, for example, educational agencies, which help shape the minds of new genera-

---

[24] There are in the USSR both state and collective farms. The collectives, "Kolkhozes," administer themselves and are under the supervision of the respective ministries of agriculture; the state farms are under direct control of the ministries of state grain and livestock farms.

tions and condition them to certain attitudes and established traditions. A long-range policy creator will inevitably have to pay
much attention to the schooling of youth in international relations;
in the majority of cases, however, he is powerless to initiate
reforms.

CHAPTER THREE

Sources of Information

MEANING OF INTELLIGENCE

GEN. WILLIAM J. DONOVAN, America's wartime intelligence director, once wrote that "no foreign policy can ever be stronger than the information upon which it is based." [1] Indeed, information is the fuel for the machinery of international relations. Without it, or without adequate intelligence material, the machinery will slow down, or idle. As a result, policy makers may well misinterpret conditions and be led to miscalculations. Worse, they may have to shoot in the dark.

Policy-formulating officials should be presumed familiar with basic historical and statistical facts concerning the areas of their jurisdiction. However, facts in themselves, indispensable as they may be, are not necessarily relevant for policy formulation, unless they have been put into the right context. Facts become articulate through additional information that indicates the direction and character of their development.

Such information may be of infinite variety, covering all possible emanations of national life, pertaining to events, conditions, factual matter, and intangibles. There can never be enough information. The more there is, the better for the digesting and processing officials, the better in the end for actual policy determination. Responsible policy makers are not supposed to read every scrap of information available about a particular country,

[1] "Intelligence: Key to Defense," *Life Magazine*, Sept. 30, 1946, p. 108 ff.

81

area, or continent. They will get only the gist of it. Rarely will intelligence come to their attention "in the raw." With few exceptions, such as cables containing news of extraordinary pertinence, information will be processed by the staff of the missions abroad, by the country specialists in the foreign office's political divisions, by officials in specialized offices such as those concerned with commercial policy, and finally by the staff of the research and analysis divisions, who may use it for immediate processing or for purposes of reference in the context of other studies.

All these contributions are like the parts of a jigsaw puzzle, the solving of which is in the hands of the division chiefs and their high-level superiors. They will co-ordinate factual statements and policy recommendations into one integrated pattern and forward it to the policy-formulating officials.

Let us repeat: there are original intelligence items of indubitable value that need no comment, but as a rule, intelligence is processed information. Thus, for the purposes of policy formulation, it is necessary

(a) to collect abroad all intelligence pertinent for international relations and foreign policy;
(b) to analyze and evaluate and relate the available material objectively and impartially;
(c) to disseminate the processed information quickly to the responsible officials.[2]

In surveying the field of intelligence, the student of foreign relations will recognize, perhaps to his surprise, that intelligence gathering is by no means an activity that bears the official mark of moral condemnation. As a matter of fact, information work is nowadays not only recognized *de facto* but also *de jure*. Reporting home from foreign posts has become an honorable occupation. When an author writes that "military, naval and air attachés are simply official spies; it would be hypocritical to call them any-

---

[2] In this volume, we are not concerned with the technique of intelligence dissemination, which is an administrative function. Obviously, an efficient code room and quick distribution service in the foreign office make incoming intelligence even more valuable.

thing else . . . ," [3] he may have put the matter rather crudely; however, actually, "official spies" have come to be universally recognized by all nations and are protected by international law. Every government knows well that other governments wish to gather as much intelligence as they possibly can obtain. The question only is to what length their agents will go to obtain foreign state secrets, and the eternal problem remains as to where a diplomat transgresses the frontiers of hospitality, taking undue advantage of his immunity, or how ruthless a free-lance secret agent may be in order to achieve his objective.

The writer has never been the member of a secret service organization and he cannot claim to know more than the average person about the techniques of collecting intelligence in a subterranean way. But he gathers from perusing whatever literature is available about secret service and espionage that more nonsense has been written in books or projected onto the screen of the movie theaters on this topic than on any other item concerning international relations. The student of foreign affairs who wants to know something about the machinery of foreign-policy making, should be mindful to look upon intelligence for policy purposes in a very unromantic way.

It may be true that attempts are being made by certain governments to pierce vital secrets with the help of espionage agents. But political secrets cannot be hidden for long. Leakages are liable to occur; implicit information may be gathered from apparently inoffensive unrestricted material, from which keen observers can discern developments and trends. All of which goes to prove that secret agents will, as a rule, concentrate upon military rather than political matter. "There is far more to be learned," wrote an espionage expert, "about a country from a careful digest of its official publications and newspapers than is to be picked up by hanging around arsenals with a 'Brownie.' " [4]

For example, Nazi Germany's geopolitical aspirations and the resulting war of aggression, could not have surprised anyone who

[3] R. Boucard, *The Secret Services of Europe*, Stanley Paul Co. Ltd., London, 1940, p. 14.
[4] R. Boucard, *op. cit.*, p. 12.

took the pains to buy and study a few pertinent books, magazines, and newspapers on the subject available at any German bookshop or newsstand.[5] Communist objectives of the Soviet government are as clear as a cloudless sky for any intelligent person who takes the trouble of studying literature on the Marxist-Leninist-Stalinist gospel. Even during the war, when censorship was at its heaviest in the Axis countries, a careful analysis of enemy newspapers and radio broadcasts used to reveal much of the aggressors' intentions, trends, and policies.

It is therefore clear that processed intelligence is of particular value for policy formulation. It is also true that much intelligence raw material can be found where only a skilled observer can recognize it (in newspapers, for example) and that secrecy of information is not necessarily the yardstick for its usefulness. Why then is it that sometimes even plain material is communicated under the restriction of high classification, be it top (or most) secret, secret, confidential or restricted? The answer is simple enough and quite significant for the character of intelligence used by foreign-policy makers. While the event in question may not be confidential at all, while it may have been discussed in the world press for that matter, the deductions drawn from it by the diplomatic staff abroad, the interpretation given to it by the area specialists, the evaluation accorded to it at home, and the policy recommendations attached to it must *de rigueur* remain confidential, as they affect national security.

Policy decisions are in themselves highly confidential. If a policy is publicly announced, it is already a going concern; all provisions to protect its execution have been taken. So long as this is not yet the case, the policy makers are still trying to work out the best possible solution for their problems; therefore, their work must be done in secrecy, and information reaching them must ac-

[5] See the chart of Nazi infiltration in foreign countries, published in *The Brown Network* by an anonymous author and backed by a "World Committee for the Victims of Nazi Fascism" in 1936, Knight Publishers, New York. But the book's documentation found little credence although it contained what later proved to be invaluable intelligence material.

cordingly not come to the attention of outsiders, particularly if it contains interpretive suggestions.

This is no "secret diplomacy" in the customary sense of the word. It is simply protection for the nation's security and welfare. Like a chess player, the policy maker who knows what his opponent is up to finds himself in a much stronger position to outmaneuver him than one who does not. Such jockeying is not an end in itself, although surely many a diplomat likes the game. So long as there does not exist a world government, no national government can be blamed for wanting to do its utmost to protect its security. In wartime, obviously, the right confidential information for the general staff or its field commanders may mean the difference between defeat and victory. In peacetime, the political and economic position of a country may be in the balance, thereby affecting the standard of living and the safety of every one of its citizens. No wonder that the foreign offices of the world are most cautious in what they will divulge and what they will keep a secret. No wonder the world's governments are so intent on finding loyal and skilled representatives abroad and scholarly experts at home, so as to be kept sufficiently informed. No wonder spies from all corners of the world are trying to break codes that would make it possible for their governments to decipher other governments' messages.

GATHERING OF INTELLIGENCE

Intelligence is collected first of all by the diplomatic staff of the missions. In the form of cables, air letters, or despatches, running accounts will be sent home about current political problems—international and domestic; the general attitude of the receiving government to the sending one; analyses and interpretations of official statements as well as of press and radio publications; the social and economic implications of present policies toward and by the receiving state; the behavior and influence of the men in power and those who are regarded as potential candidates; public opinion regarding domestic questions and international problems; cultural developments of significance, and so on.

Often of importance are memorandums of conversations that took place between the officials of the sending country and the leaders of the receiving country. Exchanges of ideas with foreign officials or interviews with private foreigners frequently offer significant keys to the understanding of controversies from the opponent's point of view. Copies of specialized reports by the attachés go to the foreign office as a matter of course and economic statistics may be forwarded from consular officers. Interviews with private individuals, such as nationals of the sending country visiting the receiving country, are not always first-class sources of information but may be useful when evidence is accumulated. Of course, there may be secret reports by special agents, destined to be read by a select few only.

It is difficult to suggest a full outline of the subjects that the policy makers will want to have worked out for their information, for apart from special issues, there are always problems to be solved between two nations no matter how friendly they may be. Only when their geographic position makes them very remote from each other, when their cultures are utterly alien to each other and their commercial relations indifferent, could there be imaginable a state of affairs where no problems vex the policy makers. But few if any such conditions nowadays exist. In a shrinking world, almost every nation has definite interests in another, be they political, commercial, or social. In all these cases policies must be determined that will solve the questions in a peaceful way. For we must assume that every foreign policy is a bona fide quest for the preservation of peace and that war as an instrument of foreign policy has become very unpopular.

Reports on the development of such problems will have to be composed and annotated by the diplomatic staff, even though they might not directly concern the sending government. They may, for instance, affect a third power, yet the issue at stake could grow to be of crucial importance for an entire area of the globe and, thereby, for world peace. The behavior of a nation's controlled press may cause another country to change its attitude from friendliness to resentment, and, as a result, a planned loan may be cancelled or other action taken. Intelligence will try to trace the reason for this change of behavior and its findings may well contribute to the policy makers' decisions to withhold the loan until further notice.

Or, elections may have been faked in violation of treaties, resulting in the upset of previous ratios of political power. Or, there may be troop movements in a direction that would be indicative of a government's desire to apply pressure against a third power. This would mean jeopardizing the peace not only in a particular area but, implicitly, in the world. Last but not least, there may be indications of sympathy or antipathy toward political groups or particular countries; such emotions may be the result of propaganda; they may develop into definite attitudes and finally establish psychological conditions with which the policy makers will have to cope.

Next to the more definite and circumscribed problems concerning the direct relationship between the sending and receiving states, it is necessary for the diplomatic staff to keep themselves informed, and report home accordingly, about the sociopolitical trends in the country of their jurisdiction. The prevailing type of government, the constitutional or ideological law, the effectiveness of either parliamentary or dictatorial control, the forces jockeying for power within that country's political parties or party factions, the character of the leaders, must be the constant objects of the observers' attention. For those in power will direct the country's trends and alliances, they will color its ideological outlooks and shape its social conditions. No foreign policy can hope to meet the needs that would not attempt to cope with the internal situation of the nations with which relations have to be settled or reorganized. For the policy makers a complete picture of the political, economic, social, and cultural status of their target area must be attained. No detail is too small or too unimportant to be left out: it may be the missing part of the jigsaw puzzle.

The usual scheme of distribution of information helps to achieve integration and condensation. So great is the volume of incoming material and so much is said in it that the job of stripping it of all that is merely a variation of the theme, its condensation and co-ordination require a great many aides and much skill. But it is the only way policy makers can get to the essentials. If they would even begin to peruse the bulk of incoming material, they would never come to formulate policy.

Usually, urgent messages will be cabled and the less urgent (but not necessarily less important) ones will be written up in despatches and sent home via diplomatic pouch—which is one of the safest though not necessarily the fastest means of communication between the foreign office and its mission. Air mail has recently become another method of relatively quick connection. (Couriers use airplanes in the majority of cases.) For classified cables, codes are used. Their safety is a relative one. There is always the possibility that foreign agents may succeed in getting hold of a code; in wartime especially, this has happened often. Also, the foreign offices of the world employ experts whose task it is to break the codes if they cannot actually steal them. So frequent change of codes is advisable.[6]

Special reports from the commercial and agricultural attachés will be worked into the general political picture by the processing officials. Problems of economies or of food production are always fraught with political significance. Indeed, foreign policy may consist of an application of economic measures to existing political conditions. The Marshall Plan to help Europe to help itself could not have been evolved as a foreign policy were it not for extensive reporting on the economic conditions in European countries and on the political outlook in the event of a collapse of European agriculture and industrial output.

Military reports will first be evaluated by the intelligence sections of the armed forces. Usually, policy makers are not strategists as well; the case of George C. Marshall who happened to be both is an unusual one. Therefore, an analysis of the reports and a professional interpretation of the findings will be a vital addition to the impressions already gained by other reports. For to be realistic, even the most enthusiastic believer in peace is bound to

---

[6] For an interesting and revealing account of the U.S. State Department's code room activities before its temporary closure in 1929, see H. O. Yardley's, *The American Black Chamber*, The Bobbs-Merrill Co., Indianapolis, 1931.

recognize that in the present-day world a foreign policy is the stronger, the better the armed forces of his country are. So long as power politics and ideological aggression threaten the peace, the old Roman proverb *si vis pacem para bellum* (if you want peace, prepare for war) still has a significant validity.

Close co-operation between the foreign offices and war departments is therefore a must. The military have the obligation to instruct the men responsible for foreign relations as to what the general outlook of foreign armed forces in certain areas seems to be. Their relative strength and the reported military, naval, and air policies of the respective countries will give the policy makers valuable clues as to the sincerity of their opposites abroad.

Now all these types of intelligence may be called direct or primary intelligence. There is also an indirect or secondary intelligence available to all who are alert enough to pick it up. It can be found in a country's bookstores and newspaper stands. It can be distilled out of books, pamphlets, articles, and news angling. It can be heard on the radio and seen on the screens of the movie theaters. Gathering this type of intelligence is easy. Every mission clerk can do it. Processing it is not quite so simple; that is done by the diplomatic staff as well as by the foreign office experts. Following a nation's intellectual production, no matter whether or not there is censorship, will reveal many things to the skilled eyes and ears of analysts and monitors. They will find the social atmosphere and the political climate of the people in question just by perusing their papers, magazines, literature, stage plays, radio broadcasts, and whatever motion pictures may be seen. Secondary intelligence sources are particularly important in countries that restrict or prohibit a free flow of information.

The most significant finds, such as inspired editorials, articles in important magazines, or statistics, will be cabled in a condensed form, which is an indication of their importance. Foreign offices will have newspaper roundups sent home at regular and frequent intervals. Many governments maintain expensive radio monitoring services so as to keep their policy people informed about the tendencies emanating from foreign broadcasting.

Processing of Intelligence. The processing of this material is as necessary as is the material itself. This procedure is being carried on abroad and at home. It may overlap; it may be doubled by several agencies; but whatever the cost for a government, it pays. There is seldom enough and usually only too little of these services, which during both war and peace have proved to be of sometimes greater importance for a true picture of conditions than despatches, which cannot help being somewhat theoretical at times. Especially press and radio intelligence offers a day-to-day picture of a country's state of affairs, and by cleverly sifting and comparing facts with previous intelligence, deductions may be drawn that are of prime importance. Foreign policy is evolved not only on the basis of facts but also of trends. Indirect intelligence provides this information if enough money is allocated for an efficient operation of this kind.

It may be added to previous explanations that processing of intelligence "raw material" or basic intelligence will, in the main, take the form of condensation, analysis, interpretation, evaluation, and relating to other events past and projected. Condensation is used for quick preliminary messages, to be followed by more extensive reports. It means reducing a news item to its essentials. Analysis is a dissection of the various aspects and facts contained in the information and an investigation of their relative significance. Interpretation is an explanation of these aspects and facts and a clarification in terms of prevailing policy. Evaluation is a process of deduction, more than of explaining; it tries to find the reason for facts and events and judges them in the context of general conditions. It sometimes goes so far as to imply policy measures in order to stimulate or eliminate certain conditions.

A well-written despatch may contain most of these elements. Mailed by the envoy with a covering letter that sketches the contents of the report "in a nutshell," it is not restricted by space and it is rather free to express ideas or even to speculate so long as the envoy approves of its line of thought. Suppose a despatch is written by one of the secretaries of the mission covering the elections in one of the more unruly southeastern European countries. It would begin by recalling the recent history of elections, the attitudes of the government and people toward democracy or totalitarianism, outside pressures exercised upon the government to falsify the elections, the assistance of lawless elements to make the balloting a fraudulent one. It would then describe the government's objectives in faking the elections, the techniques of carrying out the crime, and the results. It would describe events on election day and analyze the tabulation as published by the foreign government. It would, to a degree, speculate as to the political future on the basis of the election results.

In other words, the report would contain facts, statistics, historical allusions, a narrative of events and their background, the actual and potential results from the events and speculation as to what might be the consequences. Such a despatch has already been processed more or less thoroughly; it contains digested and applied intelligence, so to say, and does not need further processing at home. It might possibly be quoted in policy recommendations and referred to by the researchers and analysts in future reports. It might supplement secondary intelligence.

The scientific aides of foreign-policy making are much underestimated in their important contributions to actual policy formulation. It must by now be clear to the reader that foreign policy cannot be produced like a rabbit out of the hat of a magician. It needs thorough preparation. Elements of uncertainty must be eliminated as far as humanly possible so as to leave little opportunity for speculation. To be sure: devising new policies is a process involving original creation, that is, a combination of solid realism based on facts with speculation based on experience. But the intangibles should be narrowed down to the closest margin, and in order to enable the policy makers to avoid overdoses of intuition and instead follow deduction, a research department staffed with first-class historians, political scientists, economists, and sociologists is indispensable for every foreign office. If not attached to the foreign office, such services will still have to be created or made available wherever they can be found.

The research and intelligence organization in the United States Department of State is relatively new. It consists of the Office of Intelligence Research, with four geographical divisions, and the

Office of Libraries and Intelligence Acquisition, with three functional divisions. Congress has never allocated enough money for this vital work. This may be a reflection of the fact that the necessity of comprehensive intelligence for purposes of policy information has not as yet been recognized properly by many Americans. For the demands of policy work in the midcentury struggle of political ideologies, the present organization is woefully inadequate. On the other hand, the creation of the Central Intelligence Agency [7] at last enables the United States government to co-ordinate foreign intelligence for the information of high government officials.

The British Foreign Office, whose organization has had little trouble with budgetary issues and therefore could develop a more co-ordinated and efficient agency, long ago recognized the essential need for political intelligence. Formerly, such intelligence was processed in the "Library," which is a very comprehensive department with many duties. Then, in 1943, two of the most important British intelligence units, the Political Intelligence Department of the Foreign Office and the Press Section of the Royal Institute of International Affairs, were amalgamated and became a new Research Department in the Foreign Office. Once organized, this Research Department co-ordinated its work with the Library, functionally and physically. The Research Department is organized along geographical lines; its foremost task is the study of historical backgrounds of current foreign policy problems for the use of the political departments. Most of its reference material can be found in the Library.

France's reorganized Ministry of Foreign Affairs has no specialized intelligence units. Its research and analysis work is decentralized and relies on the help of the Sorbonne (University of Paris). On the other hand, the Foreign Ministry of the USSR has made several provisions for concentrated effort of research and analysis. The three advisory bodies, mentioned below,[8] particularly the Soviet Academy of Sciences and the Collegium, seem to be working along these lines

[7] Cf. p. 69.
[8] Cf. pp. 148-150

in a very elaborate manner. The research organizations of the Communist Party contribute heavily as do the faculties of the nation's universities. In the Kremlin, nothing is left to intuition. There are some basic topics to be covered by everyday research. First of all, historical investigation, used partly as background for evaluation purposes and partly for the instruction of foreign office personnel. Contemporary problems can be fully understood as the outcome of historical antecedents only, and one cannot expect staff members to be familiar with every historical detail all the time. Invariably, not only political but also social and cultural developments have their historical reasons, and so have attitudes. There is no new departure in policy that cannot be related to historical causes, not even twentieth century ideologies. There is only one item that is utterly new and demands correspondingly new approaches: the atomic problem.

Research in and interpretation of the history of nations, with respect to their political, economic, and social progress, will thus be the first and foremost task of the research agencies. There is an enormous variety of contemporary issues that, in order to be properly understood, must be traced back to their historic parallels or precedents. In particular, the history of relations between two countries will have to be the special field of investigation. The researcher, in tracing this history, may well find significant aspects shedding new light upon contemporary problems, and thereby help policy makers to gain clarity about the issue at stake.

Fact finding is another task for a research organization. Thereby is meant not only the assembling of statistics, important as that may be, but careful investigation of "the facts behind the facts." Special research projects of this type are requested by the political or specialized divisions and may concern such matters as ideology, politics, sociology, economics, or cultural life. For example, there may be a request to investigate, on the basis of actual evidence or deduction, whether or not and to what extent orthodox Marxism still forms the core of Soviet ideology, what the Stalinist modifications of Leninism amount to, and whether these changes, if any, indicate significant changes in Soviet government and society. Such research requests are large orders and involve the study of a wealth of material and a careful analysis of political statements, economic plans, constitutional revisions, social conditions, and so on. Analysis of press and radio intelligence, plus information from the embassy in Moscow would also have to be used. In short, the project would be difficult and costly but might result in a clarification of issues to such a degree that the conduct of a country's foreign policy would benefit greatly from the study.

A further important task is the evaluation of information and propaganda coming from abroad. It is possible, by studying propaganda lines, to deduce an opponent's policy or, at least, his methods of policy execution. Propaganda analysis has become one of the most enlightening sources of information in regard to foreign governments' probable intentions and has become indispensable to policy makers.

It may be added that the work of research and analysis, having to deal not only with facts but also with attitudes, must be permeated with the method of psychological analysis as well. The evaluation of a people's "national character" and national attitudes demands psychological understanding. For events happen all the time that cannot be explained on the basis of known scientific facts alone. Neither can the failure or success of sociopolitical movements. Certainly the political religions of the twentieth century need a great deal of psychological understanding. Political and social sciences, it must never be forgotten, deal with human elements, too; elements that are full of surprise and apparently illogical development.

The majority of foreign offices, even though they have their own research and analysis departments, will no doubt have to seek outside co-operation from scientific institutions, universities, and individual experts. The issues of international relations are indeed so manifold and complex that a nation's intellectual resources will have to be tapped and pooled if government research cannot go far enough. There will be necessary a liaison office able to locate and bring into contact government and private groups and individuals so that particularly difficult problems may be worked out through teamwork. Moreover, liaison will enable other government agencies to co-ordinate information and experience with the foreign office since many of them have divisions handling foreign matters.

Processing intelligence, as can be seen, is a highly scientific undertaking. The better it is organized and the more time and money a government may allocate to such an agency, the higher will the dividends be, for policies worked out thoroughly, on the basis of thorough factual knowledge, penetrating analysis, and sound evaluation, are rarely wrong.

To sum it up: "Our hope for peace depends upon our foreign policy, and to determine that policy we must test the facts which bear upon the economic, spiritual and political factors involved . . . we must know at all times what is going on in the world . . ." [9]

[9] *Life Magazine, loc. cit.,* p. 108.

PART TWO

The Formulation of Foreign Policy

CHAPTER FOUR

Originating Organs

THE conduct of foreign affairs is divided into formulation and execution of policies. Since the emergence of the national states, these two branches have been recognized and institutionalized by all sovereign nations. The organization of these services and their functions is almost identical everywhere. National foreign policy originates at the seat of the government and is administered from the foreign office (or, as it is also called, the ministry of foreign affairs, or as in the United States, the Department of State) which is in charge of handling relations with foreign offices abroad. Diplomacy, on the other hand, is charged with carrying out, as well as possible, national policies in the field. It must inform the home agency of conditions abroad and look after the interests of these fellow nationals who are residing in the country in which it has accredited representatives.

The organizational differences between the world's foreign offices are less administrative than constitutional. Administratively, their duties comprise formulation of expert opinion, supervision of the foreign service, and responsibility for the day-to-day maintenance of international relations. All foreign offices have political, economic, functional, and administrative divisions; in spite of different emphases in their organization charts, they are all brothers under the skin. There is another important similarity: foreign offices may not at all times remain in charge of foreign policy. This is so under not only dictatorships, where the leaders of the party in power utilize their foreign office primarily to administer policies that they formulated. It happens also in democracies—and quite constitutionally so.

For example, the history of the United States foreign relations has frequently demonstrated such legally unassailable actions as the President by-passing the Department of State or the Congress not wanting the Department of State to assume responsibility for a particular aspect of foreign policy, as in the case of the independent agency for the European Recovery Program, the Economic Cooperation Administration. However, in all these instances, it is understood that the predetermined broad outlines of policy are followed and that the responsible men will be accountable for their decisions. They will be accountable, in the democracies, to the people as well as to their chief of state; and not only to their party, as under totalitarianism.

What really distinguishes the world's foreign offices is, first, the nature and extent of control over foreign policy that they are allowed to exercise and, secondly, their constitutionally defined relations with the executive and legislative branches of the government under which they operate.

Obviously, the nature of policy control is determined by the political philosophy of a nation and its tangible result, the constitutional law. In a dictatorship such as former Nazi Germany or the present Soviet Union, the foreign office cannot be more than an advisory, administrative department, seeing to it that decreed policies are carried out effectively and taking charge of functional activities. Foreign policy in nondemocratic states is determined and ordered by the dictator, and/or an authoritative body consisting of a few high officials from the dominating party who might be high officers of the government but not necessarily so. Contributions of such foreign offices to policy formulation remain limited to carefully co-ordinated suggestions—co-ordinated to ideology, research and intelligence, administration of home and field offices, and the safeguarding of interests of loyal citizens. In democratically governed countries, the control of foreign affairs is constitutionally circumscribed and, at least indirectly, determined by the popular will.

Constitutional issues of policy control are by no means of

domestic concern only. The position of the foreign minister, chief and spokesman for the foreign office, has of necessity two aspects: he is responsible for his country's foreign policy vis-à-vis his own people and he must also be looked upon as the fully authorized representative of his country in matters concerning international affairs; so every foreign office is at the same time a national and an international agency and is subject to constitutional as well as international law. Its objective must be to try to adjust national aspirations to international realities.

Under no political system are foreign ministers endowed with exclusive powers. They are dependent upon their heads of state, parliamentary bodies, or political parties. They carry on the business of international relations in conjunction with and under control of their government, that is, the head of state plus the ministerial chiefs plus the leaders of their various political parties. There is no direct control by the people; at best, there is an indirect influence through elections or other demonstrations of public opinion. The measure of domestic democracy is not necessarily reflected in popular control of foreign affairs, though there is usually more of it in democratic countries than under authoritarian regimes. The nature of foreign-policy making and diplomatic activities, which are mainly based upon confidential information and operated on a rather preclusive level, has up till now prevented the people in any country from exerting real influence. This is no reflection on the techniques of democracy, where co-operation of the citizens is facilitated, but is rather indicative of the full-time attention and training necessary to assimilate all the implications of even a single area of foreign relations.

The nature of constitutional control, or the extent of political pressure on foreign affairs determines the position and prestige of foreign ministers and their agencies, the foreign offices. A brief comparative survey of such controls and the ensuing organization of foreign offices in some of the more influential countries will demonstrate the point and clarify the role of the foreign offices in world politics.

UNITED STATES

THE PRESIDENT AND CONGRESS IN FOREIGN AFFAIRS

The Constitution of the United States did not expressly delegate authority for the conduct of foreign affairs to any specified agency. However, it has been inferred from the beginning and long since accepted as a fact by constitutional lawyers that the initiative for the formulation of chief foreign policies remains in the hands of the President. The Department of State, established by law in 1789, is "the legal organ of communication between the President and other countries," and therefore, the Secretary of State, the department's administrative head, becomes the official spokesman of the President and the government of the United States vis-à-vis foreign governments.

The Constitution provides that the President inform Congress about the state of the Union; that he receive accredited foreign representatives, nominate United States envoys to foreign countries and take part in the two most important prerogatives of all: the treaty-making power and the war-making power.

These powers are, however, limited by Congress. "The President shall have power," says the Constitution, "by and with the advice and consent of the Senate, to make Treaties, provided two thirds of the Senators present concur." The Senate may also accept the President's proposals conditionally, that is, it may modify treaties without rejecting their substance. But it is up to the President finally to ratify such treaties by signing them. Only thus can they become law.

Declarations of war must be passed by Congress, usually at presidential instigation. However, in practice the President, as chief executive with power to conduct foreign relations, and as commander in chief of the armed forces, can order military action before or without declaration of war by Congress. In such cases, the constitutional authority of Congress to declare war amounts primarily to official and legal recognition of already existing conditions. This is of particular significance in the age of atomic energy, supersonic speed, and radio-guided missiles. Congress could, at least in theory, affect the continuation of an armed conflict by impeaching the President and by refusing to provide funds for the conduct of war.[1]

Information about international problems may be requested from the President by both houses of Congress. The increasing complexity of international relations and the concurrently heavier responsibilities for policy decisions have caused United States presidents in recent times to seek close co-operation with advisory bodies of the Congress, notably the foreign affairs committees of both the House and the Senate. Constitutionally, the Senate has a much stronger position than the House in the determination of foreign policy since it is regarded as an advisory body of the President in matters concerning foreign affairs.

Yet the House of Representatives can exert strong influence through holding the purse strings of the United States Treasury. It can pass, cut down, or deny requests for money appropriations. In this way, it can bring about organizational modifications in both the Department of State and the armed forces, entailing serious consequences and influence on the relations between the United States and the world. While it is sometimes held that the power to rule by appropriation is against the spirit of the Constitution, there seems to be no indication that the founding fathers wanted to prevent such possibility. The House of Representatives, like the Senate, may also express its views on foreign policy by passing, modifying, or rejecting proposed laws that have a bearing on foreign affairs, such as tariffs, subsidies, or support of prices; or may pass resolutions stating its views, joint or respective, about any foreign policy, existing or proposed.

To avoid the pitfalls of appropriation cuts, the President will remain in constant touch with both houses of Congress and confer

---

[1] The Constitution is silent about ending a state of war. By practice and decisions of the Supreme Court, it is now established that war may be ended by treaty—in which case only the Senate would be involved in ratification—or by joint resolution of Congress, repealing "authorization of hostilities." (Cf. E. S. Corwin, *The Constitution and What It Means Today*, Princeton University Press, Princeton, N. J., 1947, p. 63.)

with the party leaders of both houses when decisions of great importance are to be made.

It is through Congress and the election machinery that popular control over United States foreign policy may be exercised. Yet, appealing as the doctrine of a people's control over foreign policy may be and fine as the principle of "open diplomacy" is, in the conduct of foreign affairs the security and welfare of the state do not always permit these ideals to be carried out. Many a delicate issue demands careful treatment, which public discussions could not possibly give. Furthermore, large sections of the public might not understand or have the time, training, or background of information to master the nature of the issue and the context in which it is being treated—unless much time, money and effort are spent by both the government and the citizens on an educational campaign in order to enlighten the voters on the issues at stake. In that respect, the Office of Public Affairs of the State Department does what it can within its strictly limited budget; on the other hand, the United States Congress is most suspicious of any kind of "propaganda" and has often felt that government information activities should be narrowly circumscribed by microscopic appropriations.

Yet even though it will have to remain up to the experts who have access to essential information, to analyze conditions, draw conclusions, and submit recommendations, it is nevertheless possible for the American people to exercise influence upon the conduct of foreign affairs. This position is inherent in the Constitution, which demands that the President ratify treaties with the "advice and consent" of at least two thirds of the senators voting. Senate proceedings are, of course, open, and the Senate is a directly elected representation of the people, whose will it is their duty to express.

There is, however, a way to postpone or circumvent congressional participation in presidential treaty actions. Such actions are called "executive agreements." They have been used by many presidents of the United States since the time of George Washington, who himself made use of them. The vast majority of these agreements were approved by the Senate retroactively, but there were others that were either amended or turned down, or not acted upon at all, without necessarily losing their international validity. (Executive agreements not only may concern actions initiating treaties but may also deal with the termination of existing treaties.)

Among the more famous executive agreements figure Jefferson's Louisiana Purchase, which was, of course, ratified by the Senate at a later date. Similar agreements also initiated the acquisition by the United States of the territory of Texas, Hawaii, Samoa, and the Panama Canal Zone as well as a number of Far Eastern and Latin American issues.[2] Executive agreements were concluded during World War II between the United States and the Soviet Union.

As the significance of foreign affairs is continuing to increase to the extent where it overshadows and profoundly affects domestic issues and where presidents of the United States might well be elected primarily on the strength of their foreign policy platform rather than on the basis of the attractiveness of their domestic programs alone, the Congress is more anxious than ever to maintain an adequate control over the nation's international relations. Yet although the Constitution determines the nature of the influence that the Congress is entitled to exert upon the President and its policy agencies, the usage of executive agreements—unmentioned by the Constitution—has become firmly entrenched in the practices of United States conduct of foreign affairs. "Doubtless the President, uniting with the Congress through legislative enactment expressed in a joint resolution or otherwise, is enabled to go farther than the Executive has ever heretofore seen fit to proceed."[3] Indeed, there have been important executive agreements that were never ratified as treaties, yet established such matters as the incorporation of Texas, the participation of the United States in the

[2] Cf. W. M. McClure, *International Executive Agreements*, Columbia University Press, New York, 1941, Part One.

[3] C. C. Hyde, "Constitutional Procedures for International Agreements by the United States," *Proceedings of the American Society of International Law*, 1937, p. 45.

Universal Postal Union or United States co-operation with the International Labor Organization.

THE SECRETARY OF STATE AND HIS "LITTLE CABINET"

The Secretary of State is a political appointee, whose name must be submitted to the Senate for confirmation, by simple majority. While his activities may be criticized and his policies rejected by the Congress, only the President has the power to remove him from office. He is not, like the British Secretary of State for Foreign Affairs, subject to the "confidence" of the House and his term is ended only with that of the President unless he resigns earlier, or is asked by the President to resign. If the appointing President is re-elected, the Secretary will submit his resignation nonetheless, and it is then up to the President to let him go, or reappoint him.

The Secretary of State is the ranking member of the cabinet. Until 1947, he was next in succession to the presidency, in the event of the death of both the President and the Vice-President or in case of impeachment of both or any other situation that may prevent them from carrying on their duties in the White House. This provision was changed by the Congress in June 1947, at the recommendation of President Truman, who reasoned that a Secretary of State is an appointed and not an elected official. Instead, the Speaker of the House, elected member of the majority party, will now be first in line of succession.

Nevertheless, the Secretary of State remains the ranking member of the cabinet. He is close to the President in matters of foreign affairs; he is the United States government's spokesman to the world. He is the center around which relations with foreign countries revolve; he is the head of the agency charged with the conduct of such relations. (His personal responsibility, however, is limited. If somebody is blamed, it will be the President rather than the Secretary. In this respect, his position is quite different from that of foreign ministers in other lands.)

With the growing complexity of international relations and commitments of the United States in world affairs, the Department of State, particularly during World War II, grew from a small office to a large organization, much to the dislike of economy-minded legislators who had difficulties recognizing that with the change of the United States position in world affairs, the agency administering that position was bound to change, as well. At the same time, it became humanly impossible for the Secretary —or, for that matter, for the President—to carry on without substantial expert advice. Thus an intradepartmental and informal "little cabinet" was created, consisting of the Secretary of State as chairman, the Undersecretary and his Deputies, the Counselor and the Assistant Secretaries of State. This "cabinet," in turn, receives advice from a policy-planning staff, which was set up by Secretary Marshall and headed first by George Kennan in 1947. This planning group of top-notch area experts is charged with the responsibility for working out difficult policy problems. The results of its findings are submitted to the Secretary and possibly to his "little cabinet." Recommendations of prime importance will, of course, be submitted to the President himself. The creation of this body of political thinkers was presumably the result of Secretary Marshall's conclusion that the pressure of business and the lack of personnel leave the top-level policy makers too little time to think problems through and that provisions had to be made to permit a careful consideration of the main issues of world politics by a group of men with both local and global experience. Removed from the exigencies of administrative duties, the group may turn out to develop the foremost source of policy initiative and a tremendous help to both the Secretary and the Undersecretary of State. On a lower level, there are a number of country committees, within the department, dealing with particular areas or countries, which consists of members from the political, economic, and functional divisions. Their task is to clarify specific problems, such as might arise from treaty negotiations, and to advise officials on higher levels accordingly.

In the office of the Secretary, all foreign and domestic information relative to international affairs converge. While theoretically his is a supervising-administrative rather than policy-formulating job, he will, in practice, contribute decisively to the country's political outlook and, subject to the President's concurrence, he will accept or reject policy recommendations, or suggest modifications. He will, in certain cases, initiate new policies; particularly he will order reorganizations of the department that may be instrumental for changes of political methodology. Moreover, it is the habit of most new secretaries to bring in their own staffs to one degree or another. This, of course, reflects itself in changes of policy and attitudes.

Next to the Secretary, the Undersecretary of State is the most influential man in the Department. Like the Secretary, and like the Assistant Secretaries, he is a political appointee but his nomination will be prompted by his known administrative capacity and his knowledge of, or adaptability to, world affairs. His appointment must be approved by the Senate. He becomes automatically Acting Secretary if the Secretary is not in town but, more important, his influence upon the actual process of policy making may at times be greater than that of the Secretary. In view of the British experience with the office of the Permanent Undersecretary in the Foreign Office, there is a demand for a more permanent character of the Undersecretary's office so as to ensure more continuity in national policies, since changes of office holders occur all too frequently with all the corresponding changes in attitudes and techniques.

To assist the Undersecretary in his political and administrative duties, the offices of two Deputy Undersecretaries have been created. One of the Deputies assists the Undersecretary in political matters, acts as the Department's National Security Council representative and maintains overall relations between the State Department and the National Defense Establishment. The other supervises, on behalf of the Undersecretary, the Department's general management with the help of four functional offices. Under a Director General, these offices carry out the complex business of departmental administration and organizational tasks.

The number of Assistant Secretaries varies with the requirements of world conditions. The reorganization of 1950 created eight of them. Their responsibilities are distributed as follows: (1) public affairs (domestic and foreign information); (2) economic affairs; (3) United Nations affairs; (4) European affairs; (5) Inter American affairs; (6) Near Eastern, South Asian and African affairs; (7) Far Eastern affairs; and (8) Congressional relations.

If need arises, so-called Special Assistants of the Secretary of State are named to head certain semifunctional bureaus. They do not need to be confirmed by the Senate and are usually experts in their field. After the reorganization of 1950, there remained only two Special Assistants, one heading the Department's research and intelligence bureaus, the other handling the Secretary's press relations. However, such positions may be abolished at the direction of the Secretary, whenever they have outlived their usefulness.

The office of the Counselor, slightly ranked by that of the Undersecretary and not to be confused with that of the Legal Advisor, is of considerable importance. As the name indicates, the Counselor's task is to advise the Secretary on policy problems. The choice of a Counselor will depend mainly upon the need for a man whose background and experience may be of particular value for coping with prevailing political issues.

Another important office within the Department of State is that of Legal Advisor. The function of this office is to clarify the legal aspects of foreign relations for the benefit of the policy makers and diplomatic representatives abroad. The foreign offices of all states have legal advisors although they are not always a part of the foreign office organization proper.

The office of the Assistant Secretary for Congressional Relations was created in 1949. Since international relations have become a paramount issue, affecting the nation's political and economic existence, both houses of Congress showed an increasing interest in the management of foreign affairs by the State Department. When the former machinery of liaison between the Congress and the department was found to be insufficient under the circumstances, top-level liaison was established. It is the principal task of this Assistant Secretary to achieve congressional and administrative co-ordination of views in political as well as budgetary questions.

THE DEPARTMENT OF STATE

Foreign offices are subject to constant changes in organization either as a response to a shift of political emphasis due to the change of international conditions or as an attempt to improve efficiency and effectiveness. The U. S. Department of State is no exception. Since its creation in 1789, it has undergone innumerable reorganizations and has grown from a staff of a half dozen clerks into a full sized agency with thousands of employees.

The spirit of the men and women who make up the department has changed, too. There is still a widespread popular belief that foreign offices are breeding places of snobbishness, stuffiness, and immovable conservatism. This prejudice has come down from that period of history when foreign affairs were conducted by monarchs and their aristocratic representatives. In answer to the need for generally accepted procedures the ceremonial of international relations for foreign offices and diplomats was established;[4] and for a long period, the intercourse between nations and governments was characterized by such rules. Quite a few of them have continued to be useful and have survived. They may be discovered, in a modernized form, in the work of the protocol divisions of the world's foreign offices as well as in many of the daily practices of diplomacy.

Today, however, the equalitarian trend in the United States, never sympathetic toward "striped pants," and the inner growth of American democracy have eliminated much of the typical foreign office atmosphere. Congressional control and the election of progressive presidents have further discouraged the policy of exclusiveness. Not as often as formerly can political pull or personal fortune push a man into a departmental office if he does not merit the appointment. Political appointments of amateur envoys still occur but few men are picked who are not capable representatives of the United States. Ever since World War I, personnel policies have considerably improved, and one may state

---

[4] It was the French Court of Louis XIV that created diplomatic "fashions," which were imitated all over the world.

ORGANIZATION OF THE
EPARTMENT OF STATE

JANUARY 25, 1950

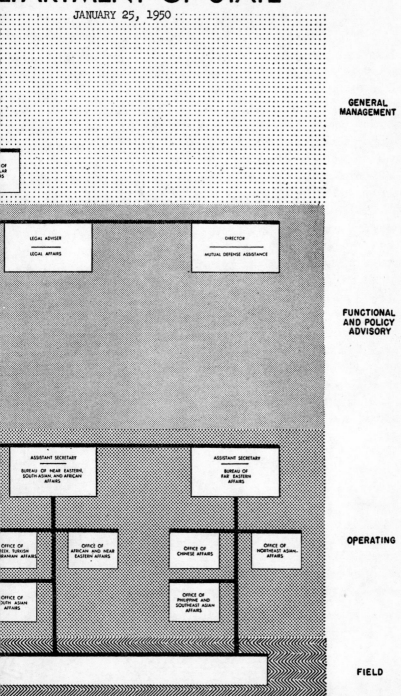

GENERAL MANAGEMENT

FUNCTIONAL AND POLICY ADVISORY

OPERATING

FIELD

OF
LAR
RS

LEGAL ADVISER

LEGAL AFFAIRS

DIRECTOR

MUTUAL DEFENSE ASSISTANCE

ASSISTANT SECRETARY

BUREAU OF NEAR EASTERN, SOUTH ASIAN, AND AFRICAN AFFAIRS

ASSISTANT SECRETARY

BUREAU OF FAR EASTERN AFFAIRS

OFFICE OF
REEK, TURKISH
RANIAN AFFAIRS

OFFICE OF
AFRICAN AND NEAR EASTERN AFFAIRS

OFFICE OF
CHINESE AFFAIRS

OFFICE OF
NORTHEAST ASIAN AFFAIRS

OFFICE OF
OUTH ASIAN
AFFAIRS

OFFICE OF
PHILIPPINE AND SOUTHEAST ASIAN AFFAIRS

GENERAL
MANAGEMENT

FUNCTIONAL
AND POLICY
ADVISORY

OPERATING

FIELD

that World War II swept away many of the last vestiges of these former vested interests. In spite of the fact that salaries, especially for top-level officers, are still insufficient, and that organizational improvement is a continuous objective, the Department of State, in the middle of the twentieth century, has become a vigorous, rejuvenated agency, staffed with men and women from the professions, who have injected new blood and fresh attitudes into those organs of the agency that needed it most.

The department is comprised of two separate entities: the departmental offices and the foreign service. The distinction between these two bodies is indicated by the fact that departmental personnel is under Civil Service while foreign service officers and clerks are under Foreign Service. Officers and Clerks of the Department of State are stationed in Washington mainly, certainly not outside the continental United States; none is assigned abroad except for a special temporary mission. The Foreign Service, however, embraces all those officers and clerks whose job it is to represent the United States abroad.[5]

The Department of State is organized in four "layers." On top are the offices of the Secretary of State, the Undersecretary and his Deputies, the policy-advising Policy Planning Staff, the Counselor and the four administrative offices of the Director General. The second layer contains such functional units as the intelligence bureaus, the economic offices, the legal and public affairs (information) offices, the bureau of the Assistant Secretary for Congressional Relation and that of the Director of Mutual Defense Assistance for the Atlantic Pact countries. The third layer embraces the vital bureaus dealing with political affairs along geographic lines and the fourth consists of the Department's overseas organization, i.e., the diplomatic and consular missions and the delegations to international organizations.[6]

---

[5] Cf. p. 187 ff.

[6] The major units of the functional-administrative area of the Department of State are called "offices" or "divisions," the latter being subdivided into "branches" or "staffs" as the case may be. The geographic area, however, is parceled out in "bureaus" which, in turn, are subdivided into "offices." Each office consists of a group of "country desks." Such groups, organized along regional interests, are supervised by an "officer in charge."

From the day-to-day policy-making point of view, the politico-geographical offices are the most important ones. They are contained in six bureaus five of which are supervised by an Assistant Secretary while the Bureau of German Affairs is under a Director. The bureaus cover (1) European Affairs, including the British Commonwealth, Northern, Eastern and Western European areas; (2) Inter-American Affairs, dealing with East, North and West Coast Affairs and Middle American Affairs; (3) Near Eastern, South Asian and African Affairs, with the offices covering Greek, Turkish and Iranian Affairs, African and Near Eastern as well as South Asian regions; (4) Far Eastern Affairs, responsible for China, Northeast Asia, Southeast Asia and the Philippines; and (5) the Bureau of United Nations Affairs which will be discussed below.

Each of these geographic offices consists of a number of "country desks," staffed by officers who are charged with the responsibility of either one particular country or several small countries of one region; or, they may be working with other desk officers on one of the more important countries. For example, the Office of Eastern European Affairs has individual desk officers to handle matters concerning the USSR, Poland, the Baltic states, Albania, Bulgaria, Hungary, Rumania, Czechoslovakia and Yugoslavia. While each of the smaller countries may be handled by a single officer, affairs concerning the Soviet Union are handled by several desk officers since obviously it would take more than one desk to handle the ramifications of United States-Soviet Union relations.

The desk officers carry the heavy burdens of the day-to-day policy work. They must be familiar with all departmental activities concerning their area and also be fully informed about the domestic conditions and international position of the countries of their responsibility. They are in close and continuous touch with United States diplomatic representatives in those countries for which they are responsible and know exactly what United States interests and objectives in those areas are. They must read correspondence, official and private, concerning "their" countries, study all incoming cables, reports, and despatches and give information to other departmental offices if need be, on "their" countries. They have to be in constant touch with the commercial and technical divisions as to the conditions that affect the area of their responsibility. They must recommend policies and procedures to their office chiefs, whose task it is to co-ordinate such recommendations for the entire region and submit them to the Assistant Secretary in charge.[7]

The newly established offices of Regional Affairs, set up in the bureaus of European and Inter-American Affairs, are to facilitate integration of policy where it applies to problems involving countries of more than one geographic office of the bureaus.

For the development of foreign policy, the geographical offices can be considered the nucleus of the State Department. Close to them are the three offices of the Assistant Secretary for Economic Affairs. They are somewhat stronger in the U.S. State Department than in other foreign offices, at least from the policy making point of view, for the simple reason that many countries have organized ministries of overseas trade; there is no such organization in the United States.

The reorganization of 1950 provided for three economic offices: Office of International Trade Policy, Office of Financial and Development Policy, and Office of Transport and Communications Policy. All these units develop the economic aspects of United States foreign policy in close co-operation with the geographic bureaus. Major special foreign economic programs will not only be so co-ordinated but also integrated with both United States domestic and foreign economic policy.

The responsibilities of the Office of International Trade Policy are carried out by staffs developing commercial policy, petroleum policy, international business practices, and economic resources. The Office of Financial and Development Policy handles monetary affairs, investments and economic development, Lend-Lease, and surplus property. The Office of Transport and Communication Policy deals with shipping, inland transport, aviation, and telecommunication policy. Of singular importance for the formulation of foreign policy is perhaps the Commercial Policy Staff

[7] About routine processing of incoming documents, cf. p. 157 ff.

which formulates, negotiates, and administers commercial treaties and international agreements such as reciprocal trade agreements and treaties of friendship, commerce, and navigation.[8]

The most important units providing essential technical facilities for the State Department are the Office of Operating Facilities; the Office of Consular Affairs under whose supervision are the Visa and Passport divisions; the Office of Personnel with divisions handling matters concerning both departmental and foreign service personnel; and the Office of Management and Budget.

Problems of international organization are handled by the Bureau of United Nations Affairs. Its four offices are in charge of matters concerning the United Nations.[9] Not all United Nations issues come under the responsibility of this office, however. For example, UNESCO affairs are conducted by the Assistant Secretary of Public Affairs, who also directs the Department's domestic and foreign information program. The Office of Public Affairs is charged with domestic information on foreign affairs for the enlightenment of the American public. The Offices of International Information and Education Exchange have the task of informing foreign countries about United States policy, civilization and ways of life.[10]

This description of the U.S. Department of State's organization is based upon its status as of January, 1950.[11] In the course of future reorganizations, offices and divisions may be abolished and new ones added. The House of Representatives' Committee on Appropriations recommended on May fifth, 1947, a "reorganization looking toward a consolidation of closely allied functions, with a corresponding reduction of the number of offices and divisions." However, whether the extraordinarily difficult situation in foreign affairs will permit a reduction is open to doubt. The U.S. Department of State is probably one of the most understaffed and overworked foreign offices in the world even though

---

[8] Cf. the description of the former Division of Commercial Policy, in "The Department of State of the United States," U.S. Government Printing Office, Washington, 1942, p. 15.

[9] For a detailed description of this bureau, see below p. 243 ff.

[10] For the issues of foreign information, cf. p. 206 ff.

[11] See chart opposite p. 110.

it was forced to quadruple its personnel "from 5,420 in 1939 to 20,000 on July 1, 1947." [12]

In general, the constant shifts and changes in international relations require a great deal of flexibility in foreign offices which will be compelled to initiate frequent reorganizations in order to cope with new tasks and conditions. The reader should keep this in mind when perusing the descriptions of foreign office organizations. But he need not be overly concerned that such changes may becloud his understanding, because they will not, as a rule, alter the fundamental principles of foreign policy formulation and administration. In fact he will notice that foreign offices the world over have a great deal in common; changes are most often of implementation or emphasis rather than of organization.

The real difference, it will be found, may be seen in the type of constitutional control over the final policy decisions and it is here rather than in the foreign office organization where basic divergencies appear.

GREAT BRITAIN

THE CROWN, THE CABINET, AND PARLIAMENT IN FOREIGN AFFAIRS

Although Britain is a parliamentary democracy like the United States, control of her foreign policy is in the hands of the crown and the cabinet rather than of Parliament. One may say that for this very reason the conduct of foreign affairs in Great Britain is somewhat less democratic than in the United States. The people have little influence upon their country's foreign policy except, in a rather general way, by voting for parliamentary parties.

Constitutionally, the crown, that is the King, possesses the sole

[12] B. Bolles, "Reorganization of the State Department," *Foreign Policy Reports*, August 15, 1947, Vol. XXIII, No. 11, p. 134.

By January, 1950, the State Department employed approximatly 18,000 people, both at home and abroad. Approximately one third of this personnel serve in the United States (most of them in Washington, D.C.); the rest are employed abroad.

power for the conduct of foreign affairs. He delegates this power to his responsible ministers, notably the Prime Minister and the Secretary of State for Foreign Affairs (Foreign Secretary).

With the growth of parliamentary government and popular power, the kings of England have been increasingly careful not to make personal use of their constitutional prerogatives concerning foreign relations. Queen Victoria may have insisted on being informed about the developments in relations with other nations and did make it very clear in a letter to Lord Palmerston that she wished to be let in on policy formulation. King Edward VII, who anticipated war with Germany and loathed his cousin, Emperor William II, is credited with the building of the Entente Cordiale to counter German expansionism and competition; but ultimate responsibility has always been with the cabinet. The crown could hardly expect a cabinet to last unless the Prime Minister and his Foreign Secretary retained the power of fundamental policy decisions, for which they are fully responsible to Parliament.

The Prime Minister is the most powerful official in the British government. Like the United States President, he can select or dismiss the members of his cabinet and, if he desires, shift them around if a reshuffle might avoid the dissolution of the whole cabinet and the loss of the men he wishes to work with. He will retain that power so long as his party remains the majority party in the House of Commons and continues to sustain him. "He is, in fact, though not in law, the working head of the State, endued with such a plenitude of power as no other constitutional ruler in the world possesses, not even the President of the United States." [13] This power can only be broken by a defeat at the polls or by a vote of nonconfidence, which would mean a defection within the party and indicate the end of that cabinet. Realizing this, prime ministers have been known to insist on substantial majorities in Parliament and have been inclined to look upon close votes as an indication of insufficient support in Commons.

The Prime Minister selects as Foreign Secretary a man whom

[13] R. Muir, *How Britain Is Governed*, Houghton Mifflin Company, Boston, 1935, p. 83.

he regards as one of the most capable and experienced members of his party and who also commands a prominent position in it. No approval of his selection by either house of Parliament is necessary; only the King is required to give his consent to the cabinet as submitted by the Prime Minister, which consent is usually only a formality. The Prime Minister may be assumed to be familiar with his Foreign Secretary's political views and, at least in fundamentals, to agree with him.

The Foreign Secretary, being a political appointee, is a member of the majority party (although in coalition governments this may not be the case) and acts as such when he appears before the House of Commons to answer questions—such as he consents to answer —and to defend "His Majesty's Government's" policies.

Parliament has no way of compelling the Foreign Secretary to divulge information if he insists that such information would be against the nation's interests. Neither he nor the Prime Minister can be legally compelled to outline their policies or submit the minutes of treaty negotiations.[14] The extent of such secretiveness on the part of the Foreign Office depends upon the general political outlook of the party in power. To generalize, the Conservatives are inclined to be more tightlipped than the Laborites, who, whenever in the saddle, have sought to free Parliament from the shackles of traditional diplomatic restrictions and let Parliament discuss foreign policy questions in a more outspoken manner. The elasticity of English constitutional law makes it entirely possible that such practices will gradually become more usual if the Labor Government succeeds in remaining in power for an extended period and continues its policy of comparatively open discussion.

Whatever the practice, however, the British Foreign Office is much more powerful than the U.S. Department of State. In the United States, as we have seen, the treaty-making power is in the hands of the President and the Secretary of State but controlled by the Senate directly and by the House indirectly. In Britain, this power is nominally in the hands of the King but actually is

---

[14] Theoretically, the House of Commons can force the resignation of the cabinet, or submit to dissolution and re-election, if the cabinet insists upon withholding desired information.

wielded by the Prime Minister, the Foreign Secretary and, in extraordinary cases, the cabinet. This constellation does not change even in the event of a declaration of war. If the cabinet finds that it must exercise the King's war-making power, all it needs is the King's assent. There is no legal need for parliamentary ratification and the only two ways for the house to object would be either a vote of nonconfidence or a refusal to pass money appropriations. In practice, the cabinet would refrain from using its war-making power unless Parliament agrees in advance: "No British Government would consider a declaration of war against a great power without the support of the people." [15]

The British foreign secretary is considerably freer in making his decisions than is the American Secretary of State. He will decide many important questions upon his own authority and confer with the Prime Minister only in major issues. If conditions force him to depart from traditionally established policies that might affect the fate of the Commonwealth, he would consult with the entire cabinet. In pursuing established policies, however, he is free to make his own decisions. He will, of course, rely heavily on the expert advice of the Foreign Office staff of permanent officials, who are a highly selected group of experienced civil servants, comparatively well paid, and in practice are secure from parliamentary attacks and protected from extreme budgetary fluctuations.

THE SECRETARY OF STATE FOR FOREIGN AFFAIRS (FOREIGN SECRETARY)

The office of the Foreign Secretary has a long history in England: it was first established about 700 years ago by Henry III. The Secretary is officially responsible, to the crown and to Parliament, for the conduct of foreign affairs, but then, the cabinet as a whole is collectively responsible, too. Lack of confidence in the Foreign Secretary usually means lack of confidence in the

[15] W. I. Jennings, *The British Constitution*, Cambridge University Press, London, 1941, p. 189.

entire cabinet except in cases where the Prime Minister dismisses and replaces him of his own volition. If the Prime Minister supports the Foreign Secretary's policies, he may appear before Commons and call for a test vote. Parliament may then decide to give the cabinet its way, particularly if the government has, in domestic matters, acted according to Parliament's desires. If it does not, the cabinet will resign *in toto*. This is in conformity with the British parliamentary practice (contrary to the American) of general cabinet responsibility.

Like most ministers of foreign affairs, the Foreign Secretary is a co-ordinator rather than a creator. His burdens of work and responsibilities are so heavy that he must, in most cases, delegate his powers to subordinates. Contrary to his American colleague's duties, his are not exclusively confined to the administration of Britain's international affairs. As an important member of a highly integrated and mutually responsible cabinet, he must pay attention to national as well as to international politics; as a prominent member of the majority party, he must be ready to appear before Commons and defend His Majesty's Government's policies. He has his formal duties toward the crown. He will have to sell his conceptions to members of the Commonwealth and Empire all over the globe, for British foreign policy vitally affects Dominion foreign policy and the Crown colonies. He must see to it that the policies of his party, and particularly his party's ideas about world politics, are presented in an acceptable form to the voting public.

He must rely, to a large measure, on the assistance of the four highest officials of the Foreign Office, immediately responsible to him: the Minister of State, the Permanent Undersecretary of State for Foreign Affairs, the Permanent Undersecretary for German Affairs and the Parliamentary Undersecretary of State for Foreign Affairs. They are about equal in rank but not in importance, for so far as foreign policy is concerned, the Permanent Undersecretary of State for Foreign Affairs is the most important man in the British government.

The Minister of State somewhat resembles the "ministers without portfolio" in many continental governments. The post was created during the World War II. The responsibilities of the Minister are not rigidly fixed; in fact, he is a roving official who may be acting for the Foreign Secretary in the latter's absence or may be entrusted with work on special political affairs, such as developed after the war. He is a member of the majority party and a political appointee. In actual policy formulation he is not nearly so influential as the Permanent Undersecretary, who is a career official, unaffiliated with party politics, and whose position is not affected by the change of cabinets or even by the shifting of governing power from one party to the other.

Endowed with ambassadorial rank, being a man of vast experience and knowledge in world affairs, enjoying a social and professional standing that sometimes even surpasses that of the Secretary himself, the permanent undersecretary is a decisive factor in the formulation of British foreign policy. Foreign policy is his field and no Foreign Secretary ignores his recommendations.

To "check and balance" his influence, there is the office of the Parliamentary Undersecretary, who must be a member of Parliament. The extent of the latter's influence depends upon his own personality. Though not necessarily an expert in foreign affairs, he may well be instrumental in initiating foreign policy if he has the ear of the Foreign Secretary and if his parliamentary standing is high. On the other hand, he may be not very much more than the mouthpiece of the Secretary before Parliament and, like the Minister of State, be sent to answer questions in Commons. Principally, his is a liaison task, bridging the gap between the Secretary and Parliament. The reorganization of the Foreign Office in 1947 created the new office of a Permanent Undersecretary of State for German Affairs. The setting up of a considerable number of departments dealing with German political, economic and security matters necessitated the supervision by a top official who could give his full and exclusive attention to these problems. Apparently, the British Government believes that it will have to deal with German issues for a long time to come; therefore the title of Undersecretary for German Affairs carries the attribute of permanency. However, the "regular" Permanent Undersecretary, the Parliamentary Undersecretary and the Minister of State outrank the Permanent Undersecretary for German Affairs.

Supervising the work of the politico-geographical divisions and the economic and functional offices are a number of Assistant Undersecretaries of State for Foreign Affairs. They are experienced career officials and have been in the diplomatic service for considerable time. Between them and the offices of the Undersecretaries, two Deputy Undersecretaries serve as a co-ordinating link, one being concerned with political, the other with economic affairs.

There is no legal department proper in the Foreign Office. Legal advisors are not executives of the Foreign Office; their work is purely advisory in matters of English or international law. There are five Legal Advisors.

Mention should be made of the private secretaries to the Secretary of State who are officials of considerable importance. There are four of them whose duties are manifold. They insure proper liaison between the Secretary and other government agencies as well as the royal household and the cabinet secretariat. They act as intermediaries to the representatives of foreign governments in London and are the Secretary's aides in connection with Parliament. They may be compared to the cabinet of the French Foreign Minister rather than to the Executive Secretariat of the United States Secretary since the latter is a secretariat proper.

THE FOREIGN OFFICE

Like the U.S. State Department, the Foreign Office has been compelled to expand greatly since World War II. It used to be a comparatively small but efficient organization. The fact that its staff consists mainly of permanent civil servants (whose security is not, as is the case in the United States, constantly threatened by budgetary troubles, insufficient pay, or eternal abuse by Congress and the public) has contributed much to its expert working organization.

Altogether, the British Foreign Office consists of forty-nine departments, not counting the offices of the Secretary, Undersecretaries, Assistant Undersecretaries, and Legal Advisor.[16]

Like other European foreign offices, the British Foreign Office consists of four main groups of "departments": (1) the top level offices as described above; (2) the political (or geographical) departments; (3) the functional, technical and administrative departments, including those offices that deal with specialized "subject" matter; (4) the information departments. It is noteworthy that, in contrast to the U.S. State Department, information and cultural relations bureaus have acquired considerable status in the British Foreign Office—as in all other European foreign offices—and now constitute an integral and major instrument of British foreign policy.

Inasmuch as foreign trade and questions of commercial policy are handled mainly by the Board of Overseas Trade, in co-operation with the political departments of the Foreign Office, there are comparatively few economic departments in the Foreign Office, only five of them altogether. There is, however, a Deputy Undersecretary of State in charge of economic affairs who is also in charge of economic problems in the United Nations so far as British representation is concerned.

The politico-geographical departments are organized in groups, most of them being under the general direction of an Assistant Undersecretary. There is no such clear-cut regional division into coherent areas as in the State Department. For example, there is one group of departments comprising the following areas: Eastern Department (including Iraq, Iran, the Persian Gulf area, Saudi Arabia, Israel, the Lebanon, Jordan, the Yemen and Palestine); African Department (including Egypt, Tangier, Liberia, Ethiopia, the Anglo-Egyptian Sudan and the various colonies); Middle East Secretariat (charged with political, social, and economic affairs of the Middle East); and the United States Section of the American Department.

The Latin American Section of the same Department, which is responsible for all countries south of the Rio Grande, is at-

---

[16] Most of the departments in charge of German affairs may be considered temporary and will presumably be merged or liquidated in the future.

tached to another group of geographic bureaus, comprising the Northern and Southern Departments. The Northern Department includes the Scandinavian countries, Finland, Iceland, the Baltic States, Czechoslovakia, Poland and the USSR. The Southern Department deals with Turkey, Greece, Trieste, Yugoslavia, Hungary, Bulgaria, Rumania, Albania, and Danubian problems in general. Under the Western Department which is grouped with the German Political and Internal Departments, come the Iberian and Benelux countries, France, Italy, the Vatican and Switzerland. This important Department also works on issues regarding the Brussels Treaty, the Western Union, the North Atlantic Pact and European problems in general. Some additional departments deal with German problems, such as German economy, commercial relations, finances and personnel of the British occupation, education, and information.

The Far Eastern areas are organized in two major geographic units: the Far East Department (including China, Japan, Korea, the Philippines, and general Pacific questions); and the South-East Asia Department (including Singapore, Thailand, French Indo-China, Nepal, Tibet, Indonesia, Afghanistan, Burma, India, Pakistan, and Ceylon); this department also co-ordinates policies in the political, economic and administrative fields of South-East Asia. A third unit within this group is the Commonwealth Liaison Department, organized for the purpose of maintaining liaison on foreign policy between the government of the United Kingdom and the Commonwealth governments.

Most of these groups of departments are supervised by an Assistant Undersecretary of State.

As in the U.S. State Department, the political detail work is done by experienced "desk" officers who have served in the countries of their jurisdiction. They are in constant and close touch with the functional departments such as the Economic Intelligence and Economic Relations Departments, the European Recovery Department, the General Department (communications), the United Nations Departments,[17] the Information Departments and others.

[17] Cf. p. 248 ff.

There are five information and cultural relations departments in the Foreign Office, namely, the Departments of Information Policy, Information Research, Information Services
(operational), Cultural Relations, and German Education and
Information. The Information Policy Department is geographically organized and represents the Foreign Office on the official
interdepartmental Overseas Information Services Committee,
which combines under its supervision all media of international information and cultural relations: (1) the information
services attached to the Foreign Office; (2) cultural relations
(handled by the semiofficial British Council for Relations with
other nations); (3) travel (in conjunction with the Board of
Trade); (4) the British Broadcasting Corporation (BBC), also a
semiofficial agency of the British Government though not a part
of it.[18]

Particularly important is the Library of the Foreign Office,
whose functions are much more essential than its name indicates.
Supervised by a "Director of Research, Librarian and Keeper of
the Papers" it is "in fact one of the most important administrative
departments of the British Foreign Office."[19] The reorganization of the Foreign Office in the middle forties left its privileged
status untouched and strengthened it further by attaching to it a
new Research Department.[20] This is because nothing has proved
more essential for an agency dealing with world affairs than background knowledge, expert information, and documentary evidence.

As mentioned above, the Foreign Office was a comparatively
small ministry before World War II, in fact, hardly more than
the headquarters of the British Foreign Service (which in principle it still is). When it was reorganized in 1943 there was created
an amalgamated Foreign Service consisting of the officers of the
Foreign Office, the Diplomatic Service, the Consular Service and

---

[18] Cf. p. 209 ff. on information and cultural relations.
[19] H. K. Norton, Foreign Office Organization, *Annals of the American
Academy of Political and Social Science*, Supplement to Vol. CXLIII, May 1929,
p. 8.
[20] Cf. p. 92.

the Commercial Diplomatic Service. Different from the U.S. State Department, where there still is a sharp differentiation between departmental personnel and foreign service officers and clerks, the British Foreign Office personnel is interchangeable throughout. At the same time, the agency expanded considerably, owing to the vaster and more complex international problems; it also democratized its foreign service by amalgamating diplomatic and consular services and by drawing personnel from more varied social groups, thus vigorously rejuvenating the once proverbially old-fashioned staff.[21]

FRANCE

CONSTITUTIONAL ISSUES REGARDING CONDUCT OF FOREIGN AFFAIRS

In October, 1946, a new constitution was adopted by the French people, superseding the old one of 1875, which for all practical purposes had already been killed by the inglorious intermezzo of Vichy.

The conduct of foreign affairs in the Fourth French Republic, according to the new constitution, has been changed considerably. Of almost a hundred articles, only five deal directly with foreign relations but they clearly express the desire on the part of the framers of the constitution that popular control over French foreign policy be brought under strict control of the National Assembly and, therefore, under the supervision of the political parties for which the people voted and which supposedly represent the people's will in matters concerning the position of France in the world.

Under the constitution of the Third Republic, the President of the Republic was a mere figurehead. He presided in sessions of the Council of Ministers but could not vote. He had to sign laws and treaties—in fact he had to ratify treaties just as the English King does—but he had even less actual power than the British

[21] Cf. p. 190 ff.

monarch. The constitution of 1875 gave the President control over treaty negotiation and ratification "subject only to the requirement of informing the Chambers as soon as the interest and security of the State permit and the further requirement of securing the consent of the Chambers for all treaties affecting peace, commerce, territory, finance and the personal and property rights of French nationals abroad," [22] really quite complete and effective limitations of presidential power. Such treaties had to be countersigned by the responsible minister. The minister, and not the President, assumed responsibility, however, so that the President's signature was a mere formality. Just as the British government rules in the name of the King, so the French government used to act in the name of the President of the Republic.

In the new constitution, these presidential duties were further curtailed. He will be "kept informed about international negotiations" (Art. XXXI); he has to accredit "Ambassadors and envoys extraordinary to foreign powers; foreign Ambassadors and envoys extraordinary are accredited to him." (Art. XXXI.) There is no further reference to his activities in foreign relations, for the war-making power (Art. VII) and the treaty-making power (Art. XXVI-XXVIII) are clearly put up to the Chambers for approval and ratification.

The constitution of 1946, however, did not appreciably change the executive powers of the cabinet except perhaps that it gave the Chambers somewhat more influence, although this grant is not intended to be used to the detriment of governmental continuity. It is stated in this constitution (Art. XLVIII) that the cabinet is collectively responsible to the National Assembly (the former Chamber of Deputies) but not to the Council of the Republic (the former Senate). But provisions in Articles L and LII are made to avoid the all too frequent changes in the administration due to cabinet crises which made prewar France an easy prey to disorganization and instability. The Constitution also established a penal responsibility of the ministers, a provision never before incorporated in any democratic constitution (Title Seven).

[22] F. L. Schuman, *War and Diplomacy in the French Republic*, Whittlesey House, McGraw-Hill Book Company, New York, 1931, p. 19.

The Premier designate, officially called President of the Council of Ministers, is asked by the President to form a cabinet just as the King of England charges the Prime Minister with a similar task. But while in Great Britain the list of ministers is subject to approval by the King only, the French President must wait until the National Assembly confirms the Premier's selection. If the Assembly confirms, the President will sign. In other words, the cabinet cannot function, nor has it the right to start working, before the Assembly has given the go-ahead signal. The ministers, being party members and, of course, political appointees, have the right to be heard by the Chambers at any time and may appear in the Chambers whenever they so desire.

In view of these circumstances, the relationship between the French Premier and his Foreign Minister resembles that between the British Prime Minister and his Foreign Secretary. The difference lies in the degree of power at the disposal of the respective foreign offices, and there is no doubt that the French Ministry of Foreign Affairs is now much less powerful and much more subject to parliamentary control than is the British Foreign Office.

Whether or not the French Chambers had in fact influence upon the formulation of French foreign policy during the period of the Third Republic is debatable. Such an expert as Frederick L. Schuman does not believe that for practical purposes the influence was a strong one,[23] in spite of the constitutional provisions that the Chambers were to be informed on treaty negotiations unless the security of the state was endangered; that it had to approve peace treaties and commercial agreements; that it was supreme in matters of financial appropriations, territorial changes and, of course, declarations of war. However, the power of interpellation, that is, the raising of policy questions in public debate, may be regarded as a strong instrument of democratic control over the conduct of foreign affairs; failure to furnish satisfactory answers has shortened the lives of many a cabinet.

Presumably the framers of the new constitution knew that the prewar Chambers could not exercise enough control over French

[23] See F. L. Schuman, *op. cit.* pp. 24-26.

foreign affairs, so they strengthened the hold of the National Assembly over the government and thereby logically over foreign policy decisions. In no other democratic country have political parties, as represented in a parliament, so much actual and potential power over the government as in France. How this power will be used and whether it can be used to the advantage of French relations with the world remain to be seen.

THE MINISTER OF FOREIGN AFFAIRS AND HIS CABINET

As has already been indicated, the position of the Minister of Foreign Affairs resembles that of the British Foreign Secretary in that he is the responsible agent for French foreign relations and his responsibility is shared by the Premier and the cabinet. However, so far as his co-operation with the Chambers is concerned, his duties may rather be compared with those of the United States Secretary of State. Like his American and British colleagues, he is a political appointee rather than a foreign affairs expert. This means that he, too, must rely upon expert advice. Yet, contrary to American practice, he can commit the nation in a way that would make it extremely awkward for the National Assembly to turn him down and, as a consequence, let it appear that the nation's foreign commitments cannot always be regarded as definite. As a result, his power is considerable although the new constitution has strengthened popular supervision over international treaty obligations.

The French Foreign Minister has at his disposal an official cabinet, which, in the way it works, is a unique institution. Created in 1912, it is hardly comparable to the "little cabinet" of the United States Secretary of State. It is presided over by a Director of Cabinet, who has a Chief of Cabinet (*"chef de cabinet"*), assistant chiefs, and diplomats of all grades who have had much experience in foreign affairs. Attached to the cabinet of the Foreign Minister is a bureau of couriers and a special telephone and cable service. The cabinet has a variety of duties, all designed to ease the load of the Minister and to cushion relations between him and the Chambers, the press, and the public. For example, it takes care of the Minister's personal correspondence, handles diplomatic visas and passports, takes care of relations with the Chambers, arranges for press conferences, gives information, and co-ordinates official foreign travel, especially via air and by boat.

It may be assumed that most of the members of the Minister's Cabinet are known to the Minister personally; they act as his "personal office staff" but it is denied by French officials of the Ministry that the Cabinet is to be a buffer between the Minister and the permanent officials of the Ministry on whose activities it is supposed to check.[24]

Equally important from the point of view of administration but certainly more influential in political respects is the office of the Secretary General of the Ministry of Foreign Affairs, the French version of the British Permanent Undersecretary. He is the highest expert on foreign affairs in the ministry, a career man on whose advice the Minister has to rely heavily. All the political, functional, economic, and administrative offices of the ministry are under his supervision. There is close collaboration between him and the Legal Advisor.

This office consists of three specialized secretariats. One deals with particular problems outside routine business (*Secrétariat Particulier*); the second is the secretariat of conferences (*Secrétariat des Conférences*), whose task it is to prepare international conferences, documentation of peace treaties, and, most of all, liaison between the French government and the United Nations, including the affairs of UNESCO. This secretariat also handles matters concerning war crimes. Finally there is the ministerial secretariat (*Secrétariat du Ministère*), supervising the organization of functional services such as that of the couriers, registration of incoming reports, and general administrative centralization. This secretariat is designed to give the Secretary General co-ordinated information on what is going on in the ministry and to check up on the efficiency of its organization.

[24] H. K. Norton, *op. cit.*, p. 13.

THE MINISTRY OF FOREIGN AFFAIRS

On the whole the organization of the French Foreign Ministry, like the British and American foreign offices, may be roughly divided into top-level offices, political and economic divisions, and functional-administrative departments. There are, however, a number of interesting differences between the French and the Anglo-Saxon foreign offices.

Next to the offices of the Secretary General, there are four main *Directions générales* of (1) political affairs, (2) economic, financial, and technical affairs, (3) administrative affairs, and (4) cultural relations. As the name indicates, each of these offices is headed by a director general, whose position approximately corresponds with that of an American Assistant Secretary or a British Assistant Undersecretary.

The Office of the Director General for Political Affairs comprises five directorates. The position of the director is roughly equivalent to that of an office director in the U.S. Department of State. There are four political directorates and one for press and information services. The political directorates are subdivided into subdirectorates and, in certain cases, into divisions or bureaus. In view of the changes of the French Ministry of Foreign Affairs after the end of World War II, a somewhat detailed account of its new organization, as of 1948, will be given below.

European Directorate. This handles political problems and correspondence concerning the political situation in the world in general and in Europe in particular. It works on issues of national defense and international law concerning European countries. It deals with economic, administrative and cultural questions, in so far as their nature is also political. It co-operates with the specialized departments of other ministries and supervises the work of the military, naval, and air attachés abroad.

The Subdirection (*Sous-Direction*) of Northern Europe is charged with affairs concerning Great Britain, Ireland, Belgium, the Netherlands, Luxemburg, Scandinavian countries, Finland, and Iceland.

The Subdirection of Central Europe handles Germany, Austria, Hungary, and Liechtenstein.

The Subdirection of Southern Europe deals with Spain, Portugal, Italy, Switzerland, the Vatican, Monaco, and Andorra.

The Subdirection of Eastern Europe works on relations with the Soviet Union, Poland, Czechoslovakia, Yugoslavia, Rumania, Bulgaria, Albania, and Greece.

Attached to the European direction is a so-called *Bureau d'ordre*, a centralized file and documentation section for the use of the European offices. A similar bureau is attached to each of the directorates.

Asia-Oceania Directorate. This handles all political questions concerning countries and territories in Asia and the Pacific, except the Hawaiian Islands and Asia Minor. There is only one subdirection and two divisions (apart from the *Bureau d'ordre*): Subdirection of the Far East; Pacific Division; Central Asia Division.

Africa-Levant Directorate. This office takes care of the political problems of African and Levant states and territories but also is concerned with the political direction of the protectorates of Morocco and Tunisia.

The Subdirection of Protectorates is charged with the political affairs of Tunisia, the French zone of Morocco, the French Zone of Tangier and Libya. There are two divisions dealing with Morocco and Tunisia.

The Subdirection of the Levant and Arab states deals with Egypt, Turkey, Syria, the Lebanon, Trans-Jordan, Iraq, Saudi-Arabia, the Yemen, and Israel.

The African bureau deals with Ethiopia, Union of South-Africa, Liberia and European possessions in Africa.

American Directorate. The Subdirection of North America deals with the United States (including Puerto Rico, Alaska and Hawaii), Canada and Newfoundland.

The Subdirection of South America comprises all Latin American countries south of the Rio Grande.

Director of Information and Press Services. The importance attributed to this directorate is demonstrated by its incorporation with the political offices under the general supervision of the Di-

ORGANIZATION OF THE FRENCH FOREIGN MINISTRY

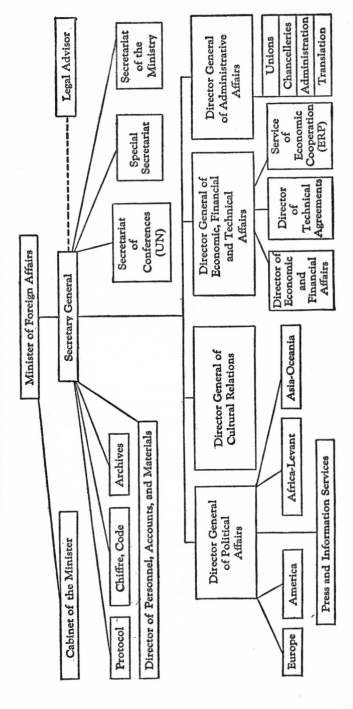

rector General of Political Affairs. Its general duties are: maintenance of relations with the press and the public; specific and general information on foreign relations; study and analysis of the French and foreign press, press agencies, and radio; liaison with the Ministry of Information and the official French press and radio agencies, as well as with political writers in the French press and French correspondents abroad; accrediting of foreign correspondents; maintenance of a press file for documentation and reference. The five special sections are:

> Section of the French Press
> Section of the Foreign Press
> Section of Foreign Services
> Section of Press Agencies and Radio
> Section of Documentation
> Administrative Section

The second *Direction Générale,* dealing with economic, financial, and technical affairs, is subdivided into two directorates: the Director of Economic and Financial Affairs whose three divisions handle geographically delimited areas, and the Director of Technical Agreements, whose two divisions are charged with problems arising out of French goods in foreign countries (including restitution of those seized by the Germans) and negotiations concerning international transport and foreign goods in France in accordance with international conventions.

It is not necessary here to describe in detail the work of the third *Direction Générale* for Administration. However, the fourth one, concerned with cultural relations, is of particular interest. The French governments have always rightly presumed that dissemination of French culture abroad created prestige that helped the French to reach their political objectives. To this end they have consistently worked to have France and Paris be considered the light and epitome of Western Civilization. The Fourth Republic has strengthened rather than weakened this conception and, as a result, seen to it that cultural relations work is prominently organized in its foreign office. Thus a Director General, one of the four highest officials under the Secretary

General, is in charge of the responsibility for cultural relations with foreign countries and the presentation of French achievements abroad. The office recommends credits for French instruction and art abroad, works for the distribution of books and the sending abroad of cultural missions, organizes art exhibits and artistic demonstrations of French achievements in other fields of art and handicrafts, participates in international cultural conventions and subsidizes cultural organizations that promote French culture.[25]

The remaining four offices deal with protocol, cryptography and codes, archives, and personnel. (It is noteworthy that the Department of Protocol has, even in France, lost much of its former importance and influence. This is especially interesting as the prestige of the French language as "the language of diplomacy" was to a significant degree based upon the leadership of the French in developing the amenities of diplomatic courtesy. While today the elaborate protocol has changed into a more businesslike approach in international relations, and moreover, the balance of power has changed, the French language has lost its paramount position, and there is no longer one language of diplomacy, but many.)

The four offices are also under the general supervision of the Secretary General.

The personnel of the Ministry is interchangeable with that of the diplomatic and consular services.

NAZI GERMANY, A POST-MORTEM

Nazi Germany, of course, is no more. Many years may pass before Germany will be able (and permitted) to organize a new foreign office. Yet for the student of the machinery of foreign-policy making, a brief post-mortem of the Nazi Ministry of Foreign Affairs offers a variety of instructive insights into totalitarian techniques of handling relations with other countries. After all, Nazi Germany was the leading country of rightist

[25] Cf. p. 218 ff.

totalitarianism; the conceptions of international relations professed by the Nazi hierarchy offer significant pointers that may be useful for comparison with other types of totalitarian policy making establishments.

CONTROL OF IDEOLOGICAL DICTATORSHIP OVER FOREIGN RELATIONS

The much maligned Weimar Constitution, the first honest attempt at democracy in Germany, contained provisions that sought to guarantee popular participation in deciding Germany's position in the world. Following their established practices, the Nazis ignored this constitution; instead they decreed that all war and treaty making power should remain in the hands of the Fuehrer. It was up to him to decide whether to use expert advice from his Foreign Ministry or to rely on his "intuition."

Consequently, Hitler alone was primarily responsible for foreign policies. Ribbentrop, his Foreign Minister during the last years of the Third Reich, no doubt recommended a number of actions that were accepted, but they were accepted only because they coincided with Hitler's own ideas and conceptions. The German rubber-stamp "parliament," the *Reichstag*, was only convoked to hear what Hitler wanted to say to the world; it had no influence upon decisions.

Thus, the Foreign Minister became a minor official charged with being the mouthpiece of the Fuehrer and the Party and a type of glorified global messenger for his chief. His responsibility was restricted, in fact, to the administration of the Ministry, which, in turn, had become a technical-administrative agency with little political influence but with an exceedingly thorough organization and a complex system of bureaus, divisions, and subdivisions.

THE ORGANIZATION OF THE NAZI
FOREIGN MINISTRY

There were ten offices in the Ministry, each subdivided according to geographic areas and subject matter. (It will be recalled that the foreign offices in the United States, Britain, and France do not use this double organization but limit themselves to politico-geographic distinctions.)

The ten offices dealt with political, economic, legal, cultural, press, radio, protocol, personnel, and domestic affairs. (There were two "Inland" offices.) [26] The list or table of organization of these offices with their double-divided branches and sections was as follows:

Political Affairs, subdivided into the following two groups of divisions:

Geographic	*Subject Matter*
1. British Commonwealth and Ireland	1. History of prewar and war periods; postwar organization; general information
2. France, Belgium, Netherlands, Switzerland	2. Technical boundary questions; map service
3. Spain and Portugal	3. Special section on interdepartmental collaboration on the USSR
4. Italy and Vatican	4. Examination of literature on foreign affairs
5. USSR and Poland	5. Liaison with armed forces
6. S.E. Europe (Balkans)	6. Press section
7. Scandinavian Countries	7. Preparation of peace treaties
8. Turkey and Near East	
9. Far East	
10. United States and Latin America	
11. Africa	

[26] See p. 139.

Economic Affairs. The divisions and subdivisions of this office dealt mainly with commercial treaties, customs, laws, international treaties, inasmuch as commerce was concerned, and exhibitions and fairs abroad. It may be presumed that its geographic divisions prepared Germany's economic penetration of satellite or conquered states.

Geographic Divisions	*Subject Matter*
1. British Commonwealth and USA	1. Office of Foreign Trade (in collaboration with Commerce Dept.)
2. Southern and Western Europe, subdivided into: (a) France, Belgium, Netherlands; (b) Spain and Portugal; (c) Switzerland, Liechtenstein; (d) Italian Empire	2. Raw material supply
3. Southeastern Europe, subdivided into: (a) Slovakia, Hungary, Croatia; (b) Serbia, Greece, Albania; (c) Rumania, Bulgaria	3. Mails, transportation agreements, air travel, railroads
4. USSR, Poland, Baltic States	4. Shipping
5. Scandinavian countries, Finland	
6. Near East (Turkey, Iran, Iraq, Egypt, Afghanistan, Syria, Lebanon)	
7. Far East (Japan, China, Manchuria)	
8. Middle and South America	

Legal Affairs. (The organization of this office was adapted to wartime functions.) It is of interest to recognize Nazi politics in the distribution of responsibilities throughout the twelve divisions:

1. General questions of international law
2. International civil law; matters concerning registration of births, marriages and deaths abroad (sic!) of people they considered German
3. Consular law; patents; international criminal law; extraditions
4. Intervention on behalf of German nationals abroad; financial support of families of German nationals abroad
5. Drafting into the army of German nationals abroad
6. Passports and visas for diplomats
7. German property in enemy countries; enemy property in Germany
8. Relations with protecting powers and international aid societies relating to civil internees in Germany
9. Relations with protecting powers and international aid societies regarding prisoners of war (subdivisions handling British, American and French prisoners)
10. German prisoners of war abroad
11. Internment matters in neutral countries; medical traveling commissions
12. Exchange of prisoners of war and civilian internees

Cultural Affairs. This office, too, was divided into two groups of divisions. Those dealing with subject matter were concerned with general questions of cultural policy; preparation of informative materials; examination of German literature as to its use abroad; theater, films, music, exhibitions; scientific questions; encouragement of the German language abroad; university questions; budget of the cultural divisions. The second group of divisions worked along geographic lines for the "improvement of cultural relations" and was separated into United States, Latin-American, Southeast European, Scandinavian, Italian, Spanish and Portuguese, French-Belgian-Swiss, British and British Commonwealth, Turkish, Near and Far Eastern, and African sections. It should be noted that there was a distinct separation between the cultural and press divisions.

Press Affairs were also organized along geographical and subject matter lines. Next to the geographical divisions, which were divided in much the same way as the cultural divisions, there were divisions concerned with: press information for German embassies, legations and diplomatic missions; issuance of a daily political report; technical direction of the receiving of press representatives; observation of the foreign press, and dissemination to the higher officials in the Foreign Ministry of information on the results; liaison with German and foreign newspapermen; liaison with newspapers and periodicals for foreign workers in Germany; organization of journeys of foreign newspaper reporters; passport questions. It is interesting and very significant that cultural and informational communications were treated in a highly specialized manner.

Radio Affairs. In addition to the divisions covering cultural and press affairs, there was also a specialized office dealing with radio affairs. It maintained close liaison with the press divisions and was responsible for giving radio information to German diplomatic representatives (and German spies and intelligence operatives) abroad. It was organized along geographic lines and monitored radio transmissions from the British and Commonwealth senders and those in France, Belgium, Netherlands, Switzerland, Southeastern Europe, the Soviet Union, Scandinavian countries including Finland, the United States, and the Far East. There was attached to this office a unit charged with recording foreign radio emissions.

It is not necessary here to examine the offices of personnel and protocol, but it seems worth while to refer to the two "Inland" sections. Group Inland I was responsible for liaison with the Nazi Party authorities and domestic public organizations; for questions concerning foreign laborers within the competence of the Foreign Ministry; for liaison with the highest Church authorities in Germany and German churches abroad. Group Inland II maintained technical liaison with the Ministry of the Interior, dealt with the exemption of Jewish foreigners from internal measures, and collaborated with the police authorities regarding such interventions; it also worked on problems of German minorities within the competence of the Foreign Ministry.

The tremendously detailed hierarchy of the Nazi Foreign Ministry did not make for a creative agency; instead the Foreign Office carried out the details of a policy that was created outside its own offices, by the Fuehrer and the Nazi Party. This tends to indicate that it is not so much the organization of foreign offices but the spirit behind them that is of importance. From the experience available it would seem that in some way, such a situation is bound to recur everywhere under totalitarian or one-party systems.

SOVIET UNION

CONTROLLING POWERS AND IDEOLOGICAL FACTORS

Soviet foreign policy has acquired the reputation of being "enigmatic." Yet for students of Soviet government and politics who have followed the ways of the Kremlin since the early thirties, there is not much of a riddle involved. The question as to who actually controls Soviet foreign relations can be answered as unequivocally as in the case of either democratic or fascist systems. There are many factors determining Soviet foreign policy but the Ministry of Foreign Affairs in Moscow is not the most important of them.

Constitutionally, the Supreme Soviet, as highest legislative body of the Union, possesses treaty, war, and peace making powers. Article 14 of the Constitution says that the

> jurisdiction of the USSR, as represented by its highest organs of state authority and organs of the government, covers:
> (a) representation of the Union in international relations, conclusions and ratification of treaties with other states, and the establishment of the general procedure governing the relations of Union Republics with foreign states;
> (b) questions of war and peace; . . .
> (h) foreign trade on the basis of state monopoly . . .

Actually the powers of the Supreme Soviet [27] are in the hands

---

[27] The Supreme Soviet is the parliament of the USSR, led and presided over by a presidium, which carries on the Supreme Soviet's legislative functions while it is not in session.

of its presidium, which is responsible—as the Supreme Soviet is rarely in session—for ratification of international treaties. It also "appoints and recalls plenipotentiary representatives of the USSR to foreign states" and "receives the credentials and letters of recall of diplomatic representatives accredited to it by foreign states." (Art. 49, paragraphs m and n.) The Presidium can also proclaim "a state of war in the event of armed attack on the USSR, or when necessary to fulfill international treaty obligations concerning mutual defense against aggression . . ." whenever the Supreme Soviet is not in session. (Art. 49, m.) Since experience has shown that the Supreme Soviet is nothing but a sounding board for the Soviet leaders and therefore does not in fact assume the functions of democratic parliamentary bodies, the measures of the Presidium of the Soviet parliament and the handling of foreign affairs by the leaders of the USSR will hardly be affected by possible divergent opinions in the plenary sessions of the Supreme Soviet. Thus popular control of foreign relations in the organization that allegedly represents the people is virtually eliminated and whatever appears to exist is purely academic.

But the Presidium of the Supreme Soviet itself is only a reflection of the greatest power in the USSR, the Communist Party. For the party rules the country. It has assumed a "guiding and directing role" in all Soviet government agencies. Andrei Vyshinsky himself has stated so in particular reference to Soviet foreign relations.[28]

This does not mean necessarily that Communist Party members within the Soviet Ministry of Foreign Affairs (Minindel) [29] wield much influence in policy making. Just as in other Soviet government agencies and establishments, party representatives work in the Minindel, too. They have even organized a so-called "Active," which is permitted to submit suggestions concerning foreign affairs but which apparently has never carried any ap-

[28] A. Vyshinsky, *Sovietskoye Gosudarstvennoye Pravo*, Moscow, 1938, p. 153.
[29] Until March 15, 1946, the name of the Soviet foreign office was People's Commissariat for Foreign Affairs, abbreviated NARKOMINDEL. Then the Commissariat became a Ministry and the abbreviation accordingly changed into MININDEL, and the Commissars became Ministers.

preciable weight in policy determination. However, it does mean that the party leadership, interpreting the political ideology of the USSR according to conditions and opportunities, issues directives known as "party lines," that these orders are being followed as the law of the land, and that Soviet foreign policy and diplomacy are oriented accordingly. The Minindel gets these directives and must implement them. It does not as a rule contribute to their creation except by furnishing background studies.

While theoretically distinct, Party and Government in the USSR are for all practical purposes identical. Most top leaders of the party are top leaders in government. This is clearly indicated in the composition of the Political Bureau of the Central Committee of the Communist Party, or abbreviated, Politbureau. Since May, 1941, its Chairman, Stalin, was also Prime Minister; its presumed Vice-Chairman, Molotov, Foreign Minister. Some of the other members are at the helm of important government agencies. The same principle is demonstrated in the membership of the Council of Ministers [30] or in the Presidium of the Supreme Soviet. In former years, this was not necessarily so; Moscow's Foreign Ministers, of the twenties and thirties, Chicherin and Litvinov, had no standing in the party whatever, but since the collapse of "collective security," the leading foreign policy officials have been party members of high standing. In this way, they are in a strategic position to recommend and defend policies. The Minindel has profited by their leaders' importance in the party. While its relative influence is limited, it is still the second most important government agency in the Stalinist hierarchy, ranking just behind the Ministry of Defense.

When important foreign policies are to be formulated, the Politbureau assumes an all-decisive power. It will listen to the views of the Council of Ministers and the Foreign Minister; it will consider the opinions of other high party or government officials but finally make up its own mind and transmit its orders to the Presidium of the Supreme Soviet and the Council of

[30] Consisting of the heads of the various government agencies with predominantly technical rather than political functions.

Ministers. There is no way of opposing or influencing the Politbureau's decisions, and the Supreme Soviet has always and will in
the future obediently vote for the recommended legislation if it
is in session, or give its ex post facto consent as required.[31]

The Constitution further provides that the active conduct of
Foreign Affairs be vested in the Council of Ministers and the
Minindel, with the Supreme Soviet or its Presidium having con-
firming or ratifying powers. This sounds very democratic indeed
but actually, Soviet foreign policy is but a part of Soviet over-all
ideology. Therefore, Soviet foreign policy remains subject to
ideological factors, of which the Politbureau is the supreme
guardian.

The concept of the position of the USSR in the world is
naturally shaped by modified Leninist-Stalinist Marxism. Since
Trotsky's theory of "permanent revolution"—which was tantamount to a permanent state of war against non-Marxist powers—
was discarded in favor of consolidation of the Soviet territories
(Stalin's dictum of "socialism in one country"), the non-Soviet
world has been led to believe that in international relations a
"co-existence" of the socialist Soviet Union (which has not as yet
reached the stage of a communist classless society) with the non-
Marxist states was possible. Indeed, the co-operation between
Russia and the democracies during World War II seemed to
demonstrate such a possibility. In the democracies, the frequent
clashes with Russian policies, methods, and unfriendly propaganda
were taken as necessary evils, which did not really reflect upon
East-West collaboration. More of this collaboration was expected
in postwar years, particularly through the United Nations
organization.[32]

---

[31] Little is known about the way the Politbureau arrives at policy decisions. It
is probably a mistake to believe that Soviet policies are formulated in unanimous
harmony by the members of this highest council of the USSR. Frequent speculations about a "moderate" and a "radical" faction, battling each other, with
Stalin making final decisions as the supreme arbiter, may or may not be wrong;
one could, however, deduce from events such as the rift between the Yugoslav
Tito regime and the Kremlin-directed Cominform that Soviet foreign policy is
not altogether monolithic.

[32] Cf. K. London, *op. cit.*, p. 245 ff.

However, the years following the end of World War II clearly demonstrated that the original Marxist dogma concerning capitalist countries and their eventual downfall as against the rise of communism continued to dominate Soviet foreign policy. It appeared that from the point of view of the Communist Party, the doctrine of a possible "socialism in one country" was but a temporary expedient for the strengthening of the Soviet state. The nature of Soviet foreign policy and action inside and outside the United Nations made it clear that the Politbureau had only suspended, never abolished, its consistent views on the ultimate and unavoidable struggle between the communist and capitalist worlds.

In view of this principle, which until recently was minimized by the world's foreign offices, Soviet foreign policy had to develop in a two-pronged fashion. The *official* policies were announced through the Narkomindel, the *unofficial*—though real—ones through the Communist International (Comintern).

The Comintern, as will be recalled, was an aggressive attempt at organizing Communist infiltration in foreign countries so as to undermine the stability of foreign governments and nations by way of ideological Trojan Horse tactics. Thereby the position of the Soviet Union was to be strengthened as the Communist world center and base for future actual warfare against non-Communist countries. The abolition of the Comintern in 1943, which was greeted with enthusiasm throughout the non-Marxist world, did not mean that the Soviet government intended to abolish the underlying ideas of that organization. It felt that the activities of the Comintern had served its purposes and that it could transfer Comintern objectives to different agencies without changing its aims. In view of its ideological foundation, Soviet policy has been quite successful at achieving several goals with one policy; the liquidation of the Comintern, apparently a gesture to win the confidence of Russia's capitalist wartime allies, proved to be nothing but the closing of a series of offices whose foreign branches could not be maintained during the war, and the incorporation of the duties of these offices into other organizations.

But in one respect, the liquidation of the Comintern was

important: Soviet foreign policy became at last consolidated. Formerly, foreign office and Comintern policies were often at loggerheads and confused the world, particularly during the years when men like Chicherin or Litvinov tried to make the USSR respectable in international diplomacy. Then the Comintern, directed by Bolsheviks who did not believe in the possibility of reconciliation between the two worlds, threw obstacles in the way of the Narkomindel and repeatedly set out to ruin whatever confidence the Narkomindel had been able to build up.

The years of war silenced Bolshevik aggressiveness somewhat. But when the war was won and the Soviet Union had become a world power second only to the United States, the Communist party leaders did not see any further reason for holding back and changed their tactics again. This time, they frankly superimposed the party's foreign policy upon the Minindel's foreign policy. Or perhaps one should say that the policy of the party destroyed whatever had remained from the pre-Molotov era. For the first time, Soviet foreign policy was single-minded. Leading members of the Comintern's former executive committee had now become leading statesmen in countries like Yugoslavia, Bulgaria, Rumania, Albania, Hungary, Poland, and Czechoslovakia, or influential oppositionists, some of them as members of the government, in countries like China, France or Italy.

The establishment of the Communist Information Bureau (Cominform) in Belgrade, Yugoslavia (which after the Tito government's schism from Moscow-led orthodox Communism was transferred to Bucharest, Rumania) revived officially the activities of the Comintern though in a different form and for different purposes. The Cominform will execute rather than formulate policies outlined in Moscow. The Soviet Union, having established itself as a world power and having become supreme in Eastern Europe, no longer needed two policy agencies. Communist and "national" foreign policy have become one and the same in the Soviet orbit.

There is yet another aspect of the organization and control over Soviet foreign policy: the position of the Union republics. During the history of the USSR the status of these republics with regard to participation in international relations has changed two times. Until 1923, each of the republics was permitted to maintain foreign relations of its own. From 1923, an all-Union Narkomindel took over and represented the Union as well as the republics. Emissaries of the republics, appointed by the Council of People's Commissars of the individual Union republics, represented the views of their governments at the Narkomindel. In a reverse manner, these emissaries instructed their "state" governments about possible obligations concerning international treaties that might be of special interest for the respective republics.

Again, in February 1944, this system was changed and the Union republics were permitted to enter into negotiations with foreign governments directly. As a result, there are now theoretically 16 foreign offices in the USSR, two of which are recognized members of the United Nations (Ukraine and White Russia). This does not mean that the Union republics in practice initiate business with foreign nations without first being advised to do so by the Moscow central authorities. All treaties concluded between the Union republics and foreign powers must be approved by the Supreme Soviet of the Union republics and that of the USSR. One may safely assume that any such treaty negotiation would not even get under way without preliminary permission from the Politbureau.

This apparent autonomy of the republics has affected Soviet foreign relations in several ways. First, it has created a larger representation of Soviet views on the international forum of the UN.[33] Second, it has relieved the Minindel of the USSR of minor issues or of embarrassing problems that could be sidetracked through Union republic intervention. Third, it has emphasized the independence granted by the USSR to the constituent republics in the fields of foreign relations, foreign trade, and national

[33] This was agreed upon at the Yalta Conference in 1945 in view of the fact that the participation of the British dominions and that of the Latin-American nations were looked upon by the Soviet government as strengthening the British and American positions respectively. While such a comparison was rejected, Stalin's request for the admission of the Ukraine and White Russia was granted by Prime Minister Churchill and President Roosevelt.

defense. Fourth, it has provided an attractive propaganda item for domestic consumption by arousing both nationalistic and ideological fervor.

These are, very briefly, some of the more important aspects of control over Soviet foreign relations. To realize their meaning it must never be forgotten that "the summit of Communist hopes and aspirations is, in the last analysis, today as in Lenin's time, a complete change of the world's political, economic, social and cultural set-up, and at the base of Soviet foreign policy lies the desire to make the world safe for communism or sovietism." [34] In this sense, Soviet foreign policy is but a tool of global class warfare on a gigantic scale, and its machinery is organized accordingly.

THE FOREIGN MINISTER AND HIS ADVISORY BODIES

The position of the Foreign Minister is not predicated upon the fact that he is chief of the Minindel but depends upon his standing in the Communist Party and his connection with the Politbureau. Thus Molotov who was not only a senior member of the Politbureau but also Vice-Chairman of the Council of Ministers and whose standing in the party hierarchy is high, exercised a much greater influence upon the formulation of foreign policy than did men like Litvinov, who, for all his astuteness and diplomatic talents, was never influential with the party and was even looked upon with suspicion.

Next to the Minister, the second most important man in the Minindel is the First Assistant (or Deputy) Foreign Minister, whose position may be compared, to a degree, with that of the United States Undersecretary of State. But his influence, too, depends upon his standing in the Party. Andrei Vyshinsky, First Deputy Foreign Minister before succeeding Molotov, who was not a member of the Bolshevik party when the Russian Revolution started and is not a member of the Politbureau, happens to be in

[34] *"Trends in Russian Foreign Policy Since World War I,"* prepared by the Legislative Reference Service of the Library of Congress, U.S. Government Printing Office, Washington, D.C., 1947, p. 65.

good, though not high, standing. His influence, while consider-able, will not be comparable to that Molotov enjoyed.

Under these two men, there are a number of Deputy Ministers, whose number appears to vary as do their duties. Presumably, there are about four or five of them working on a regional basis, but at least one specializes in information and is regarded as the Minindel's mouthpiece. Some of the Deputy Ministers, particu-larly those who are supervising regional offices, are sometimes sent out to perform special missions of diplomatic nature. Unlike the United States, there is no distinction between departmental and foreign service personnel; anyone in the Minindel may be assigned at home or abroad.

Some other Assistant Foreign Ministers are not in charge of specific routine tasks but form, together with foreign affairs experts, an advisory body, a sort of brain trust for foreign affairs problems. They constitute one of three consultative bodies that are furnish-ing the Minindel and the top-level party leaders with thoroughly worked out recommendations and research papers.

The second advisory body is the so-called "Collegium of Diplomacy." This "College" has existed for many years. Its members are said to be appointed by the Council of Ministers and some of them are Assistant Foreign Ministers. It is not regarded as influential with the Party but with the higher echelon of the Minindel officials only. Very little is known about its organization and the type of its work. Not much more was known about the workings of the third advisory body, the "Institute of Economics and World Politics" whose head was the influential economist Dr. Eugene Varga. However, about the end of 1947, Varga was dismissed because he disagreed with the Politbureau's views on capitalist economy. His institute was absorbed by the Soviet Academy of Sciences and some of its activities transferred to the Moscow University's school of politics.[35]

The Collegium has certain rights that the Varga Institute did

[35] Varga did not believe, as did the official party doctrine, that an early collapse of capitalist economy is in sight. On the contrary, he warned that certain modifi-cations of capitalism might strengthen rather than weaken it for the time being. When the party rebuked Varga for such heresy, he would not recant.

PRESUMED ORGANIZATION OF THE SOVIET MINISTRY OF FOREIGN AFFAIRS

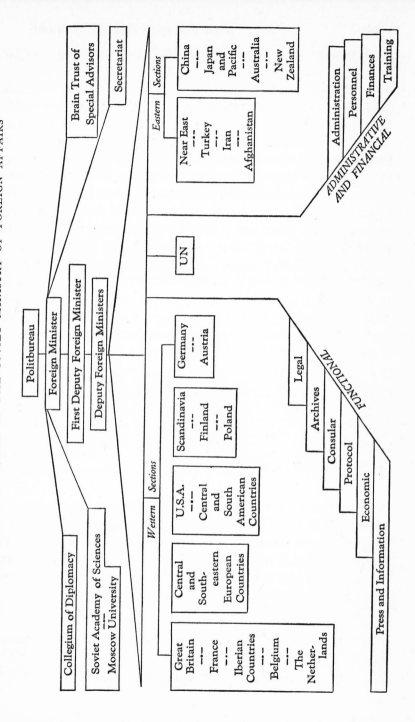

not appear to enjoy: If, for example, the Foreign Minister sees fit to reject the recommendations of the Collegium, and its members feel very strongly about it, the Collegium might appeal to the Council of Ministers which, in turn, may sustain the Collegium and void the Minister's decision.

It seems as though these advisory organs do much of the work that ministerial committees are charged with in the Western foreign offices. They demonstrate, moreover, that the Soviet government tends to resist hasty decisions, that all its policies are well founded on the basis of thoroughly worked out plans. Much time and money is spent for thinking and research, and it should never be assumed that Soviet policies have ever been formulated on the spur of the moment. Probably no other nation pays so much attention to expert analysis and evaluation of all possible available material. But this does not mean that the officials of the Minindel or their advisory bodies may actively participate in the formulation of Soviet policy. It is up to the Politbureau to accept or reject their findings. Men like George Kennan or Charles Bohlen in the United States have considerably more influence than their opposite numbers in the Soviet Union.

However, the value of Soviet intelligence and analysis is prejudiced by the necessity for Soviet representatives abroad and officials at home to conform, and continue to conform, to the accepted Marxist doctrine.

THE ORGANIZATION OF THE MININDEL

According to a resolution of the Third Session of the Central Executive Committee on November 12, 1923, the work of the Narkomindel was legalized for the following duties:

1. Protection of the foreign political and economic interests of the USSR, and protection of Soviet citizens abroad;
2. Fulfillment of regulations set down in treaties and agreements with foreign governments;
3. Direction of the execution of treaties and agreements con-

cluded with foreign governments and co-operation with the appropriate institutions of the USSR and the Union republics;

4. Supervision of the fulfillment of the treaties, agreements and acts concluded with foreign governments by the appropriate organs of power.

This was a relatively narrow program, a situation that can be understood in the context of world politics in 1923 when the USSR was still regarded as an outlaw nation. Since then the task of its foreign office has greatly broadened and the recent edition of the "Great Soviet Encyclopedia" states the tasks of the Minindel as follows:

> "Diplomatic protection of the political and economic interests of the U.S.S.R. abroad; establishment and maintenance of diplomatic relations with foreign countries; supervision of Soviet diplomatic activities abroad; preparation of international agreements and the conduct of negotiations for such agreements as well as the supervision of their proper execution; protection of Soviet citizens abroad and establishment of close cultural relations with foreign nations." [36]

The Soviet government has never published a chart of the Minindel's organization. Its reconstruction in this chapter is therefore conjecture, based upon the consensus of experts. While the Minindel has presumably changed frequently since it was first set up, such changes are probably not fundamental when one considers that the basic objectives of Soviet foreign policy have been rigidly maintained; only the methods of implementation have varied. A major reorganization may have been carried out after official and unofficial (Comintern) foreign policies were merged (in 1943).

It may be assumed that the Minindel comprises, apart from the top echelons and the advisory bodies, the conventional groups of politico-geographical, functional, and administrative offices. The economic sections are not believed to be strong, probably for the simple reason that the Ministry of Foreign Trade takes care of international commerce, which is a state monopoly in the USSR. The determination of economic policy is made by the Politbureau,

---

[36] *Bolshaya Sovietskaya Entsiklopediya*, Vol. 41, p. 207.

with recommendations submitted by a number of interested ministries, of which the Minindel is only one.

So far as the political divisions are concerned, the Minindel seems to distinguish, from the point of view of Russian geography, between two broad groups: the western and eastern sections. The western sections deal with Europe as well as the American countries; the eastern sections are responsible for the Near and Middle East and the Far East. There are said to be at least four sections in the Western Division. Section I probably contains the Scandinavian countries, Finland and Poland, Section II the countries in Central and Southeastern Europe; Section III the western European countries such as Great Britain, France, Belgium and the Netherlands, Italy, etc. It is possible that an additional section is occupied with the German-Austrian problems. The last section probably comprises the Western Hemisphere in its entirety.

Of the two eastern sections, one presumably deals with the countries in the Near and Middle East and with India, the other with China, Japan, the Philippines, Australia, and New Zealand. To what extent political considerations are superseding geographical ones, in influencing the organization of the Minindel is difficult to say. It is conceivable that the inside organization takes into account the degree to which a country submits to Soviet ideological pressure. Most probably, the satellite countries in the Danubian area (Section II) have been singled out for special treatment.

The functional divisions appear to comprise the office of the Legal Advisor, a press section, a small economic and a protocol section, administrative offices, and personnel and training divisions. Those other ministries which have sections dealing with foreign countries are obliged to co-operate closely with the Minindel.

Moreover, the Minindel has organized a bureau to handle United Nations affairs.[37] Its Press Division is of perfunctory importance only because it is a mere cog in the wheel of the enormous propaganda machine of the Soviet government, which

[37] Cf. p. 250 ff.

permeates every government agency and is directed, in the last analysis, by the Politbureau. The Minindel's training and personnel divisions, though in the administrative section, are considered to be very important for the development and education of a new generation of Soviet diplomats.

CHAPTER FIVE

Techniques of Policy Formulation

It is true that fundamental attitudes toward foreign countries are conditioned by history and experience, and that a nation's peculiar situation determines the range between its minimum and maximum aspirations. In normal times, it would not be too difficult to adopt policies to needs and conditions. For example, French foreign policy during the past century and a half has been primarily motivated by the quest for protection against Germany; or (another example) United States foreign relations during most of the same period were characterized by the determination to avoid joining "entangling alliances" but nevertheless to guarantee the safety of the Western Hemisphere against possible European infringements.

The fundamental change of world conditions resulting from two world wars has rendered obsolete many traditional policies and compelled all nations, the United States not excepted, to revise their viewpoint in world affairs. Therefore, the formulation of new policies, or the modification of former ones, is one of exceedingly difficult ramifications. The men who determine policy cannot be compelled to follow routine procedures, such as may be in force for the research or functional work of minor officials or, to a degree, for the duties of area experts, the "desk officers." High-level policy decisions involve all the elements of scientific speculation or artistic creation and entail the heaviest responsibilities imaginable. For policy makers must anticipate history, which not only presupposes factual knowledge, deductive capacities, and a talent for synthesis but also a great deal of human understanding, psychological finesse, an astute sense of political, social, and economic climates and, last but not least, much courage. This is a large order and few men command all these talents, which accounts for so many mistakes committed by policy makers of all lands. Moreover, mistakes in the conduct of foreign affairs no longer concern only the country whose statesmen blunder. They have chain reactions.

OVER-ALL CONSIDERATIONS

Roughly, the process of formulation of foreign policy consists of four phases: recommendation, modification, crystallization and final decision. Normally, the area experts recommend; their ideas are invariably modified by the reviewing officials; they may be rejected and returned for rephrasing or they may be recast by the superior officials themselves. When an agreement in principle has been reached by the experts and chiefs of the political—and if necessary by the economic or functional—offices, the recommendation will be whipped into final shape and thereby "crystallized" to the extent that it can be submitted to the high-level policy makers. There may be additional modifications but then, finally, the policy is formulated and approved, rejected or tabled. It can become "law" and be transmitted to the respective missions; it may be announced officially. In events of particular importance, the final decisions may not be made in the foreign office but left to the chief of state or government, and/or to the parliamentary bodies.

This procedure occurs daily, in many variations. It is simpler when policy decisions have to be made that do not change the over-all picture of established foreign relations. It may be far more complex if issues are at stake that concern the welfare and future security of the nation.

In the main, issues of fundamental significance will be initiated on the highest level. For example, it seems beyond doubt that the decision of the Soviets to carry out an outspoken anti-American policy was originated in the Politbureau. Or, it may be assumed that the so-called Marshall Plan to help Europe to help itself

stemmed from the top levels of the United States government.
This does not necessarily mean that the area experts are excluded
from collaboration. On the contrary, once a new policy has been
conceived as such, the country specialists of the political and
economic divisions and the technicians of the functional divisions
will be requested to provide their chiefs with as many ideas, facts,
analyses, and evaluations as possible.

When it comes to the final acceptance of the policy, techniques
and habits are different in democratic and in totalitarian countries.
The Soviet leaders will hardly find much opposition to the
acceptance of their policies once the one-and-only party has en-
dorsed them. The Supreme Soviet will be properly coached and
vote for any proposal the Politbureau wants them to vote for, or
its Presidium will confirm the policies in its name if it is not
convoked. The government will be charged with the execution
of the policy and told what methods to use: it has no recourse and
will do what it is told.

In the United States a policy that involves the security or prosperity of the nation may be announced by the President or the
Secretary of State but cannot be looked upon as definitely in force
until the Congress consents and votes the necessary funds. Congress may overrule the experts and establish its own estimate, or
requirements. Its decision, if agreed upon by the President, will
be carried out by the State Department, which, in contrast to the
Minindel, is empowered to do the job as it sees fit.

Once in a while policy changes are introduced that are so basic
that the normal course of events in the foreign offices is upset.
Even then, however, decisions on policy formulations are the
product of team work; a small team in totalitarian countries, a
larger one in the democracies. This process is bound to be the same
anywhere because there is no single man in his right mind who
can dare decide his country's foreign policy all by himself. Hitler
and Mussolini tried it and in the end failed disastrously. With
all his influence and power, even a Stalin cannot decide major
foreign policy issues unless he has the support of the majority of
his advisers. He may have often persuaded the members of the

Politbureau to follow his views but he probably cannot force them to do what he wants unless they believe he is right.

Where so many people have to meet so many contingencies, there can be no rigid system or method of work. There must be flexibility and adaptation to conditions. Only on the lower and middle levels, in the research and analysis sections and the regional divisions, can there be anything like an outlined "job description" or set office procedures. Yet even on their level, more latitude will have to be granted to foreign affairs officers than to employees in any other government agency.

The evolution of policies from recommendation to acceptance cannot be altogether systematized; it is too changeable because the nature of policy issues changes constantly. Even in routine business, hardly any two problems are alike; if it is attempted in the following paragraphs to describe procedures, the reader must be ever mindful that such a description can only generalize so as to give an approximate idea of political work in the foreign offices.

Inevitably, foreign affairs issues will originate in one particular country. However, they cannot be examined in the light of their own area merits only; they will have to be considered in the light of the entire region within which the respective country is situated. They will, eventually, have to be evaluated on the basis of global policies. It is the complexity and variety of the innumerable problems and aspects involved that make it so difficult to present a clear picture of policy formulation.

AREA WORK

The preceding chapters have mentioned the great variety of source material that is routed to the desk of the country specialist. The majority of it is informational and does not require immediate action.

The cables from the missions abroad are most important. Written by the diplomatic and consular staff, the envoy included, they are a running account of events, conditions, and developments in the country to which the mission is accredited. They also include evaluations of that country's relations with other countries.

Within the range of these reports fall the messages of the attachés, sent to their respective agencies (defense, commerce, agriculture, and so on), copies of which go to the foreign office area bureaus. These cable messages are supplemented by air mail letters and despatches, containing detailed reports on current problems or specialized matters that rarely require action but keep the foreign office staff informed on pertinent matters. They are sent home either by courier (via diplomatic pouch) or by air mail.

Further information for the interested offices will be furnished in reports containing interviews with fellow citizens or foreigners who are familiar with certain aspects of the country in question and volunteer to reveal their views. There are reports from traveling newspapermen,[1] intellectuals and artists, businessmen and technicians who may have worth-while observations to make. There is always some information to be obtained from the diplomatic representatives of the country with whom the area specialist is in touch and with whom he may exchange ideas. Sometimes surprisingly good information can be distilled from the most obvious and easily accessible sources such as foreign newspapers, radio broadcasts, books, and motion pictures. All these details are supplemented, organized, analyzed, and evaluated by the research bureaus in order to make sure the area expert is provided with a solid body of facts. He will need this knowledge for his recommendations of policy, for unless he knows the past and can appraise the present, he will be unable to speculate upon the future. Policies, of course, are formulated upon assumptions of future developments.

The messages from the envoy must be considered as the most important source material of policy making. It is known that the influence of an envoy of recognized experience or intellectual standing upon area policy formulation is great, second only to that of the foreign minister and his immediate advisers. But not always is the envoy's advice accepted. If policies are determined

---

[1] Reading of newspapers, domestic and foreign, is of great importance. In the free countries, the study of such papers as the New York *Times* or *Herald Tribune* in the United States, the *Times* in Britain or *Le Monde* in France, to mention only a few examples, is a must for every foreign affairs official, since these papers have the best overseas news service.

against his recommendations, the reason may well be that, being concerned with one exclusive area, he may lose his sense of proportion when it comes to regional or global policy formulation. In any event, most serious consideration is given to his messages. As for all other information, the area expert will have to evaluate the reliability of the sources and the soundness of the envoy's political analyses with care and objectivity. Most foreign affairs officials have developed, after years of practice and experience, a fine sense of judgment and discriminating evaluation. The steady flow to their desks of reports and documentary evidence will produce a full enough picture for them to help distinguish between reliable, questionable, and unreliable information. Accumulated evidence of past mistakes in judgment or accuracy in deduction will further help them to arrive at a close familiarity with the area under their jurisdiction. It takes years of training for a foreign affairs specialist to become an expert, and any government that lets such experienced men go for no other than budgetary reasons wastes the taxpayers' money.

Let us now imagine one of the most routine events in any foreign office, the arrival in the mail receiving and distributing center of a cable from one of the embassies abroad. In most cases, it will be a classified message and therefore coded. Consequently it will first have to be decoded and then transmitted to the geographic office concerned. The higher the cable is classified, the smaller will be the list of distribution because it is of utmost importance for every foreign office to avoid leaks. Lack of security constitutes a grave danger for any nation's position in the world.

Suppose the cable arrived in the foreign office of Country A, written by that country's Ambassador accredited to Country B. It contains information about impending changes in the government and political make-up of Country B, indicating a move from moderation toward radicalism. As a result, it forecasts the shift from a free to state-controlled economy. The cable therefore concerns both the political and economic area experts of the foreign office and, in some countries, those of the ministries of overseas trade. It would obviously be brought to the attention of the top-level policy makers, who must be informed about such important and pertinent trends and developments. It should also be of interest for the intelligence sections of the armed forces inasmuch as the indicated changes may be expected to change the defense policy of Country B by way of new alliances or new enmities. For the time being, however, the politico-economic aspects of the message would appear to be the most important ones. Since the political considerations are basic, the cable should be answered by the political area division concerned.

The reaction to the Ambassador's cable must necessarily differ according to Country A's political and economic ideas. If that country happens to be a liberal democracy attached to a free economy, the possible changes in Country B would raise serious questions of a political or economic nature. There may follow a deterioration of relations between the two countries. This century of ideological crusades has left little chance for compromise between diametrically opposed ideologies. Thus the officials of Country A's foreign office will have to examine whether the change in Country B requires a change in Country A's policies toward Country B in particular and Country B's geopolitical region in general. It may well be that the policy makers of Country A have relied upon a long standing friendship between A and B and made this relation the cornerstone of their regional and perhaps even global policies, which now may have to be changed. On the other hand, if Country A were a defender of a controlled economy and inclined to applaud the introduction of political radicalism in Country B—with whose previous governments it had not felt especially sympathetic—the shift in Country B's conceptions would clearly initiate a period of closer co-operation between the two countries on the basis of ideological affinities. If Country A is a capitalist democracy, it may cancel credits; if A is ruled by a socialist or Communist regime it may grant credits to Country B. If Country A is democratic, it will tend to discourage state monopolies and be reluctant to deal with them; while a leftist-totalitarian Country A will do all it can to further nationalization and state trade monopolies in Country B.

In either case, the responsible desk officer of a foreign office would receive the cable for his immediate attention, would think the matter over—if he has time to think!—and then take it up with his "opposite numbers" in the economic or functional divisions. He would ask for more detailed background material from the research bureaus and finally discuss the matter with his superiors. In some foreign offices, country or area committees are set up for the clarification of current policy: in this case he would consult them to be informed and to inform them. Eventually, having reached certain conclusions, he would draft an answer to the cable if a specific answer is to be given at this juncture. The Ambassador's message need not, however, require immediate action. He may have sent it for the purpose of clarifying and detailing previous information, or to contribute new information and thereby keep his government on the alert for major political and economic changes in Country B. On the other hand, the Ambassador may feel that the impending crisis will necessitate a new policy approach or different methods of executing existing policies, and he may wish to receive instructions as to the course to follow if the predicted change does take place. He may himself recommend definite policies or suggest the general direction of policy he considers advisable.

In studying the Ambassador's cable, the country specialist will have to exercise objective and discriminating judgment. Neither he nor his superiors are compelled to accept the Ambassador's views as infallible, although they will take his situation report to be reliable. In fact, the officials of the area division concerned may find themselves in disagreement with the Ambassador's interpretation and overrule him.

If the country specialist considers the situation as not alarming or wishes to wait for further developments, all he may do is to acknowledge receipt of the cable and possibly indicate whether or not the foreign office will take appropriate action, and when it may do so. If, on the other hand, action is considered necessary, a variety of ways and means is at the disposal of the officials concerned. Subject to approval of the high-level policy makers, the following steps to be taken may be recommended: (1) the publication of an official policy statement by the government of Country

A; (2) the announcement of the cancellation or granting of a loan according to the political beliefs of Country A; (3) a note of protest from the government of Country A to that of Country B or a note of encouragement and offers of moral support or actual assistance; (4) the putting out of inspired stories by radio or newspaper. These are just a few examples; the variety of political action is as great as is the variety of circumstances with which policy makers must cope.

It is understood that in most of these cases, the recommendations of the area experts must be approved by the foreign secretary and his advisers, if not by the chief of government. But nevertheless, the range of action for desk officers, at least in democracies, is considerable. None of them will be under the illusion that their work is more than preparatory or that they furnish more than an indicator toward a direction in which a foreign policy may ultimately develop. They know that it cannot be more than that, not because their recommendation may be lost in the hierarchical protocol but because they must concern themselves with strictly specialized areas. This means that their findings and suggestions must be looked upon as part of a more comprehensive policy issue, that of regions, continents, and the entire globe. Only when coordinated with the broader policy issues, and with domestic capabilities and temper, can their policy recommendations be appraised —can they be either used, or modified, or rejected.

The entire procedure involves a great deal of nervous tension and emotional strain. In an organization as complex as a foreign office, whose decisions may be of vital importance for the welfare of the nation and the peace of the world, frustrations of the staff members are daily fare and spare no one, from the foreign secretary down to the lowliest clerk. However, the area specialists are probably the most frustrated and distraught of individuals. They are exposed to pressures from above and below. Their work is affected by the cumbersome machine of a paper-pushing bureaucracy, which may deprive them of vital documents. Their ideas are watered down by their superiors through the mere fact that local recommendations have to be subordinated to regional or global considerations. Protocol may prevent them from defending their views in the front offices; and they may encounter a lack of co-operation and understanding on the part of other bureaus of their office or other government agencies.

REGIONAL AND GLOBAL CO-ORDINATION

As a rule, the chiefs of the area departments under whose super-vision the country specialists work are administratively responsible for a group of countries in the same general area with similar po-litical problems. It is their main task to co-ordinate individual policies into one greater whole. Approaches recommended toward individual nations will have to be adjusted to over-all regional policy or, perhaps, to a policy of universal validity.

It goes without saying that such co-ordination under a common denominator is the rule in totalitarian countries where sociopo-litical ideologies determine over-all policy. Consequently, the work of the country specialist in such countries as the USSR must of necessity remain one of research and intelligence rather than of policy recommendations; in the same way the co-ordinating job of regional chiefs is mainly one of adjusting policy to the ob-jectives of the ruling ideology. It may be presumed that the area and regional officers in the Minindel are discouraged from making policy recommendations and that their duty is to state facts rather than to say what they would propose to do about them. Even if their range of work were larger, they would want to avoid sticking their necks out—which, by the way is "popular tactics" in all for-eign offices. For nobody likes to assume responsibilities unless his position is so high that accepting the blame is part of his job, as well as the acceptance of the harvest of plaudits in case of success. Totalitarian officialdom has reason to be more afraid than demo-cratic government workers. The worst that can happen to the latter if they are incompetent is to be dismissed; the worst that can happen to the former is concentration camp or death.

To return to our case in point: the chiefs of a geographic region in trying to co-ordinate the recommendations submitted by their country experts, will then confer with the next higher officials in the hierarchy, those who are in charge of continents or wider areas such as Europe, Near East, Middle East, or the Far East. These may be office directors or assistant (or deputy) foreign secretaries. In case of disagreement, the higher ranking officials have the last word under authoritarian regimes; they are not necessarily passed over by their superiors in democratic countries where, as a rule, the minority opinion is heard as well. Obviously, if it seems that no agreement is possible, the Secretary himself, or his deputy, will have the last word. But it should be clear that democratic procedures are followed in democratic countries even in policy formulation.

Matters of regional or global policy are, of course, far more intricate than policy on a country or area level. Policy objectives concerning one country or a limited area with similar problems must be examined in the light of conditions that concern large parts of the globe if not the entire globe. For example, western policy toward a country like Hungary cannot be separated from issues affecting the USSR, central, eastern, and southeastern Europe. Policy connected with Greece would, in addition, have to be considered in the light of questions connected with the Near and the Middle East and the Mediterranean area in general. Policy toward France is linked not only with western Europe, Africa, and Asia (where French colonies are a factor) but also with France's internal conditions—with a consideration as to whether or not she may be able to stand up against Communist penetration.

This necessitates co-operation of a considerable number of offices and officials. The political personnel alone cannot submit recommendations without first consulting the economic and functional divisions. Special intelligence studies will have to supplement the theses defended by responsible policy makers. In other words, the middle and higher echelons of the entire foreign office will now deliberate as to the final policy lines to be recommended to the foreign secretary. Policy which is being developed in this way, that is, from the lower to the higher levels, may be expected to remain within the bounds of traditional concepts. Digressions will rarely happen, except in emergencies. This means that the chiefs of offices and divisions as well as the country experts must be familiar with the over-all policies of their country toward specific countries as well as toward geographic areas. The clearer this policy is, the better will the men who prepare policy recommendations be able to adapt local and regional policies to global policy.

GLOBAL ASPECTS

Policy on a global scale can not be decided by only the foreign ministers; it must be reviewed and approved by the head of government or state. If the latter is prudent, he will take into consideration the recommendations of his advisors, who, in turn, should have developed their point of view on the basis of expert opinion in the political and economic fields.

When it comes to decisions concerning the fate of the nation, not one single agency can and should be responsible. For example, the policies framed by the United States government toward the Soviet Union and the resulting policies regarding the United States attitude toward problems like Germany or Korea are the result of co-operation between the White House, the State Department, the agency dealing with the European Recovery Program, the defense agencies and possibly still others. Similar procedures exist in Great Britain where the Prime Minister, the Foreign Secretary, the Chief of the Board of Overseas Trade, the Imperial Defence Council, and a variety of economic and functional offices will co-ordinate their efforts, the final decision being up to the crown.

In determining policy, national leaders have to face global issues in two ways. One is related to their nation's interests in a world of ideological conflict and technical dangers; the other is connected with the international body which was created to solve disputes peacefully: the United Nations.[2] The adjustment of national foreign policy to the issues connected with the maintenance of international peace has become the object of the most serious attention of statesmen throughout the world. But even here, differences in attitude between totalitarian and democratic

[2] For a more detailed analysis of this specific problem see p. 229 ff.

governments are striking. In view of its ideological objectives, a totalitarian government will conveniently compromise with trends toward international co-operation only so long as it feels that it is not strong enough to oppose world opinion. For we must not forget that, from its point of view, the company of nations it has to put up with is not very desirable. Therefore, while it co-operates when it feels that by doing so it does not prejudice any of its principles, a dictatorship may not be expected to recognize the right of majority opinion. It will veto any compromise when possible and boycott decisions that cannot be vetoed. Meanwhile, the dictatorial group, representing the ruling party, will formulate its policy along ideological lines, regardless of the will of the majority of nations. Its decisions cannot be appealed and *post-mortem* approvals by rubber stamp "parliaments" serve primarily as window dressing.

Under democratic constitutions and governments, policy decisions of worldwide import must have the approval of the chief of state or of government and, directly or indirectly, of the parliamentary bodies. In the United States, this principle of universal approval of basic policies by Congress, particularly through the foreign affairs committees of the House and the Senate, is more strongly upheld than ever. The introduction of bipartisan policy as a direct consequence of global complications has only led to a further increase of frequent and close consultation on foreign affairs between the administration and representatives of Congress.

The initiative and responsibility remain, however, in the hands of the policy makers. Whether they be chiefs of state or ministerial officials, they are human beings and their final determination as to what kind of policy is to become national principle depends not only on all those factors discussed or mentioned in previous chapters but also on their human qualities, their backgrounds, prejudices, and sympathies. It will depend upon their feelings for foreign statesmen whom they may know. It will, of course, be largely influenced by their ideological conception of how the world should be fashioned. The foreign affairs officials in the lower and middle levels have their prejudices, too, but in the process of elimination, their possible bias will be resolved into a more realistic and objective attitude.

To be sure, policy decisions of leading officials will not be biased a priori. They will be influenced by (a) well grounded views of the political or economic advisors, (b) the views by chiefs of state and parliamentary bodies, (c) the views of the mission chiefs abroad. But it still remains a fact that the machinery of foreign policy is driven by human beings and that human elements cannot be entirely dismissed. Indeed, they may outweigh careful professional preparation. There are, for example, little tricks of fate that through human imperfections play havoc with policy decisions: the messenger service may have broken down just when its exact functioning was vital; an official may have missed seeing a document that was hidden by an absentminded secretary or misrouted to the wrong office; interoffice or interagency co-ordination may have failed simply because responsible individuals demonstrated the fickleness of human nature.

Beyond such inevitable events, there is the ever-remaining problem of the lack of time. The working day of a foreign minister (and his top aides) is not long enough for him to go into more than the most vital questions, and even then he has to be briefed because he has no time to do any extensive reading. Thus very much depends upon the skill with which his subordinates can present issues to him orally or in summary written form. Much depends also upon the personal views of the briefing officials and the way they themselves have been briefed by their experts, or were able to study the problem in question.

Foreign policy on a global scale is beyond the sole concern of "technical" policy formulation and therefore of the organs, instruments, and agents that are connected with the business of international relations. It is a matter of national concern for the entire government and whatever popular institutions of self-rule a people possesses. In decisions reached at conferences between leading statesmen, foreign affairs experts can do no more than advise and recommend. To a considerable extent, even the democratic chiefs of government, sitting at the conference table, must be expected to exercise a great deal of autonomy. As has so often been claimed, the last decisions affecting relations among nations are made among a handful of men who are not necessarily foreign affairs experts.

And at this juncture, the area experts can only hope and pray that their chiefs will not frustrate their efforts, but will cover their weaknesses and use their strength to drive a good bargain. The fundamental issues will invariably remain the same even though they may come up in different forms: security, freedom, prosperity, and respect for international law and morality.

PART THREE

The Execution of Foreign Policy

CHAPTER SIX

Executing Organs

THE MEANING OF DIPLOMACY

DEFINITIONS of diplomacy are as numerous as the books that have been written about it. It may be said, however, that diplomacy is the art, or technique, of maintaining relations with sovereign states by way of negotiations. Diplomats are government officials to whom is entrusted the execution of their country's foreign policy in a given area by way of negotiations. This delicate task requires not only knowledge and experience but also tact and patience, not only intelligence but also discipline, not only salesmanship but also dignity, as well as the ability to observe and interpret accurately.

Diplomacy is an ancient institution. Of its two branches, the diplomatic and consular services, the consular is the older. The maintenance of relations with foreign governments or vassal states, through temporary and occasional sending of envoys, was already a time-honored custom in the ancient Roman, Hellenic, and Asiatic Empires. While the Dark Ages checked rather than stimulated the development of temporal political institutions, the end of scholasticism in Europe gave new impetus to commercial and cultural contacts. City states like Venice and Florence developed a vigorous program of contact with Christian and Moslem countries and, as a result, diplomatic activities flowered. Certain bilaterally accepted principles concerning the status of the envoys, (for example his inviolability and immunity) forecast later agreements that, between the Peace of Westphalia and the Congress of Vienna, grew into international law. The regulations covering diplomatic ranks and precedences, signed in Vienna in 1815 and Aix-la-Chapelle in 1818, have remained in effect ever since, with only minor adjustments to the changing world.

Although the organization of the diplomatic hierarchy has remained more or less static, the character and technique of modern diplomacy have undergone considerable modifications. These changes pertain to constitutional, technological, and organizational matters.

The envoys of past times were personal representatives of their monarchs and accredited to foreign sovereigns. Modern diplomats represent their governments and, thereby, their peoples (in certain cases their political parties).

Before departing for his post, the envoy of past times received detailed written and oral instructions, but once he had left, his independence was almost complete and his power of decision uncontested. It had to be that way because communications were slow and the exchange of messages by courier was not only time-consuming but also unsafe. The modern diplomat, although he receives over-all instructions before departing, remains in close daily touch with his foreign office by radio, telephone, cable, teletype, or fast travel. As conditions change and policies require daily adjustments, the envoy's policy must remain flexible in response to the flow of information and instruction that reaches his desk.

In earlier times, the envoys were "plenipotentiary" not only in name but also in fact. They were the negotiators, and they alone; it very rarely happened that two sovereigns met, and if they did, they still left the details of a general agreement on policy up to their ambassadors. The contemporary diplomat is meticulously guided by his foreign office and is not independent in his decisions at all. He cannot decide crucial issues; he can only explore them initially to the point where the heads of state and the foreign ministers may meet in conferences with the envoy attending in an advisory capacity. The new concept of diplomacy by conference that has developed in the twentieth century has greatly contributed toward a deflation of the envoy's influence.

Diplomacy has lost much of its glamor. Conference methods

and social changes have altered its aspects and the job it has to do has become harder and more grueling if more mundane than ever before. A diplomat is not limited to the task of maintaining and fostering relations between the sending and receiving states. He must also be the "eyes and ears" of his government. Diplomatic (and consular) representatives must report to their foreign offices about the political, economic, social, and cultural conditions of the receiving country and evaluate their findings as evidence for the policy makers at home. The U.S. Department of State presents its view of what an efficient member of a diplomatic representation should be able to do thus:

"To create good will and common understanding, and, with restrained and critical leadership born of mature experience and profound knowledge of men and affairs, use these as instruments for enhancing international confidence and cooperation among governments and peoples.

"To promote and protect the interests of the United States and its citizens.

"To negotiate, with tact, sound judgment and intimate knowledge of conditions at home and abroad, protocols, conventions and treaties, especially regarding international intercourse, tariffs, shipping, commerce, preservation of peace, etc., in strict conformity to Government instructions.

"To establish and effectively utilize personal contacts in farsighted ways for the benefit of his Government and of American citizens.

"To analyze and report on political and economic conditions and trends of significance to the United States.

"To exercise skill in following prescribed form and routine procedure when possible; and display discriminating judgment, as may be necessary in more complicated situations requiring investigations, careful accumulation of information, or professional understanding of laws, customs, conditions, etc.

"To administer an office in a business-like and efficient manner." [1]

This American description of an ideal diplomat is quite ade-

[1] "The American Foreign Service," State Department Publication 235, pp. 4-6. See also under Foreign Service Organization, below, p. 189 ff.

quate for universal application. Harold Nicolson, defender of a "moral" diplomacy, describes an "ideal diplomatist" as possessing "seven specific virtues, namely, truthfulness, precision, calm, good temper, patience, modesty, and loyalty." [2] And this list does not count traits that the author takes for granted: "intelligence, knowledge, discernment, prudence, hospitality, charm, industry and even tact." [3]

As diplomacy has become, in the twentieth century, a hard and burdensome profession and as, at the same time, world conditions have deteriorated economically and socially, the modern diplomat is rarely that motion picture specimen of brilliant social living. He must accept his government's foreign policy and must try his best to carry it out even though he may not agree with it. The alternative for him, should there be no compromise between his views and those of his foreign office, would be resignation. Often, he will be blamed for failures just as he will be credited with successes that are not really of his own making.

However, with all the instructions, orders, or recommendations from his government, the envoy must be free to choose his techniques of persuasion and negotiation. He must know when the time has come to request or recommend new instructions or top-level conferences. Conditions abroad are always somewhat different from what they appear to the analysts in the foreign offices and changes of these conditions occur so frequently that theoretical reasoning may well result in assumptions that do not correspond to reality. When such a condition becomes too pronounced, the diplomat must draw the attention of his home office to this.

Diplomats nowadays must be clear-thinking, level-headed, and scholarly. No longer are social graces, as such, decisive for diplomatic success. Fortunately, high birth and personal fortune have lost much of their former magic. To be sure, a man who knows how to be popular and to impress foreign officials favorably is preferable to one who has an unfortunate personality. But much

[2] H. Nicolson, *Diplomacy*, Harcourt, Brace and Company, New York, 1939, Chapter V.
[3] *Ibid.*, p. 126.

more important for success in implementing policies are sound political judgment; talent for quick acquisition of knowledge of the country to which the diplomat is accredited; ability to adapt to that country's psychological climate; understanding of the problems concerning the general area in which that country is situated. There are few things more dangerous than an amateur diplomat who knows too little or relies on half-truths.

Comparatively speaking, the democratic diplomat possesses more freedom in applying his government's policy than does the representative of a totalitarian state, who will come to the conference table with a rigid set of orders that only his superiors can modify. Therefore, diplomatic conferences between democratic and totalitarian envoys or foreign ministers are bound to fail in their objectives unless there happens to be a coinciding political interest. If a compromise cannot be reached, a horse-trade might be substituted, although even here ideology seems to have unfavorably influenced the carrying out of such agreements. This is one of the fundamental differences between *then* and *now;* formerly diplomatists, defending their country's interests, were fundamentally very much alike. They understood each other and in their debates they were silently agreed upon the common denominators of Western civilization. The onslaught of political ideologies has changed this aspect and thereby started a new phase of diplomacy, whose organization may have superficially remained the same but whose spirit has greatly changed.

ORGANIZATION OF THE DIPLOMATIC CORPS

In former times, that is, before 1815, the problem of precedence of diplomats in political and social affairs caused much feuding and often brought dynasties to the brink of war. Ever since there was a semblance of diplomatic activities, as far back as in the sixteenth century, strict orders of precedence were needed for peaceful negotiations or ceremonies. Usually, the representatives of the Pope came first, those of the Holy Roman Emperor and his heir apparent next, followed by the envoys of the kings of France, Spain, Aragon, Portugal, Britain, and Denmark in that order.

In modern times, particularly since the few remaining monarchies have been constitutionally limited, these problems are no longer taken quite so seriously. Countries are created and vanish; the political power of existing states changes. Today protocol must be flexible, adjust itself quickly to prevailing conditions, and set up precedence accordingly. Furthermore, round-table conferences make the seating order illusory; and the realistic attitude of contemporary diplomats keeps them from crying wolf should there be a mistake of protocol. Diplomacy has become less ceremonial and more businesslike.

Nevertheless, the diplomatic body (or, as it is called in the former language of diplomacy, the *corps diplomatique*) in any capital is still subject to certain accepted customs. The *corps* consists of the heads of the missions and their counselors, secretaries, attachés and, in certain cases, consuls. The honorary head, the *doyen* (dean), is usually the oldest of the envoys present or the one who has served longest in the particular capital; however, if there is a papal nuncio he is usually made *doyen* regardless of his age or the time he has served.

The *doyen* represents the diplomatic body at important functions that do not involve problems of political relations between the countries but concern the *corps* itself. He is the "supreme guardian of the immunities and prerogatives of the whole corps . . . but in all other matters his authority is limited." [4] Before speaking for the *corps*, he must consult with its leading members.

In accordance with international conventions, the members of the missions are given a number of privileges, the most important of which are: (1) extraterritoriality, (2) inviolability, (3) immunity. Extraterritoriality is the concept of regarding the premises and equipment of diplomats as being outside the territory to which they are accredited and the fiction that their premises constitute part of their own territory. Consequently, diplomats are exempt from direct taxation. Inviolability means that even in the event of war between the sending and receiving powers, the safety of the diplomats would be guaranteed. Im-

---

[4] Translated from R. Genet, *Traité de Diplomatie et de Droit Diplomatique,* Paris 1931/32, Vol. 1, Chapter 370, p. 398.

munity signifies the exemption of diplomats from the criminal and civil courts of the receiving country.

The mission is granted exemption from the receiving state's laws, a concession which is based upon reciprocity and therefore does not infringe on any country's sovereign rights. The envoy and his diplomatic staff and their families are extraterritorial and so are the grounds of the mission, its furnishings and archives, and the property of the diplomatic staff. Inviolability is, of course, the logical consequence of extraterritorial rights. Immunity means exemption from the jurisdiction of the receiving country. Diplomats who are granted immunity cannot be summoned into the courts; they are also exempted from taxes and released from customs duties.

(A much debated question is the so-called "right of asylum" for political refugees in an extraterritorial mission. Opinions about this right vary; there is no clear-cut international agreement, subscribed to by all civilized nations. The United States has, in the past, not encouraged the universal acceptance of this right but it has, on the other hand, not overly hesitated to grant asylum to political persecutees whose only crime was a political conviction.[5])

The appointment and recall of envoys is handled in accordance with internationally recognized procedures; however, every state appoints its envoy in its own constitutionally determined way. For example, in the United States, the President nominates a candidate and the Senate has to confirm him by simple majority. The consent of the Secretary of State before the publication of the nomination is a foregone conclusion. In the United Kingdom, the Foreign Secretary submits the name of the candidate to the King, whose approval means ratification of the appointment. Here, too, it is unlikely that a candidate's name is submitted without the assent of the Prime Minister. In France, the Foreign Minister recommends an appointment and the Chambers must approve or decline; if they approve, the President signs a decree, making the

[5] Asylum was granted by the United States Legations in Sofia (Bulgaria), Bucharest (Rumania), and Budapest (Hungary) in the years of 1946 and 1947 to moderate political leaders who were persecuted by their respective Communist dominated governments.

appointment official. In the defunct Nazi and Fascist dictatorships, the Fuehrer or Duce made his own choice of the envoy and no ratification was needed. In the USSR, envoys are nominated by the Presidium of the Supreme Soviet but it goes without saying that without the assent of the Politbureau, the Supreme Soviet would hardly dare pronounce a confirmation.

Once the candidate has been approved by all his own authorities, a so-called *agrément* is sought from the government to which he is to be accredited. For no government need accept an envoy it does not want. If it refuses the agreement, there is no choice for the other country but to look for a new candidate; and relations might well become strained for some time. In such case, the envoy-to-be is a *persona non grata*. If, however, he is a *persona grata* and the agreement is granted, he can proceed to his post. A nomination will, as a rule, be made public only after the nominating authorities have made certain that the agreement will be given. Therefore one may take for granted that the publication of the candidacy of a new envoy implies consent of the government to which he will be accredited. That government may, on the other hand, reverse itself and request recall of the envoy (or of any other member of the diplomatic staff) if it feels that the activities of this person have made him, in foreign eyes, *persona non grata*.

If all domestic and foreign provisions have been fulfilled, the new envoy will officially start his work by first conferring with the head of his state, his foreign minister, and the chiefs of the political divisions of his foreign office. Then he will review the material in the foreign office files concerning the country or area in which he is to be accredited. He will then wait until his predecessor has left and, if possible, confer with him before departing. Once arrived in the capital of the receiving country, where ceremonies are now at a minimum, he will seek an audience with the head of the receiving state in order to submit his "letter of credence." Formerly, this state visit was a very elaborate affair; nowadays, it is comparatively simple. The envoy, in handing to the head of the receiving state a letter from his own head of state, makes a brief speech, stressing his desire for friendly and peaceful collaboration. In accepting the letter, the head of the state, aided by his foreign minister, answers in a similar vein. The speeches have almost never any political importance as it is considered bad form to touch upon political problems or disputes during this ceremony; moreover it is usual practice to exchange these speeches in writing before the oral presentation in order to avoid initial surprises.

By this presentation of his credentials and the acceptance by the head of the state, the envoy is fully accredited. A copy of the letter has already been sent to the foreign minister and it is he upon whom the new envoy will call first when he starts his courtesy visits. He must meet the most influential leaders of the receiving government and he must, of course, visit his colleagues of the diplomatic *corps*.

The recall of an envoy is even less ceremonial. Whether or not the resigning envoy will pay visits to the leaders of the receiving government depends upon the degree of his personal attachments rather than upon political expediency. Sometimes he may travel home "for consultation" and not return; sometimes he is withdrawn for political reasons and leaves the capital during a period of tension.

No formalities at all are used for foreign service personnel. None of them needs to be accredited; all they must have is a diplomatic passport with the visa of the receiving government. The only other foreign service officer who must have official consent from the receiving government is the consul.

THE DIPLOMATIC HIERARCHY

It was pointed out above that the most important agreements of the Congresses of Vienna (1815) and Aix-la-Chapelle (1818) were regulations covering the hierarchic ladder of the diplomatic personnel. These regulations, codified in the so-called *règlement*, are still the basis of contemporary classification of foreign service personnel.

The *règlement* distinguished between four classes of heads of mission:

1. Ambassadors, legates and nuncios
2. Envoys and ministers accredited to the sovereign
3. Ministers resident, accredited to the sovereign
4. Chargés d'affaires (*ad hoc* or *ad interim*), accredited to the foreign minister

In modern times, this list has been reduced to three categories. Ambassadors still top the grades. Legates and nuncios are Papal envoys; a legate, always a cardinal, is sent for special missions; a nuncio is a permanently accredited diplomat, who is never a cardinal.

A merger of the second and third grades has gradually developed through the past century. Ministers, who rank under ambassadors, are now usually called "Envoy extraordinary and Minister plenipotentiary." The former distinctions between envoys, ministers, and ministers resident,[6] the last being lowest in rank, were created for the sake of precedence. The words "extraordinary" and "plenipotentiary" were added to enhance the dignity of the title and thereby to achieve precedence but then this method was emulated by almost every state until these adjectives became stereotypes.

There are two types of chargés d'affaires. A chargé may be assigned to do a special job (chargé *ad hoc*, or *en titre*); he may also substitute for the envoy during the latter's absence (chargé *ad interim*). Usually a counselor or first secretary takes over the duties of the envoy when the latter is out of town or incapacitated. He also heads the embassy or legation during the time from the resignation of the old to the arrival of the new envoy.

There are, moreover, two types of high-level diplomats that political necessities have added to the ranks of diplomacy. One is temporary, and called "chief of mission," with the rank of minister. He may be found in countries where embassies or legations had for some reason not as yet been established but where diplomatic relations seemed desirable. For example, the United States

---

[6] A minister resident's duty was observation rather than negotiation. Since envoys nowadays take care of both tasks, and since diplomatic precedence rarely disturbs the sleep of envoys in this time and age, there is no need for a minister resident.

has sent missions to some of the former German (now Soviet) satellites in southeastern Europe. The missions' purpose was to represent the United States and observe conditions until the time when the peace treaties were ratified and permitted regularization of relations. The second case is the elevation of the number two man of important embassies to minister-counselor. In other words, the ranking staff members of some of the political key representations were promoted to the rank of minister as the pressure of business made it necessary for them to substitute frequently for the ambassadors. These ambassadorial representatives are given the rank of minister-counselor when it is considered desirable that they be high-ranking officials in their own right.

The rank of ambassador or minister is also often conferred for a limited time to persons who are sent abroad to fulfill important tasks of specialized nature. They may take with them a staff of their own but they do not necessarily fall under the categories of the *règlement* and therefore any special status granted to them is a matter of courtesy rather than of international law. Such envoys do not have to present their credentials. For example, the American mission to Greece in 1947, charged with the responsibility of supervising the spending of American credits, was headed by Gov. Dwight Griswold, whose diplomatic rank was that of ambassador.

Next to the heads of missions, the following diplomatic ranks are internationally recognized and used:

Counselors (of embassy or of legation). They are not necessarily part of a mission but if they are, they rank highest among the diplomatic staff members. In certain cases, they are elevated, in important embassies, to minister-counselor so as to confer a higher rank to a man who will be chargé d'affaires if the head of the mission is not present.

Secretaries (of embassy or legation). They usually rank first, second or third Secretary. Their actual importance in the mission does not, however, depend upon their personal rank. First secretaries may be chargés d'affaires and third secretaries may fill a key post in the work of the mission.

Attachés. They may be specialized experts or junior officers of the mission. In many countries, newly appointed foreign service officers start out as attachés. However, the experts of commerce, agriculture, army, navy, and air, although "attached" to the mission, and under the general supervision of its head, are more or less independent observers of developments in their fields and are charged with maintaining personal and professional relations with their "opposite numbers" of the receiving countries. Usually a commercial attaché would be responsible to the ministry of commerce rather than to his foreign office; an agricultural attaché to the ministry of agriculture and the military, naval, and air attachés to their respective agencies. They are, however, obliged to submit to the mission's discipline and scheme of things, and copies of their reports will be transmitted to their government's foreign office.

As to the special functions of the attachés, suffice it to say that the commercial attaché is expected to collaborate with the consular services that specialize in matters of commerce, trade, and transportation. Thoroughly familiar with his own country's economy, the commercial attaché will have to explore the economy of his host nation, report home about its aspects and try to find out how his own country's economy could profit by collaborating with that of the foreign country. In this way, he will be furthering good relations between the two nations and working toward the economic well-being and prosperity of each.

Agricultural attachés keep themselves informed about the development of food production of the receiving country and will be ready to exchange views and techniques with foreign agriculture officials. They may advise them or receive advice; like the commercial attachés, they will foster relations between the two countries by co-operating to mutual advantage. This post became increasingly important after World War II when world food production suffered a severe setback.

Military, naval, and air attachés are first of all technical advisors to the chief of their mission. Obviously, the state of the armed forces at home and abroad must be known to the ranking diplomats, for the strength of armies, navies, and air forces— coupled with the estimate of the willingness and ability to use them—often determines the degree to which diplomatic negotiators will insist upon their point of view. Second, these attachés will report to their respective ministries about the conditions, strength, and morale of the armed forces in the receiving country. It is up to them to secure such information; they will, in the majority of cases, hardly rely upon official information provided for them but try to get their source material from personal contacts. They are not by any means "spies"; every government is well aware of the nature of their activities and accepts them on the basis of reciprocity. They represent their country at official military displays and attend whatever conferences have to do with problems concerning the armed forces. They are expected to study the general organization of the receiving country's armed forces and ministries of defense; the development of new arms on land, on the sea, and in the air; the system of recruiting and how it works; the public attitude toward national defense; the ways and means of military instruction; the morale of the armed forces; whatever they can find out about approaches to strategy and mobilization; the present defenses of the national territory and the military geography.

Among the other specialized officials of the mission, the cultural and press counselors or attachés have come into prominence. The importance and effectiveness of foreign information and cultural exchange as a new arm of foreign policy has been universally recognized and almost every government has created organizations dealing with this problem. Up to the end of 1947 the Congress of the United States had not seen fit to maintain such services on any significant scale; whereas most other nations, large and small, have elaborate home and foreign service organizations dealing with the matter. Because of the importance most countries attach to their information and cultural affairs, personnel for such activities have now become part of the missions and have significantly been granted diplomatic status.

The rank of the missions differs with the importance attributed to the receiving country by the sending government. The embassies (headed by ambassadors) are of course of highest rank, then follow the legations (headed by ministers) and finally come the temporary missions (headed by a chief with ministerial rank).

The designation of the rank of representations is a matter of reciprocity. As a rule, it depends upon political and economic considerations rather than upon the size of national territories. Therefore, many a small country is host to an embassy. For example, the United States maintains an embassy in Prague, Czechoslovakia, in spite of the small size of that country. After World War II it was felt that Czechoslovakia's key position as a "bridge" between East and West made it politically important out of proportion with its actual resources. In reciprocity, Czechoslovakia maintains an embassy in the United States. Both countries had only legations before the war.

There is no limitation as to the number of officers and clerks of the missions that may be sent abroad.[7] While diplomatic and consular representation, according to international agreements, is strictly confined to the recognized business of maintaining relations with the government to which they are accredited, it is well known that the ranks of their foreign representatives were swelled by totalitarian governments, who sent specially trained propagandists, political organizers, and agitators abroad in the disguise of diplomatic agents, thereby violating the codes of international law. In a number of cases, these agents were uncovered, declared *persona non grata* and forced to leave. But the majority of such agents, including those working in the commercial fields, cannot be exposed because they skillfully conceal incriminating evidence and are careful to follow, on the face of things, the rules of diplomatic behavior: "The minimum requisite of correct behavior (aside from staying within the limits prescribed by international law) is to refrain from public criticism, at least, of any of the institutions or the governing personnel of the receiving state."[8]

The main office of the mission is, naturally, in the capital of the receiving country, which is the seat of that country's government. There may be branch offices of the mission in other important

---

[7] The Soviet Union and some of its satellites effectively limit the numbers of foreign diplomatic personnel by delaying visas and failing to furnish adequate quarters.

[8] B. Akzin, *Propaganda by Diplomats*, The Digest Press, American University Graduate School, Washington, March 1936, p. 6.

cities. Such offices may, however, not deal with political matters but are either consulates or information centers, whose tasks will be outlined below.

THE CONSULAR SERVICE

The consular services are part of the foreign service but are distinct from diplomacy. Although diplomatic and consular personnel is interchangeable in most countries, the duties of the consular branch are different from those of the diplomatic branch of the foreign service. Their international status is different, too. Consular services are much older than diplomatic activities, owing to their concentration on commercial relations on the one hand and protection of nationals on the other.

Strangely enough, in spite of the vital importance of consular work, international law has treated consuls not so well as diplomats. Whatever immunities are accorded to them are either based upon mutual agreements between the governments exchanging consuls or are granted to them by courtesy. Therefore, while the extent of consular immunity has always been debatable, they are well enough protected and in certain cases, where diplomatic personnel is not available, are given all the privileges of diplomats. There is no question that consular offices and archives are regarded as extraterritorial and that many of them enjoy exemption from taxes and customs duties. No such immunities are granted, however, to noncareer consuls, who may or may not be nationals of the receiving state.

Consular services have no part in diplomatic work but their reports on commercial conditions may well influence the shape of their governments' commercial policy and thereby indirectly their foreign policy. Reporting, however, either voluntary or upon request, is only a small part of consular duties. Among the host of other duties are: answers to private inquiries regarding economic problems and assistance of nationals in their business (if such business is being transacted in the respective consular district); the creation of conditions favorable for exports from the consul's country into the receiving country and the promotion of their sale there if such promotion is possible or necessary; the protection of fellow citizens, particularly those who become stranded, entangled with foreign courts, or land in foreign jails; the authentication of documents, registration of births and deaths of nationals, and issuing of visas and passports; decisions concerning citizenship; jurisdiction over vessels and seamen of the home country if they are in a port belonging to the consular district. In fact consular services take care of about every problem arising within their district, except diplomatic business. Consulates naturally work closely with their diplomatic missions even though their offices are often separated from those of the diplomatic mission.

There are two kinds of consuls: career consuls and honorary consuls. Only the career consuls belong to the foreign service. There are four different ranks of consular career officers: the consul general, the consul, the vice-consul, and the language officer (interpreter). Honorary consuls are often called consular agents; they may be nationals of the receiving or sending countries and receive only a token salary. They are neither extraterritorial nor inviolable but subject to the laws of the land in which they function.

The consul general, being the principal career consular officer, is in charge of all the consulates of his government in the country to which he is accredited. For example, the American consul general in London supervises all United States consulates in the British Isles. In some oriental countries, the consul general may also have to fulfill diplomatic functions provided there is no diplomatic mission present. If there are other consulates general in the same country, as may be the case for commercial reasons, then such consulates general remain under the supervision of that in the capital of the receiving country.[9]

The duties of consuls are of similar nature if they are in charge of the consular offices in a given country where there is no consulate general; also, they may be subordinate officers in charge

---

[9] Usually, consul generals reside in the capital of the receiving country. In the United States, however, where the capital is not a major trade center, they reside in New York, the nation's largest and commercially most important city.

of specialized work. If there is a consulate general in the same receiving country, consulates are given certain districts to which their jurisdiction is limited.

Vice-consuls are usually junior foreign service officers, but although they are young and at the beginning of their career, they may well have to do very responsible work, particularly in smaller consular offices. (There are also noncareer vice-consuls, promoted from the ranks of clerical personnel for the execution of specialized duties.)

Before a consul takes office, the government to which he will be accredited must agree to receive him and grant him the privileges he may claim. This agreement is called *exequatur*. It is for the consul what the *agrément* is for the envoy. An *exequatur* must also be granted to an honorary consul or consular agent who is a national of the receiving state. As in the case of envoys, inquiries are made as to whether the consul to be named is *persona grata* in the receiving state before the appointment is actually published. The request for an *exequatur* is sent by the foreign office to the envoy accredited to the receiving state who, in turn, transmits it to the foreign office of that state.

An amalgamation of diplomatic and consular duties has often occurred in places where there is only a small diplomatic staff or none at all. While the governments have the right to refuse recognition to such a combination of activities, most of them in practice do not object.

In places where there are consular representations from other nations, there exists a consular body (in the manner of a diplomatic body) with a *doyen* heading it. A newly appointed consul would have to get in touch with the *doyen* for reasons of international courtesy just as his diplomatic colleagues would address themselves to the diplomatic corps.

FOREIGN SERVICE ORGANIZATION

The diplomatic and consular branches of the world's foreign offices are part of their foreign service organization. The diplomatic and consular establishments abroad cannot be effective *per se;* it is the personnel who either fail or succeed. It is the rank and file of diplomatic and consular officers and clerks who make the work of the envoy possible and therefore, by implication, the execution of their country's foreign policy. The governments of the civilized world are well aware of this fact, more now than ever before. They are striving to select the best among the interested of their young men—at times young women, too—for their foreign service organizations.

Until World War I this profession was universally presumed to be the prerogative of wealth and noble birth. There were historical traditions for such discrimination; the diplomatic representatives of monarchs used to be wealthy aristocrats who were willing to pay the heavy ceremonial expenses involved. Salaries for diplomats, if they were paid at all, were quite insufficient and the envoys invariably spent more than they received. They were willing to do this because it meant increased prestige and power for them.

In Britain, until the beginning of the World War I, candidates for the foreign services were only admitted to examination if they could prove they had an independent income of at least $2000 per year, because they would not receive a salary during the first two years of their service, and later on their income would need supplementation. It was not quite so bad in the United States even before the Rogers Act of 1924 modernized the American foreign service. But salaries were small, and for aspiring young men, family wealth and political connections were at least as important as intellectual achievements and character.

In the France of the Third Republic, the motto of the Republic notwithstanding,[10] the diplomatic service had remained more or less in the hands of the rich upper middle classes and those aristocrats whose fortunes had not wasted away. In Imperial Germany, foreign service was exclusively in the hands of the aristocracy and high reserve officers of the army and navy; the Weimar Republic tried to change this state of affairs but did not achieve much of a democratization, and, in fact, never got a

---

[10] "Liberty, Equality, Fraternity."

foreign service law through the *Reichstag*. In Imperial Russia, foreign service was a prerogative of the aristocracy to the extent that even sons of very wealthy merchants were discouraged from entrance into the Ministry of Foreign Affairs if they had any ambitions to become high-level officials. Only between the two world wars did conditions begin to change.

Gradually, provisions were made for any young man of outstanding intelligence and character to become a foreign service officer in either the diplomatic or consular branches. In the United States, the Foreign Service Act of 1946, amending and improving the Rogers Act of 1924,[11] raised salaries (though not sufficiently for top positions), established an impressive security system and established the Foreign Service Institute for the specialized training of selectees. A candidate must pass an examination, consisting of achievement and character tests. If he passes, his name will be put on an eligibility list and he will be offered an appointment as soon as a vacancy occurs. Having been appointed, he will have to go through a training course at the institute before receiving his first foreign assignment. Indeed, in the United States, the democratization of the foreign service has made great progress; the "spoils system" is nonexistent for career foreign service personnel, and political appointments are limited to some, but by no means all, chiefs of diplomatic establishments.

While the Rogers Act had already merged the diplomatic and consular branches of the foreign service, the Foreign Service Act of 1946 failed to make departmental and foreign service personnel interchangeable. Thus the United States is probably the only nation where the officers of the State Department are not automatically foreign service officers. According to the Foreign Service Act, no officer under its jurisdiction may be permitted to remain more than four consecutive years in the United States, after which he must be given a new assignment abroad. "He may not again be assigned for duty in a Government agency until the

[11] The Rogers Act of May 24, 1924, legalized the first major reorganization of the United States Foreign Service under this name, combining the diplomatic and consular services and introducing the merit system for career foreign service officers.

expiration of a period of time equal to his preceding tour of duty [12] on such assignment or until the expiration of two years, whichever is the shorter.[13]

It is regrettable that the distinction between foreign and departmental personnel has not been eliminated. Most other foreign offices have long since recognized the disadvantages of such differentiation and abolished it. At present, American foreign service officers may be given the chance of serving at home at infrequent intervals and during short periods of time, whereas departmental officers will be sent abroad in exceptional cases only and stay there for a few weeks or months. A rotation of the entire staff would not only produce better information and more political wisdom but would also utilize available manpower to a fuller extent.

In Great Britain, far-reaching changes in the foreign service organization have occurred since the beginning of World War I. With the abolition of the clause that candidates must prove that they have independent means, the selection of aspirants was democratized and a new salary scale created. On the other hand, the requirements of the examination to be passed implied that the candidate, apart from a good deal of savoir-faire, would have to have not only a university training but also possess thorough knowledge of two major languages, a knowledge which in truth could only have been acquired abroad. In other words, there was still not much chance for an intelligent candidate whose parental finances were limited.

It was not until 1943 that the so-called "White Paper" recommended modifications in the foreign service laws, which were then enacted into law. The paper stated frankly that

> the conditions which the Diplomatic Service originally grew up to meet no longer exist unchanged in modern international affairs. Economics and finance have become inextricably interwoven with politics; an

[12] Section 572 of the Foreign Service Act of 1946 determines that "every Foreign Service Officer shall, during his first fifteen years of service in such capacity, be assigned for duty in the continental United States . . . for periods totalling not less than three years."

[13] Foreign Service Act of 1946, Part H, Sec. 571 a.

understanding of social problems and labour movements is indispensable in forming a properly balanced judgment of world events. The modern diplomat should have a more intimate understanding of these special problems, and greater opportunities to study them than he usually possessed in the past. His training and experience must be wider. By introducing the reforms . . . it is intended to re-equip the Foreign Service to meet modern conditions and to create a Service which, by its composition, by the recruitment and training of its members, and by its organization, shall be better able to serve not only the interests of the nation as a whole, but also to deal with the whole range of international affairs, political, social and economic, and so constitute an adequate instrument for the maintenance of good relations and mutual understanding between the United Kingdom and other countries.[14]

As a result, the language requirements that proved to be an unassailable hurdle for aspirants without foreign travel were removed. If a candidate has passed the initial test and has been accepted, he will be sent abroad for 18 months at government expense. He will then, under due supervision, study the languages (usually French and German for diplomats; French for the consular and commercial diplomatic services) as well as history and economics; when he passes the language tests after 18 months, he becomes a full-fledged member of the foreign service. The main examination is competitive just as in the American Civil Service, and those permitted to undergo the tests are chosen "on the basis of their records, of their showing before an interview board . . . and of a written examination in the English subjects."

Just as the United States Foreign Service Act of 1946 permits the appointment to the foreign service of older men on the basis of service needs and candidates' distinguished records, the British reform, too, makes it possible to permit entry of candidates above the normal age limits ". . . who, by their record since completing their education, have shown themselves specially suitable for the Foreign Service."

The British reform, moreover, eliminates the branching of the foreign service into diplomatic, commercial-diplomatic, and con-

[14] "Proposals for the Reform of the Foreign Service," (Cmd. 6420) London, 1943, H.M. Stationery Office.

sular services by amalgamating them all into one and thereby making them interchangeable with the staff of the Foreign Office.

In France, conditions in the foreign service were hardly any different from those in prewar United States or Britain until the Third Republic collapsed. Although in that republic there were no actual obstacles for aspirants it was presumed that each of them who applied for an examination had already graduated from the famous *Ecole Libre des Sciences Politiques.* Such study was no small matter for families of modest means; it presumed university graduation and maintenance for the time of studies at the *Ecole.* The demands on students were heavy; famous statesmen considered it an honor to lecture and the intellectual standard of students was supposed to be of the highest. There was little possibility to "work one's way through college." Preparation for foreign service was a full-time undertaking and to do it, one had to have money. There is little doubt that the Fourth Republic will try to effect a change and distribute scholarships to deserving candidates. The *Ecole Libre* became a victim of the postwar upheaval. In its place, an Institute of Political Science has been set up at the Sorbonne. Graduates of this famous university who desire to enter the foreign service must pass a competitive examination to be admitted in a new School of Administration. This is a compulsory postgraduate school for all future public servants but offers specialized courses on diplomacy for foreign service candidates.

In totalitarian countries aspirants for foreign service are bound to be loyal members or future members of the party in power. This, and this mainly, makes them eligible for candidacy and entrance examination. In Nazi Germany, personal fortune was not required if a man had the support of the Nazi Party. Their training bred a new type of foreign service man, propagandists and spies rather than diplomats, who were gradually to replace the old-school diplomats still on duty.

In the Soviet Union the government had to rebuild the foreign service from scratch. This was made easier by the fact that recognition of the USSR by other governments was granted only gradually during the first quarter century of its existence. Meanwhile, the Soviets were able to train a body of young diplomats who have shown themselves reliable and efficient in the Soviet way. The Soviet government does not save money in staffing their missions: it is well known that the Soviet embassies and legations are the most voluminously staffed of all.

The selection of candidates is handled with great care in the USSR. Since the life of Soviet citizens is an open book to the government, since their reactions and tendencies are recorded from the time they are brought to the "cradle" (day nursery, *crèche*) as infants while the parents work, it is easy enough to judge a candidate's character and loyalty on his record. However, scholarship is required, too. One may assume that a candidate has had a university education and attended courses in special schools of both political and academic character. If the authorities hear about a promising aspirant whose education has, however, not been up to par, they will make it possible for him to fill in the gaps of knowledge so that he may proceed, in time, to pass the tests. Yet only the very best students will be selected; only "A" students would be able to receive the stipends which make free university and postgraduate study possible for them.

The character of Soviet foreign service officers is very different from that of their non-Marxist colleagues. While western diplomats and consular officers will naturally mingle with the people to whose government they are accredited, Soviet diplomats keep to themselves. They have preconceived ideas about their host nations and they are not permitted to investigate the merits of these nations by personal experience. Therefore, the character of Soviet foreign service assumes a purely administrative and office routine. Improvement of relations between the USSR and capitalist countries is not sought; rather there seems to be a tendency to keep them on a day-to-day working basis, not more, not less. Moreover, since it is considered dangerous and disloyal to think of or report on ideas or conditions contrary to the preconceived Communist doctrine, the USSR personnel in the field tend to send back reports that corroborate the opinions at home. The fact that most of these reports are liable to be unrealistic constitutes a great danger for the development of relations between the Soviet Union and the western powers, in fact for world peace.

CHAPTER SEVEN

Techniques of Implementation

THE most ingenious policy is only as good as its application. Political thought of the highest intellectual caliber remains idle theory unless it can become a living principle of a nation's relations with other nations. The value of a policy formula is determined not only by its depth of conception and the accuracy of forecasting; it must also be founded upon practicability of application.

The failure of a policy to meet with response does not necessarily mean that the policy makers have come to the end of their rope. It does not create a *casus belli*, nor does it even have to result in a break of diplomatic relations. It is a rare occurrence indeed if a policy, once introduced, succeeds immediately just as it has been envisaged. As a rule, the attempt to apply a policy will lead to modifications of the policy itself and of the methods planned for carrying it out. In some respects, relations between two nations may be likened to those between two business concerns: each will try to obtain the most favorable conditions and each one will, in the course of bargaining, adjust its interests to those of the opponent. If a government decides to reject a compromise, then the opposing government must decide to what extent, in the interest of peace, it can make concessions, without sacrificing its security, prosperity, and prestige.

DIPLOMATIC COMMUNICATIONS

The agents traditionally charged with the execution of their countries' foreign policy are the diplomats. But with the many changes that occurred during the first half of the twentieth century, diplomacy's task and the scope of its work have changed. Rarely is the influence of leading diplomatists of so decisive a character as was the case before technology and ideology changed the aspects of international relations. Diplomats now compete with the activities of their chiefs, the foreign secretaries, and the heads of government. Presidents, prime ministers, and foreign secretaries of negotiating governments meet in person—a revolutionary development in international relations. True, there had been occasions when such gatherings of heads of states took place. The Vienna Congress of 1815 is the classic example. But it used to be the exception rather than the rule. Diplomacy by conference, that is, the meeting of chiefs of government and foreign offices whenever difficult problems arise which can not be settled through normal diplomatic channels, now overshadows traditional diplomacy.

In the heyday of diplomacy communications were slow and often hazardous, and the envoys, representing their monarchs, had an almost absolute power to negotiate. They often enough created foreign policy and were the dominant figures in international relations. The closer an advancing technology brought the diplomatic staffs abroad to the supervision of their home office, the more did they become instruments of policy execution rather than policy creators, and the more did it become their primary job to be the "eyes and ears" of their government abroad. Being able to be in daily contact with their home office, the envoys find their field of initiative obviously limited. The problems of the country to whose government they are accredited are only a small segment of regional or global conditions; so their policy recommendations, valuable as they may be in themselves, are bound to remain restricted in over-all application.

However, traditional diplomacy is still irreplaceable for routine handling of international relations, for official reporting, and for the protection of nationals. Diplomacy by conference is active in dangerous crises, emergencies of an international character and, of course, within the framework of international organizations such as the United Nations. At this juncture, the ways and means at the disposal of traditional diplomacy will be briefly surveyed inasmuch as they are designed to carry out policy.

Diplomatic action does not come exclusively from the initiative of the missions abroad. A government's announcement of foreign policy, the way in which it is announced, or reiterated, or even the omission of an official announcement may emanate from that government's capital city but definitely constitute a diplomatic action. It was mentioned before that the announcement of a policy amounts to the confirmation of the fact that it has already been introduced. The statement and its form and timing are part of the policy and are in themselves a method of application.

Official proclamations on policy, made by such personalities as the United States President, the British Prime Minister (or the King in his speeches from the throne at the opening of Parliament), the French Premier or the Prime Minister of the USSR, are made to emphasize such policies of the respective countries as are likely to commit a nation to a course of action and to make clear the motivation of this action for the international record. At the same time, the pronouncement serves to propagandize the policy at home and abroad, and it serves the envoys abroad as a political platform to which in their negotiations they can freely refer.

The form of such statements is limited only by the ingenuity of their announcements but some usages have developed that are recognized throughout the world. For example, public speeches may be occasioned by some internal holiday; speeches may be directed to the domestic audience but meant to be for foreign peoples' attention; letters may be written by chiefs of government to some high personage or, as in the case of Stalin's letter to an American newspaper correspondent, to convenient interrogators; questions may be asked in press conferences the answers to which are meant to be policy statements or interpretations.

Inasmuch as foreign policy must inherently be flexible to the utmost, the problem of interpretation is of prime importance and is, in official announcements, tantamount to a policy declaration. This is true also of interpretations of treaties whose provisions are contested. The interpretation of what are "German Assets" in formerly German-occupied countries according to the Potsdam Agreement of August 2, 1945, is different in Washington than in Moscow; an official account of the Washington view would have to be looked upon as United States policy.

In addition to such unilateral statements by the highest officials of the government, policy may also be executed in negotiations between foreign envoys and the foreign secretary of the receiving country. It is true that this envoy cannot, as a rule, commit his country before having consulted his government. The answer or suggestion will come to his embassy or legation, but before it arrives, it may have been preceded by negotiations between that government and the envoy of the country with whose foreign office he is in touch. The complexities of such criss-cross negotiations are somewhat alleviated by modern means of communication, but in important issues personal consultations between the two foreign secretaries with their respective envoys participating may be indicated. In such cases, the diplomats, who are to be distinguished as such from policy makers and administrators, play an important though subordinate advisory role. Their task begins in earnest when the load of responsibility for policy implementation is fully put on their shoulders.

The execution of foreign policies by the way of traditional diplomacy has essentially two forms: the written and the oral negotiation. Official written communications between governments are called "notes." Such documents may be passed on by the receiving government to the envoy of the sending government for transmission to his foreign office—which is invariably done by cable. Or, the sending government may cable the draft of a note to its envoy, giving him considerable leeway in rephrasing the text and timing its submission to the receiving government in accordance with (a) prevailing conditions that cannot be exactly judged by his home office, (b) political events to which the note may refer, (c) similar notes submitted by other governments, (d) publication dates in the press stipulated by the communicating countries.

There are two types of diplomatic notes: the *note* and the *note verbale* (verbal note). The former has the form of an official letter, signed by the envoy of the sending country and directed to the foreign minister of the receiving country, or signed by the foreign minister of the receiving country and addressed to the envoy of the sending country. The Note Verbale, however, is not signed but carries the official seal of the sending agency and is not directed to any particular person but to the receiving agency. For example, an embassy would send a verbal note to the foreign office to which it is accredited or a foreign office would send such a note to the embassy. It is customary that diplomatic communications are not sent from one foreign office to the other but that the foreign missions are the agencies through which official correspondence must be channeled. Personal letters exchanged between the heads of state are not regarded as diplomatic notes but rather as "private" correspondence between the leaders regardless of the importance of such letters or the fact that they may be published.

In addressing a foreign minister or a political or diplomatic agency, certain formalities of style and formulas must be observed. The beginning and the end of notes are written in standard phrases, slightly varied according to the degree of good or bad relations between the corresponding countries. While meaningless in themselves, their omissions or modifications would be looked upon as a serious violation of the diplomatic code. In view of the importance of correspondence between two sovereign nations, a certain elevated and sometimes florid style, so often ridiculed by the public, should be understandable. The composition of a note is not an easy task; it requires much thinking and a great deal of literary capacity for the transformation of political thought into high-level and diplomatically acceptable language.

Notes are, as a rule, not lengthy communications. If more extensive briefs or presentations of fact are required, a memorandum is more suitable. In diplomatic terms, this is also called *aide memoire,* or *exposé.* In a memorandum, there are no formalities required nor are courtesies obligatory. It consists only of factual material which, in most cases, will be attached to a note or a verbal note.

The form of a collective note is rarely used. It is a document signed by several or all of the diplomatic corps accredited to the government to which the note will be sent. Also, a collective note may be sent by the representatives of a number of nations who desire to accept or reject the suggestions of another nation. (One of the most famous collective notes was directed by the Allied powers to the German Government on June 16, 1919, rejecting Germany's representations against the Treaty of Versailles.)

One of the grimmest of all diplomatic notes is the ultimatum. It stipulates a definite time before which the receiving government must have taken certain action to the satisfaction of the sending nation—or else there will be a state of war between the two countries. Since in the majority of cases national pride or conviction of a righteous position will not permit a government to comply, an ultimatum amounts to a proclamation that war is about to break out. The ultimatum is, however, a form of international courtesy, sanctioned by international law. In the twentieth century, few ultimatums have been sent before armed conflict started.

The declaration of war, following an ultimatum, or announced without previous warning, is communicated to the respective envoy as a regular diplomatic communication, mostly as a note or verbal note. However, a special declaration of war is necessary only if the ultimatum does not constitute a conditioned declaration of war.

Among the unavoidable written communications between an envoy and the foreign government of the receiving country, there are, for example, the letter of credence marking the beginning of the envoy's activities or correspondence pertaining to the text of agreements or treaties negotiated between the two governments. While treaties of importance are mostly signed by the chiefs of government, there remain enough opportunities for the diplomatic representatives to sign as plenipotentiaries of their governments. It may be mentioned that publication of notes, memoranda, or treaties is, as a matter of common courtesy, timed according to the convenience of both the governments concerned. Only in the event of war or political crises, as has happened so often since the beginning of the thirties, may one government attempt to "scoop" the other one, for tactical reasons of applied policy.

As a rule, the number of written communications between

diplomats and governments is kept down to a minimum. It is a matter of record that personal contacts and oral negotiations are preferred by governments and diplomats. First of all, because it is easier to deny spoken words than written papers. Secondly, because it is mainly in the personal contact and exchange of views between the diplomats and the officials of the receiving government that the art of diplomacy can be applied. The dissipation of misunderstandings, the clarification of policies and the negotiation of treaties will in most cases be conducted orally. Traditional diplomacy has formalized personal consultations into such terms as declaration, notification, representation, communication, information, and simple conversation in order to typify the character of the discussion between the envoy and the foreign minister. This terminology has, however, lost most of its former importance as the relations between the statesmen have become far more informal, provided the relations between the negotiating countries are not too strained.

Among the treaties, which are usually regarded as the crowning work of policy execution, there are many types, of varying importance. Not all treaties appearing as such are termed treaties by international lawyers. For example, there are "protocols," which may mean a preliminary draft review or simply be minutes of a meeting negotiating a treaty. There are "agreements," a somewhat more informal type of treaty but not necessarily less important in its political implications. There are joint "declarations" of two or more contracting states in which the signing parties commit themselves, vis-à-vis the world, to definite policies or actions. There are "concordats," which are treaties of national governments with the papal curia. And there are the treaties themselves, which, as most other agreements or declarations, will have to be ratified in accordance with respective constitutional laws.

Treaties and agreements may be political, economic, military, or cultural. They may be bilateral or multilateral; there may be regional agreements or international covenants such as the United Nations Charter.

To be sure, contracts between nations should constitute the

foundation of international relations. It has been pointed out before that respect for the sanctity of treaty structure is tantamount to respect for international law. In fact, treaties must be looked upon as a basic part of the body of law regulating relations between governments and nations. The extreme opportunism of totalitarian policy has, unfortunately, lowered the respect for treaties, and there can be no doubt that the frequent violation of agreements and treaties in the first half of the twentieth century has considerably weakened the confidence in the value of treaties. Therefore, policy makers and diplomats are now on guard against placing too much confidence in the paragraphs of a treaty document. A treaty is only as good as the intention of the signers to fulfill its stipulations faithfully. Neither policy makers nor diplomats can and will bank on this intention without reservations.

It should be emphasized, at this juncture, that treaty negotiations do not occur very often in the course of diplomatic relations between nations. There may be modifications or even abrogations, but the real task of the diplomat consists in day-to-day routine relations with the officials of the foreign office to which he is accredited and as many officials and private individuals of the receiving country as possible. The atmosphere of exclusiveness that marked and marred old-time diplomacy, restricting the contacts of the envoy to highly unrepresentative circles, has changed. It is now recognized that one of the foremost duties of an envoy is to try and understand the people of the receiving country and it is known that as a result he will be able to give much better advice to his own government. In addition, his attempt at understanding the nation to which he has been sent will almost certainly produce a different attitude on his part and, in turn, make him more popular, thereby transferring his popularity to the country he represents.

However, it cannot be emphasized too strongly that his success or failure depends largely upon the ability of his government to formulate adequate policies, to administer foreign affairs efficiently, and to maintain continuity in politics and personnel. Without vigorous support from his government and without the unity of purpose of his nation, he cannot expect to win his objectives. Also, "however brilliant and accomplished are the ambassadors in foreign capitals, there must be coordination and direction of their efforts by a Foreign Minister at home." [15] Continuity of policy formulation and administration—such as has always existed in the British Foreign Office regardless of the political party in power—is bound to be reflected in the foreign service although it is understood that there should be limits as to the time during which an envoy may serve uninterruptedly in one post. Human nature being what it is, too long a connection with the same foreign government would tend to influence the envoy to the extent where his objectivity may be affected and his presentation of conditions be biased. Most nations have therefore incorporated provisions in their foreign service laws that make it mandatory for diplomatic and consular officers to come home and stay home for a considerable time after having served more than a number of years abroad. Only in rare cases will they then be sent back to the posts they left; usually they proceed to other stations.

DIPLOMATIC SANCTIONS

It has been said that foreign offices should be termed "departments of peace" so as to contrast their tasks with those of the departments of war. Indeed, to maintain the peace is the fundamental task of diplomats. Not a peace at any price but a peace that would insure a maximum of security, prosperity, and freedom for their nations. But even the most strenuous diplomatic attempts at a compromise may fail, and relations between two countries may deteriorate to the degree where open hostility is demonstrated. In that case, several possibilities are open to the policy makers who wish to continue striving for the prosecution of their policy or the introduction of new policy methods. There is a long way to be explored between a political deadlock and imminent danger of war.

The first step that might be taken after reconciliation efforts

[15] S. Gaselee, *The Language of Diplomacy*, Bowes & Bowes, Cambridge (England), 1939, p. 32.

have temporarily failed is the recall of the envoy. This action does not have to signify a break of relations between the two nations. The mission's work will continue and the ranking diplomatic officer will, as chargé d'affaires, administer his country's interests. Officially, the envoy may be called home "for consultations" and if the storm blows over while he is at home, he may return. In most cases an envoy's recall for consultation is an implied hint to the receiving country by the sending country that a serious situation has arisen and that measures must be taken to straighten out controversial issues before the situation deteriorates further. In a few cases, such a recall will be used to change envoys. The government of the sending country may feel that the recalled envoy did not properly interpret policy or that his methods were inadequate to cope with existing difficulties. He may be replaced by another man whose background and approach have a definite bearing upon the mission he is to fulfill. (There are, of course, many cases where diplomatic replacements have no political significance. But somehow international circles will try to interpret a recall and replacement with political implications.)

The recall of an envoy may also signal the beginning of radically new policies and not necessarily have any bearing upon existing relations. A classic example was the recall of Soviet Ambassador Litvinov, who advocated the policy of collective security. When this policy failed, the Kremlin replaced him with a younger diplomat who was less permeated with traditional diplomacy and represented Stalin's "realistic" and unsentimental opportunism which some time after Livinov's recall led to the short-lived Russo-German treaty.

It does not often happen that a government will decide to go further and break relations with another government. This means that the entire mission has to be closed. As a result, there will be no official sources for vital information. Another mission may take over the first nation's "interests" but it can deal with only a few problems such as the protection of nationals. Foreign missions, friendly as they may be to each other, can seldom, if ever, be expected to reveal part or all of their own informative material to the nation that found it necessary to break relations.

A further means of enforcing policy is the refusal to grant recognition to a new government (installed, for example, after a successful revolution) or the withdrawal of recognition from a government which was recognized before.

Let us first state that there are two types of recognition: *de jure* or *de facto,* and that that recognition to be accorded need not be restricted to governments as such but to acts of governments such as the annexation of territory. *De jure* recognition means that a government or a new state of affairs or a new policy has expressly been recognized by formal diplomatic action. *De facto* recognition means that an official statement of recognition may or may not be issued but that the new situation has been accepted as inevitable. Silence, in this case, may mean consent or toleration, and it does not matter whether or not this consent is implied with good grace or with misgivings. There is no particular diplomatic method for recognition or nonrecognition prescribed. It may be "granted expressly by a formal document or an oral declaration, or impliedly by the indication of entering into diplomatic relations" with the new state or government.[16]

Usually policy makers will be reluctant to withdraw recognition from the government of a state with which their nation has maintained diplomatic relations. For withdrawal of recognition would entail a break of relations and lead to the closing of the diplomatic missions of the two opposing nations. Withholding recognition from a new government that came to power by way of revolution, or from a newly formed state, is a similar problem. Cases such as the American nonrecognition of the Soviet government, after the Russian Revolution, for a period of fifteen years after that government's establishment are relatively rare and from a practical point of view not recommendable. The withholding of British recognition of the new state of Israel had understandable political reasons but it was still an impractical gesture, which will, in the end, hardly strengthen the British position in Palestine.

Generally, the government initiating nonrecognition is bound to hurt itself just as much as it hurts the government from which

[16] L. Oppenheim, *International Law,* 3rd Ed. Vol. I, Section 72, p. 135.

recognition is withdrawn or withheld. One of the repercussions is the loss of official intelligence sources, a serious loss indeed. The United States, however, during its diplomatic history, has frequently applied the principle of nonrecognition as an attempt at policy enforcement or political demonstration. Only in recent years have American policy makers become increasingly doubtful about its practical value.

For in general, nonrecognition is primarily a demonstration of political principles and a show of determination to stick by these principles no matter what the cost. But the effectiveness of such measures depends entirely upon its by-product, such as freezing of assets, denial of credits, suspension of loans, abrogation of treaties, exclusion of foreign nationals, stoppage of political, social, and economic intercourse. (One may refer to the fact that the application of nonrecognition toward the small and weaker states in Latin America was successful within limits for the United States while the same policy method toward the Soviet Union or Japan or Germany did not achieve its purpose. It may have helped to propagate policy lines but did not help their implementation.)

The rigors of ideological disputes have, unfortunately, left moral principles in a weakened state. Thus political demonstrations such as nonrecognition or the break of diplomatic relations are no longer effective *per se*. They must be backed by strength, determination, and domestic unity of purpose.

Nonrecognition of a government's actions or policies is possible without actual break of relations. For example, the United States did not recognize Hitler's annexation of Austria or his destruction of Czechoslovakia but did not withdraw its diplomatic representation from Germany at that time. This type of nonrecognition may be necessary for the political record.

With the exception of war as an instrument of foreign policy, the above are, roughly, the means of execution or enforcement of foreign policy through diplomatic channels. Clearly, the choice is not ample; in fact, there is often enough no choice at all. Diplomacy, as we know it, is no longer able to cope with the overpowering problems created by ideological and technological issues.

It needs new means to execute foreign policy. It needs a "new arm."

The "new arm" of foreign policy exists. It is known as information, or cultural relations, or—as many people are reluctant to call it—propaganda. However, there is no need to be frightened by the word propaganda. "It is a perfectly good Latin term, from propago, to extend, enlarge, increase, carry forward, advance, spread, to propagate, to make known, to spread an idea." [17] It is necessary to give careful consideration to the role of propaganda in the execution or enforcement of foreign policy. It may prevent a war—but it can also precipitate one.

PROPAGANDA: INFORMATION, CULTURAL RELATIONS, PSYCHOLOGICAL WARFARE

The differences between these three types of propaganda are subtle. What is information to one country may be psychological aggression to another. The exchange of cultural goods may be just that to one country but outright propaganda to another. In the democracies, news coverage presenting both sides of a dispute is information; in totalitarian countries all information that is not strictly censored and co-ordinated to the officially recognized policy is subversive propaganda.

In psychological warfare, the totalitarian governments were, at the outbreak of World War II, better equipped than the democracies and, to a degree, this is still the case. For democracy continues to strive for international information on the basis of free communications and opinions; it is intent upon stimulating mutual understanding by fostering cultural relations between civilized nations. Wars, the UNESCO Charter proclaims, "begin in the minds of men," and the hope of UNESCO is that by stimulating understanding, there will develop appreciation and, finally, respect. Whenever and wherever democracies have instituted propaganda programs, this seems to be the basic motive.

[17] J. Hargrave, *Words Win Wars*, Wells Gardner, Darton & Co. Ltd., London, 1940, p. 31.

In contrast, a totalitarian government does not wish to understand others; it only wants to have the others understand its own ideology. It is opposed to cultural exchange except if it anticipates advantages for itself. It is, in other words, unilateral; it propagandizes its party lines with psychological weapons. It regards propaganda as a foremost instrument of national policy, and significantly "the initiative in introducing propaganda as a regular instrument of international relations must be credited to the Soviet Government." [18]

In this general context, what does propaganda mean? How does it work? Which mediums are at the disposal of the political propagandists?

Directed from one nation to another, propaganda is the attempt by a government to convince a foreign people—over the heads of that people's government—of the righteousness of its policy and to imply that failure of this policy will mean calamity. Political propaganda is directed mainly to two groups: the educated leadership and the masses. It undertakes to influence the leaders intellectually and to impress the masses emotionally. It presupposes that public opinion, even in dictatorship countries, is strong enough so as to exert pressure upon the rulers. According to needs and conditions, to objectives and target areas, to methods and degrees, propaganda may appear as information, cultural relations, or psychological warfare.

Propaganda *per se* is as old as the human race. Since time immemorial, political and military leaders have tried to "soften" their opponents' morale if they could not persuade them, for people who are not sure of themselves are easier to sway. Moreover, in an age of ideological contests, where the ardent belief in a cause has become a fundamental premise for the political behavior of governments and peoples, foreign-policy makers cannot expect to succeed without propagating their convictions. It is meaningful that this recognition of the importance of propaganda is paralleled by the development of techniques and mediums that are almost as unlimited as its psychological possibilities. For

[18] E. H. Carr, *Propaganda in International Politics*, Oxford Pamphlets on World Affairs, No. 16, Clarendon Press, Oxford (England) 1939, p. 13.

foreign-policy makers to forego the instrument of propaganda is like a doctor preferring the horse-drawn buggy to the automobile.

In the introduction to a book on cultural relations among nations, Archibald MacLeish counseled that "the entire problem of the conduct of foreign affairs requires—urgently requires—re-examination . . ." and that "Foreign Offices are offices of international understanding, the principal duty of which is the duty to make the understanding of peoples whole and intelligible and complete." [19] Indeed, after World War II, most nations, large and small, organized information activities. The lessons of ever-increasing totalitarian propaganda between the thirties and forties were not forgotten. However small, however poor the nation, comparatively huge amounts of the national budget were set aside for its information services, cultural exchanges, or outright psychological warfare. The importance attributed to such activities by democratic countries like Great Britain and France is clearly indicated in the foreign office organization of these countries. It is hardly necessary to point once more to the unlimited means at the disposal of propagandists in the USSR, or to recall the establishment of the Communist Information Bureau (Cominform), the propaganda front of international Communism. [20]

The Congress of the United States, perhaps disturbed by the word "propaganda" and the fact that the dictatorships were the first to utilize it on a large scale, has not appropriated sufficient funds to establish a United States information program adequate to compete with the enormous propaganda efforts of other states, particularly of the Soviet Union. As a result, American statesmen found themselves in the disadvantageous position of not having at their disposal a strong enough organization for the dissemination and explanation of their points of view. Americans are masters of

[19] R. McMurray and M. Lee, *The Cultural Approach: Another Way in International Relations,* The University of North Carolina Press, Chapel Hill, 1947, p. x.

[20] The COMINFORM may be regarded as an organizational revival of the COMINTERN (Communist International), designed to co-ordinate Communist propaganda on a global scale and directed particularly against the anti-Communist powers in the West.

advertising, but the very word "propaganda" disturbs them deeply.

Yet propaganda has become part and parcel of modern living. Its purpose is, as the Encyclopedia Britannica ably explains, "to influence opinion and conduct." Even before the Roman Church instituted the *Congregationes de propaganda fide* (missions for the purpose of disseminating faith), so as to convert infidels, men tried to "influence the opinion and conduct" of their fellow men. In the Middle Ages, when the Church controlled the minds of men, its great propagandists of faith kept an ever-continuing stream of sermons pouring on the flock, doing just what the ideological propagandists do today for their political religions: promising paradise to the faithful, hell to the faithless, and purgatory to the fence sitters.

Today, the word can be spread in many ways and forms. With a good knowledge of conditions in the target area, with practice in applied social psychology, and the development of techniques of dissemination, an unlimited vista of possibilities has been opened. We have the radio and the newspapers, the book and the play, the motion picture and still photographs, the presentation of national art and the exchange of specialists and students. With the help of these mediums, an effect can be made-to-measure and its timing calculated. Some of the mediums are limited by censorship or outright exclusion; some defy borders and obstacles.

There is no saying where, in foreign relations, propaganda begins and where it ends. One may go so far as to claim that diplomacy has in many ways become an appendage to propaganda. Let us consider the mediums by which propaganda can be spread.

Mediums. There is, first and foremost, the radio. Long, medium, and short waves fill the ether twenty-four hours a day, in most civilized languages, year in, year out. With no impediment except the limitation of the number of receiving apparatus, almost every government is eager to clarify its policy and defend it before the world forum of the air. The radio was developed during World War I but it was not used, in its beginnings, for purposes of international propaganda. Such use would have been regarded as bad taste by traditional diplomatists, and it needed unconventional iconoclasts like the Soviets, the Fascists and the Nazis, to start sending regular programs, written for listeners in definite areas and delivered in the language of the areas.[21]

Soviet radio propaganda broadcasts were first heard in 1926, when they were received in England. However, since 1934, a network of short wave stations has been developed designed to serve "long-distance relays in the Soviet Union" and, at the same time, "the radiation of programs overseas." [22] In 1938, two 120 KW short wave transmitters were constructed that were then the most powerful short wave stations in the world. The programs were sponsored by the Comintern rather than the Soviet government and kept within the bounds of Leninist-Stalinist-Marxism. The Soviet Commissariat of Foreign Affairs had ostensibly nothing to do with them. This, of course, was still the time when Soviet foreign policy was conducted by two agencies that seemingly worked at cross-purposes: one was set up to adjust Soviet aspirations to the traditional type of international diplomacy (The Commissariat of Foreign Affairs); the other was to prepare for world revolution without outwardly interfering with official Soviet foreign policy (the Comintern).

Fascist Italy began about 1932 to disseminate propaganda by radio. By 1936, when Ciano's Ministry of Press and Propaganda was established, Fascist "information" had become aggressive and expansionist. From 1932-36, most programs were transmitted in the Arab languages; after 1936, the programs were broadcast in 18 of the most important languages. Soon, however, Mussolini was outdistanced by Hitler. His Ministry of Popular Enlightenment and Propaganda, headed by Joseph Goebbels, threw itself into the psychological warfare with enormous vigor. It started foreign language broadcasting in April 1933, three months after Hitler seized power. Soon thereafter, the Soviets perfected their

---

[21] After World War II, the Allies broadcast special programs to displaced persons in various languages, beamed to areas where these languages were not spoken. For example, Polish language shows were offered to Polish DPs in Germany.

[22] See A. R. Burrows, "Broadcasting outside the United States," *Annals of the American Academy of Political and Social Science*, Philadelphia, Vol. 177, January 1935.

own propaganda methods and joined the great contest for peoples' souls and minds.

The western powers, disdainful of such methods, remained silent for too long a time. It was not until January 1938 that the British Broadcasting Corporation began to radio foreign language programs to Arab countries. In March of the same year Spanish and Portuguese were added and in September 1938, after the Munich catastrophe, there followed German, French, and Italian language broadcasts. But not before the outbreak of World War II, when the Ministry of Information was established, did these programs assume the character of an organized propaganda effort. The French, too, waited until the war had broken out before setting up a limited foreign language broadcasting program; they concentrated on cultural relations as they had always done. The course of the war, unfortunately, did not give them much time to develop a propaganda organization but their cultural program continued, even under the Germans, to function in one way or another. The United States, as the last big nation, joined the war in the ether in 1941; however, not until 1942 was a program established, with the organization of the Office of War Information (OWI) for Europe, Asia and Africa and the Coordinator of Inter-American Affairs (CIAA) for Latin America.

Needless to say, the Japanese government had followed the practices of its Axis partners long before the outbreak of the war but had directed its activities toward the Far Eastern area mainly, where it concentrated on racial and religious "exchange," whereas its short waves beamed to America carried on psychological warfare with the help of American-educated Japanese. Of particular interest were the many societies for cultural relations organized by Japan and representatives of powers befriended by Japan. There were German-Japanese and Italian-Japanese cultural associations located in Japan, Germany, and Italy—not to forget the Japan-China Educational Association, whose primary purpose was the conversion to the Japanese viewpoint of Chinese and Manchurian students in Japanese schools.[23]

[23] Cf. R. McMurray and M. Lee, *op. cit.*, Chapter 4, "Japan: The Racial Approach," p. 78 ff.

Radio, however, remained the principal instrument of propaganda in Europe, and it may be anticipated that the steady progress in relay and beaming techniques as well as the improvements of receivers will further extend the importance of this medium as an instrument of foreign policy all over the globe. Throughout the politically crucial areas, it is already a chief weapon of political warfare and information. It knows no borders. More and more citizens, even in totalitarian countries, will be able to listen; beyond the confinement of the iron curtain considerable numbers of Soviet citizens can receive American broadcasts in the Russian language. Attempts of dictator regimes to prevent their citizens from listening are of necessity short-lived and will be circumvented.[24]

Broadcasting, whether it is used at home or for overseas consumption, constitutes the backbone of contemporary information or psychological warfare. It reaches most people and is the speediest means of news dissemination. It is a convenient outlet for governmental policy statements that are to be made widely known. It can endlessly repeat propaganda themes and hammer them into the minds of the listeners. Broadcasts can penetrate through all the iron curtains in the world no matter where they are; they can join forces with newspapers by transmitting the printed word as the papers can reprint the spoken word, thereby deepening or widening their effectiveness. There is practically no limit in radio opportunities for political purposes—except those of a budgetary nature.

The next important mediums of propaganda are the printed word and the moving picture. Both, however, are limited by foreign censorship or import restriction. Wherever they are free to be circulated without impediment, their importance increases manyfold.

From a propagandist's point of view, the motion picture is an ideal medium. The enormous impact of the movies upon the

[24] The majority of radio receivers in the USSR are equipped with short-wave receiving facilities. Many stations in the Soviet Union must use short wave because of the tremendous distances in that country. The owner of a receiving set for medium waves only cannot listen to any of the stations beyond the Urals.

thinking, character, and emotions of modern man has become evident all over the world. Language obstacles can be overcome with the help of technical devices (such as "dubbing" a film in another language or adding a translation of the dialogue, the so-called "subtitles"). There are, however, differentiations of culture complexes that, as a rule, limit the effective use of films to either occidental or oriental audiences according to their origin. For example, American motion pictures are exceedingly popular wherever Western civilization exists but their effect in Asia remains necessarily spotty and is limited to orientals who are familiar with the occident. The same is true in reverse.

Since exhibition of motion pictures in foreign countries is dependent upon a foreign government's import license, the quantitative propaganda value of films is greatly reduced. Even if a foreign embassy shows one of its nation's pictures to a number of invited persons, and these persons are greatly impressed, they cannot possibly communicate their impressions properly to other people who have not seen the film. There are few, if any, possibilities of showing pictures through the underground in countries where a propaganda effort is desired, and certainly the number of such audiences would not be sufficient to warrant the investments in money or personal safety.

In such cases, the use of the printed word is somewhat easier. Even during actual conflict, pamphlets can be dropped from airplanes or disseminated by way of artillery shells filled with printed leaflets. In peacetime, printed propaganda may be used in various forms: newspapers, periodicals, pamphlets, books; all of them supplemented with graphic or photographic illustrations if desired. Adequate translations may easily be secured; the process is expensive and of course time-consuming, but it can be done well. If budget considerations prohibit the printing of foreign language publications, news bulletins and feature material may be disseminated by the missions abroad and mailed (translated and mimeographed) to the political and intellectual leaders of the receiving country as well as to the editors of those foreign papers and periodicals where publication of the information seems desirable. Foreign censorship may not permit its extensive use but practical experience has demonstrated that such information is speedily disseminated by word of mouth and thus becomes known to a great number of people. Particularly in countries with iron curtains the "grapevine" works speedily.

Radio, the motion picture, and the printing press are the three most rapid mediums for the achievement of immediate propaganda objectives. There are additional mediums, used in the framework of what is known as "cultural relations." Since their effect concerns the well-educated social groups mainly, they are of long-range character but their ultimate effect is by no means to be slighted. They comprise the establishment of information libraries, mutual demonstrations of achievements in the fields of the arts (such as roving exhibitions, concert tours, lectures, and so on); exchange of professors, artists, specialists or students, and the organization of cultural societies fostering their respective national cultures.

The use of such cultural mediums by the governments of France through decades, if not centuries, is a classic example of the all-pervading importance of cultural relations and their lasting effects in the political and social if not economic fields. It may be stated in all frankness that the gradual decline of France as a world power throughout the past hundred years has been hidden so well by cultural propaganda that the minds of many policy makers have been distracted from the fundamental fact that post-Napoleonic France was a *"grande nation"* only in the cultural sense and not in any political aspect. By the same token, the neglect of the United States to acquaint the world in any systematic way with its growing new culture has materially contributed to a stereotype of wrong impressions abroad that have been fostered by sensation mongers, uninhibited tourists, and unrealistic Hollywood pictures. How dangerous such misconceptions may turn out to be was shown clearly when they were effectively used in anti-American propaganda, which began to become virulent under Hitler and Mussolini and became even stronger after the World War II.

What, then, is the position of the governments of some leading nations in using all these mediums of propaganda as a new arm of their foreign policy?

Missed opportunities characterize the position of the United States, whose elected representatives, deeply suspicious of all forms of government propaganda or information, consented to the establishment of the Office of War Information and the Coordinator of Inter-American Affairs only under the duress of a total war effort. Obviously, the main objective of the OWI had to be the conduct of psychological warfare. In that, it was frequently embarrassed by congressional mistrust and the reluctance of the State, War and Navy Departments to recognize the OWI as an agency administering a new form of warfare. In his interesting book *Persuade or Perish*, Wallace Carroll has vividly described these difficulties.

When the war ended, the President of the United States abolished the agency but, knowing well that certain services would remain essential for the conduct of United States foreign policy, he decided to set up (August 31, 1945) an interim organization (Interim International Information Service) to work out plans for a new information agency under the supervision of the Secretary of State. With the OWI, the CIAA was abolished, to be merged with OWI into this new IIIS. It must be mentioned, however, that in 1936, the Congress had allocated a small sum for cultural relations with Latin American nations. This was one of the implementations of the "good neighbor policy." The State Department created a Division for Cultural Relations which was to direct the ensuing activities. This division disappeared when all information and cultural relations activities were merged into the Office of International Information and Cultural Affairs (OIC), which on January 1, 1946, was established by executive order as a part of the State Department and put under the Assistant Secretary for Public Affairs. However, the agency still operated on its own budget and lacked congressional enabling legislation. Since it was a new type of operation, the Congress believed that it would have to pass upon the principle involved. A law authorizing the State Department to conduct information activities failed to pass in

1946, though some money was appropriated to keep the agency alive.

In 1947, with the enabling legislation still in abeyance, the Congress overruled the administration by cutting the requested budget for OIC to such a small amount that all the State Department could do was to maintain a skeleton staff, to weed out cultural exchange activities, to reduce the "Voice of the United States of America" (foreign language radio program) to scarcely more than a whisper and to hope for better times to come. The increasing tension between the Soviet Union and the Western powers, the endangered prestige of the United States abroad and the creation of the Communist Information Bureau (Cominform) for the co-ordination of Soviet and Soviet-satellite propaganda succeeded in changing the mind of many legislators, but did not immediately help to finance American propaganda more generously. True, in January 1948, legislation was passed authorizing the State Department to undertake informational activities in a reorganized Office of Information and Educational Exchange (OIE). But only at the end of the fiscal year, in June 1948, did the Congress appropriate funds for the organization, just enough to operate it on a very modest scale. The effectiveness of the program was hamstrung, however, through the decision of the Congress to separate information completely from cultural relations. Thereupon the mediums of radio, press, and the motion picture were organized in the Office of International Information (OII) and those concerned with educational exchange, American libraries abroad, and other long-range cultural fields were administered by the Office of Educational Exchange (OEX). Although policy co-ordination was envisaged, the fact was overlooked that propaganda, whether carried out by way of informational or cultural mediums, is indivisible: its mediums dovetail.

To prevent a possible split into its components under different administrators, the office of a General Manager was established in 1949.

The reluctance of the Congress to overcome its deep-seated suspicions against propaganda activities at a time when conventional diplomacy could no longer hope to dislodge ideological offensives—a course which left the United States practically mute during a period of concentrated Communist attempts at weakening its influence, prestige, and power—is all the more astonishing when compared with the tremendous efforts of other nations, all of them less rich and powerful than the United States.

Britain, too, was late in introducing a program of information and cultural relations. Only in 1933, was the British Council for Relations with Other Countries established "to carry on a program of cultural expansion or 'national interpretation' abroad." Significantly, the council began its activities in Paris.[25] An official announcement said that the council was organized "to promote abroad a wider knowledge of the English language, literature, art, music, science, educational institutions and other aspects of our national life, and thereby to encourage a better appreciation of Great Britain and to maintain closer relations between this and the other countries." [26]

The British Council is a semiofficial agency, financially backed by the government and subject to the prevailing policy lines but independent so far as the implementation of policies is concerned. Its work was greatly broadened during World War II and thereafter; moreover, other British organizations supplemented its activities. The Ministry of Information with its Department of Enemy Propaganda was established during the war mainly for the purpose of conducting psychological warfare. It controlled the foreign language broadcasts that were transmitted by the British Broadcasting Corporation (BBC). Like the council, the BBC is a semiofficial government-controlled organization, financed by the government out of license fees paid by owners of receiving sets.

The Ministry of Information was abolished after the war, just as was the U.S. Office of War Information. However, while some war functions were liquidated, the work was essentially carried on in the expanded information departments of the Foreign Office. Also, the BBC continued to broadcast foreign language programs. There was never a question, in Great Britain, as to the usefulness

[25] R. McMurray and M. Lee, *op. cit.*, p. 138.
[26] *Ibid.*, quoting the London *Times* of March 20, 1935.

of such operations. There was little opposition in Parliament against appropriating the necessary funds. Thus the British propaganda activities remained strong, in fact, were increased in many ways. So important were they considered by British policy makers that the economic crisis had no influence in cutting them down; rather, more money was provided to the British Council in crucial areas, and the reorganization of the Foreign Office demonstrated that cultural relations, information, and psychological warfare were looked upon by the British Government as essential means of carrying out its foreign policy.

France "first among modern nations recognized the advantages of a large-scale program of cultural relations with other countries" and "by the end of the century, France had spent more than 20,000,000 francs to 'maintain her moral influence in the Near East and to extend it to the Far East' and considered the expenditures to be well justified." [27] Whoever knows the French will appreciate that they are not inclined to waste of money, as they vie with the Scots for the reputation of being the thriftiest people in Europe. Such expenditures on the part of the French can reflect only their government's realization of the useful effects of cultural propaganda. France had many governments, far too many during the seventy years of the Third Republic, but not one of them is known to have repudiated the country's propaganda activities. The result, as has been mentioned above, justified the efforts.

As a consequence, victory in World War I did not cause the French nation to rest its case. In fact, in the year 1920, the French propaganda program was considerably enlarged. With the collaboration of the Ministries of Commerce and Industry, Public Instruction and Fine Arts, activities were controlled by the Ministry of Foreign Affairs. Its two organizations were *Service des œuvres françaises à l'étranger* (the French counterpart of the British Council) and the *Service d'Information et de Presse*.

Not even the impoverished Vichy government ceased cultural propaganda, and when the French Committee of National Libera-

[27] *Ibid.*, p. 9.

tion was founded in Algiers, it immediately started a small program of cultural relations. When the liberation had been accomplished in 1945, one of the first actions of the new government was the reinstitution of the cultural and information services. Considerable sums of money were allocated to rebuild universal confidence in French cultural achievements and thereby to re-establish French prestige, which had suffered so much. With the reorganization of these services went the establishment of more administrative and policy offices in the Ministry of Foreign Affairs, as has been described above. In 1946, the ministry's budget amounted to about four billion francs of which 1.2 billion were earmarked for the *œuvres* alone.[28] Despite the low value of the French franc, this is a tremendous sum to be spent by a nation whose economy is in a bad shape. But it seems the French people, with the exception of the Communists, share the view of their government that nothing is too expensive to restore the universal respect for French culture. For almost everybody in this harassed country recognizes that, particularly in Europe, cultural prestige helps create firm foundations for political prestige.

It seems hardly necessary to re-emphasize that propaganda in any form was a major instrument of foreign and domestic policy in the leading prewar Axis countries: Germany, Italy, and Japan. And as totalitarian policy cannot conceive of differences between domestic and foreign issues, unless on a temporary basis, the huge propaganda agencies of these nations poured out an equal amount of "information" at home and abroad. The organizations mobilized in these countries were completely at the disposal of the respective governments and used exclusively to propagate ideologically colored opinions, news, and cultural items. Such manifestations were expertly used to create a cultural veneer under which lay brutal, ideologically motivated suppression and aggression. It is clear that without such propaganda, these governments could not have achieved their temporary successes—which remained temporary only by the grace of God and the help of the Arsenal of Democracy, the United States. Armed strength alone

[28] *Ibid.*, p. 38.

could not have succeeded in keeping Hitler and Mussolini in power for such an extended period. It was predominantly the power of political religions that did that and it was the propaganda machine that disseminated the creed in many forms.

All three Axis countries had set up ministries of propaganda, and neither Hitler nor Mussolini had any hesitation in calling these agencies just that. In Japan, the various propaganda organizations had elaborate and flowery names, for example: Eastern Asia Economic Research Society, Institute of Oriental Culture, Association of Greater Asia, East Asia Religious League. There was also any number of societies fostering Japanese cultural relations with individual countries on the basis of "cultural agreements." Naturally, all these societies were controlled by the Department of Foreign Affairs. There can be no doubt that the infiltration of Asia with such propaganda was deep, just as Nazi-Fascist ideological infiltration spread far and wide in some European lands and minds. Were it not for the incredibly brutal behavior of the Nazi and Japanese soldiery, this propaganda would have been eminently successful. It is known, for instance, that the Ukrainian population did not oppose the German occupation in the beginning, but adopted a wait-and-see policy. Ukrainian nationalism had been rampant under cover and never adapted itself absolutely to the Soviet system. Ukrainians turned against the Germans only when they witnessed the terribly cruel and presumptuous behavior of the German troops and administrators. They believed, at first, in the promises of German propagandists and they were driven back to the Soviets only after they found that Nazi propaganda was unreliable or untrue.

Little is known about what the Kremlin spends for its worldwide propaganda machine. Although native Communists in many lands have taken over some of the work and pay for it themselves from their local party coffers, the investment in spreading the Marxian gospel in Soviet fashion must run to the equivalent of hundreds of millions of dollars. Propaganda so permeates USSR domestic and foreign affairs that one may presume that a very substantial part of the entire Soviet budget is spent for purposes of overt and undercover Soviet propaganda.

During the first years of their existence, the Soviets had no official, centralized foreign propaganda agency. Whatever political propaganda was disseminated came from the Comintern rather than from the government of the USSR. It was not until 1925 that VOKS (Vsesoyuznoe Obshchestvo Kulturnoi Svyasi s Zagranitsei), Society for Cultural Relations with Foreign Countries, was established. Its predominant task was to show foreigners that the Bolsheviks were about to create a strong new culture. This word, "culture," has great propagandistic importance and is full of meaning in the Soviet Union. It denotes a term of integration comprising everything from the highest in art to the clean appearance of a citizen. It has become an educational term of high significance for ideological loyalty. It is part of the ritual of the political religion, applied at home and—in the case of Soviet occupation of foreign countries during and after World War II—abroad.

After the war, the temporarily suspended activities of VOKS were re-established but, more important, war propaganda facilities were also expanded and reorganized. It should be noted that, in the totalitarian tradition, the Soviet propaganda machine is being used for both domestic and foreign audiences, often with exchangeable material. An interesting example of this double-barreled use of Soviet information occurred in 1946 when a small Ukrainian station broadcast that there was a brotherly feeling between the Ukrainians and the people of the Subcarpathian Ukraine and that there should be no border separating them. Subcarpathia at that time was part of the Czechoslovak Republic. Immediately, the broadcast became generally known and caused speculation as to whether or when the USSR would demand cession of this province from Czechoslovakia. It was not long before a bilateral agreement was announced to the effect that the Subcarpathian Ukraine would be ceded to the USSR and become part of the Ukrainian Republic.

For domestic purposes, the Central Committee of the Communist Party creates propaganda policy and initiates major campaigns to implement the Politbureau's overall policy decisions. Under it, there is an Administration of Propaganda and Agitation, which administers propaganda work on an all-Union basis. Miniature propaganda organizations are set up in every republic, region or district of the country, all of them having departments of press, propaganda, agitation, and cultural enlightenment.[29] However, foreign propaganda is not centralized in any particular agency. Its policy is determined by the men who make foreign policy and order the methods by which it is to be carried out. Since Soviet diplomacy after World War II has become a rather subordinated factor in Soviet foreign policy execution, propaganda in every form and disguise has become the primary task of Soviet diplomats and made them merely mouthpieces and glorified messengers of their government.

In matters of foreign propaganda, the Minindel's role is presumably small. Since policy formulation of the propaganda line must be identical with the party line, the nature, quality and type of propaganda will be painstakingly outlined by the Communist party leadership. In view of the fact that the entire Soviet government machinery is attuned to the party line and can be used for both domestic and foreign purposes, the Soviet leaders did not consider centralization of foreign propaganda necessary. With all conceivable mediums at their disposal, they have made propaganda a dynamic, aggressive instrument of their ideology and a highly powerful weapon fighting for the enforcement of foreign policy—which again is inseparable from ideological objectives.

In this connection, it is interesting to point out that the long-range cultural mediums are used by the Soviet propagandists in an extraordinary and skillful manner. As at home, so abroad, they utilize such subject matter as the fine arts, music, or literature in a masterful manner for the very important purposes of (1) using apparently harmless mediums for political indoctrination, (2) earning cultural prestige, specifically vis-à-vis European nations, (3) gaining the sympathies of artists and intellectuals. The support of the arts began as soon as the Soviets obtained power; it started in Soviet-liberated theaters of war when next to the smok-

[29] See "Public Opinion in the USSR," in *Public Opinion Quarterly*, Spring 1947.

ing debris of buildings the Red Army ordered the theaters, operas, and concert halls to perform.

Of the "fast" mediums of propaganda, radio is, of course, the largest. In spite of the damage done to Soviet broadcasting stations during the war, there were, in 1947, "about 130 broadcasting stations whose total power most probably exceeds 3000 kilowatts . . ." and the "Five-Year Plan which covers the period between 1946-1950 calls for the establishment of numerous transmitters and studios, and the manufacture of millions of receivers and loudspeakers." [30] Many of the more powerful senders are being used for foreign propaganda; in addition there are about 25 short wave transmitters working which are "used both for domestic and international purposes, for the transmission of home broadcasts to distant places and for international programs to foreign audiences." [31]

Newspapers, periodicals, and books are used freely. Wherever there is Soviet influence in other countries, there will be Russian language papers and Soviet-sponsored papers or magazines in the respective native languages. The Soviet radio broadcasts many articles of representative Soviet papers. Translation rights for Soviet books are easily and cheaply available.

The importance of Soviet motion pictures has sharply decreased since the twenties. During that time, the USSR created some outstanding works of film art ("Battleship Potemkin," "Mother," "Storm over Asia," or "Road to Life"). Since then, Soviet movies have deteriorated to the extent that even in the Eastern European satellite states Soviet pictures draw very small audiences. Perversions of history such as the film "Ivan the Terrible" have been recognized as crude Russian chauvinism and exposed as such among non-Communist audiences.

In the long-range media, such as exchange of students, outstanding personalities or artistic offerings, the Soviets have not been co-operative in their relations with countries beyond the iron curtain, even though they were offered reciprocity. Apparently

[30] A. Huth, "Broadcasting and Television Methods in the Soviet Republics," *Tele-Tech*, New York, Sept. 1947, p. 31.
[31] *Ibid.*, p. 33.

afraid of having to allow the presentation of the democratic point of view to their audiences, they have dropped every pretense of cultural co-operation and limited such activities to satellite areas. Anti-Communist countries, therefore, will have to rely on their own mediums of information and propaganda if they wish to be heard by the Russian people or the countries under Soviet domination.

One word about subversive activities and agitation for sabotage, which have always been and still are an important part of Soviet propaganda. Most of the leading men in the USSR have grown up using this weapon to achieve the revolution. As they found it highly effective, they continue using and developing it—in foreign countries. With the help of native members of Communist parties, and with the assistance of misguided and credulous sympathizers who are not labeled as Communists and therefore of even more value, Soviet thought may be propagated and Soviet tactics applied. Subversion may be purely ideological, that is dialectic, but it may also become an attempt at sabotaging a country's political and economic stability.

So far as propaganda devices are concerned, they are by no means exhausted in the enumeration of mediums above. A clever propagandist will be inventive enough to develop more and different techniques suitable to promote and facilitate the execution of policies. It is not necessary that every manifestation of information or cultural exchange be exported *per se*; it might well take place in the domestic sphere and reach foreign audiences by indirection. For example, demonstrations of "aroused" masses, articles in the domestic newspapers, broadcasts on the domestic radio, publications of books may conveniently become known and give foreign governments and peoples the impressions that they are expected to get. The success of a foreign policy depends very much upon its acceptance by foreign public opinion, and even in the Soviet Union this is considered to be a factor important enough for keen observation by the Soviet leaders and their propagandists.

There are, in addition to diplomacy, economic pressure, and propaganda, no other peaceful means for the execution of a foreign policy that is considered vital for a nation's existence. War is the only other way, and a doubtful way it is, for even if a war is won, so much has been lost in the process of winning it that the benefit to be derived from victory is dubitable. More and more, nations and governments have come to this conclusion and try, in their own way, to achieve their objective short of war. Traditional diplomacy, in times of crisis, cannot expect to cope with the formidable obstacles of ideological strife. And since diplomacy by conference has changed the aspect of modern diplomacy, the broad field of controversy between opposing ideas and conceptions is the struggle of words and ideas, whether it is called cold war or propaganda or information or cultural relations.

In an angry book, a British writer wrote at the beginning of World War II that "in modern war, not to use propaganda is treason" and "not to use it skilfully is to court disaster." [32] With modifications, it may be said that in the process of executing foreign policy, not to use propaganda is a neglect no nation can afford and that the failure to provide a foreign office with a sufficiently able information organization will boomerang with the failure of the policy itself.

As a new arm of foreign policy, propaganda is simply a device to gain support among the people to whose country a policy is directed. After all, foreign policy is directed toward the people, and the attempt of a government to submit its point of view to men and women abroad should be understandable, if not laudable —that is, provided the way in which the information is broadcast remains within the boundaries of objective decency. One cannot say that totalitarian propaganda has seen fit to accept such a moral standard. For this reason, informational propaganda has too often deteriorated into psychological and ideological aggression. This is most regrettable from the democratic point of view but is no reason why the democracies should not continue to build up their own propaganda methods, if only in self defense. They cannot afford to forego new techniques of foreign policy execution, however costly they may be.

[32] J. Hargrave, *op. cit.*, p. 3.

PART FOUR

National Foreign Policy and International Organization

CHAPTER EIGHT

Sovereignty and the United Nations

WHEN the meaning of foreign policy was discussed in a previous chapter,[1] brief reference was made to such policy problems as may arise as a result of a nation's membership in an international organization (for example the United Nations). Even more delicate questions concerning adjustment of national to international policies may have to be answered by nations that have not acquired such membership but must still confront the organized community of nations. This problem is comparatively new, for international organization, in the contemporary sense of the word, did not exist prior to the establishment of the League of Nations.

The League's foundation confronted baffled statesmen with a new dilemma, namely, how a sovereign nation's foreign policy could remain independent but, at the same time, abide by the League's principles even if national aims and objectives ran afoul those of the League. One cannot say that during the League's lifetime statesmen sought to solve this problem with unconventional methods except for the introduction of the international conference technique, which survived the League and gradually became a habitual feature of modern diplomacy.[2] In general, statesmen tried to mold League policies in accordance with their own government's desires and upheld their nation's sovereign rights to the hilt.

The establishment of the United Nations was a step forward

[1] Cf. *supra*, Ch. I.
[2] Cf. Lord M. P. Hankey, *Diplomacy by Conference*, Chapter I, Ernest Benn Ltd., London, 1946.

toward international community living. But although, as compared with the League, it increased the threat of sanctions against the breakers of peace, it did not abandon the principle of sovereignty. It was still this philosophy rather than that which would look upon the UN as a preliminary move toward World Government that ruled the thinking of the framers of the Charter. The question was, in 1945, whether the UN, like the League, was to be a forum of sovereign nations with all the members insisting upon their sovereign rights to the bitter end, or be an association of member peoples, willing to make concessions to the point where the sacrifice of national sovereign rights may be accepted if the common good would require it.

It is conceivable that, given time and peaceful development, many nations may have been prepared to make such concessions for the sake of an enduring peace. There are definite indications to that effect; for example, the decision of numerous governments and parliamentary bodies to submit to the opinion and verdict of the International Court of Justice. (The United States Senate, creating a precedent in American history, ratified United States recognition of the Court and agreed to submit to its findings.) However, this propitious development was severely impeded by the ideological dispute that marred relations among the United Nations almost from the time since it became apparent that the Axis powers would be defeated in the not too distant future.

The contest of ideologies has introduced a new dangerous element into international organization. More than national sovereignty, totalitarianism aspired to achieve worldwide *ideological sovereignty*. In other words, the sovereign rights of individual nations were to be subordinated to the international rule of an ideology. As a result, countries objecting to such an ideology could not help insisting on their own sovereign national laws and prerogatives. Under such circumstances, the process of adjusting national policies to international co-operation had already become platonic by the time the United Nations decided to go to San Francisco and write their Charter. Thus sovereignty, once again, became the chief obstacle to productive international co-operation, that is, the adjustment of national to world politics.

In the era of growing nationalism, sovereignty had developed into a convenient philosophy for both rulers and ruled. There was general agreement that a nation should radiate power; the only question that remained to be answered was who should represent this power and use it.[3] However, against this solid and unshakable tradition and the fact that sovereignty had become identical with nationalism or even patriotism, some opposition grew among a few political thinkers who were against the simplification of the problem. They developed the idea—which is typically democratic—that the source of national power is not unitarian but manifold, that is, that "social authority is . . . of plural character and greatly divided."[4]

These "pluralist" opponents of sovereignty and their British supporters, the non-Marxist Fabian socialists, claimed therefore that the concept of sovereignty should be abolished. But they did not suggest realistic alternatives. Their influence remained small; they did not succeed in modifying the universal attitudes toward sovereignty, much less in changing them. Yet their ideas have perhaps helped to produce a certain degree of modernization of the theory of sovereignty in the twentieth century. No longer, as in Bodin's doctrine, is it absolute and unrestrained by law. At least in a democracy, it is much more a "unified organization of authority within the community in order to provide the necessary basis for a system of legal order . . ."[5] But—and this is of prime importance for foreign policy making—whatever the philosophical ramifications, whatever the intellectual value of opposing theories, sovereignty, in this century, is as fundamentally accepted a fact

---

[3] Since in the late sixteenth century Jean Bodin developed the theory that the state is the highest power over land and people, practically unrestrained by law, a number of political thinkers have further elaborated this doctrine. Men like Thomas Hobbes, Rousseau, Bentham, Chief Justice Marshall, and Austin, to name only a few of the most important defenders of sovereignty, built up and strengthened Bodin's theory through the seventeenth and eighteenth centuries until in the nineteenth century it had become, in Chester Maxey's words, a "fixture of political thought of the world."

[4] C. C. Maxey, *Political Philosophies*, The Macmillan Company, New York, 1938, pp. 617-618.

[5] J. Dickinson, "Working Theory of Sovereignty," *Political Science Quarterly*, Vol. VIII (1927), p. 524.

as it has been since there were nations in the proper sense of the word. The growth of the nation state may be attributed to the ideal of sovereignty more than to any other single contributing factor. The League of Nations and the United Nations have made the attempt to break through the wall of sovereignty but have so far met with little success, even in the democracies.

For those who formulate and execute foreign policy, considerations of national sovereignty are of decisive import, for their policy must first of all be concerned with their nation's minimum aspirations: independence, security, and reasonable prosperity. The question then would be: to what extent is it permissible or advisable to achieve these objectives by relinquishing sovereign rights? Obviously, participation in international organizations does not *per se* constitute a violation of the concept of sovereignty. Only when it comes to actual co-operation with other nations may the problem arise whether required compromises may conflict with sovereign prerogatives.

Let us point out here that "absolute, unqualified and unchecked sovereignty is a conception of anarchy." [6] Just as the citizen in a democratic community is a relatively free agent so long as he does not harm his community, so a sovereign nation's prerogatives must, in the interest of peace, be limited lest its presumptuous behavior toward its own citizens and toward other members of the international community give cause to disputes and even to open conflict. "Every government knows that it is a member of a community of nations with well recognized rules of conduct, and is subject to the obligations in order to be entitled to the advantages of this membership." [7]

This acknowledgment of international obligations among nontotalitarian nations seems to indicate that absolute sovereignty is no longer possible or profitable in a society of free and equal nations. Ever so often will makers of foreign policy find themselves compelled to consider the relaxation of one or the other of their nation's sovereign rights if they really want to participate

---

[6] J. T. Shotwell, *The Great Decision*, The Macmillan Company, New York, 1944, p. 202.
[7] *Ibid.*, p. 203.

in any international organization. The representatives of totalitarian governments, realizing this dilemma of their nontotalitarian colleagues, merely pretend to co-operate. True, their membership in an international organization seems in itself to be a proof of their willingness to collaborate, but they are bound to find themselves in opposition to those powers whose ideologies are not theirs. They must, therefore, evade the issues; if the conclusion of an agreement cannot be prevented, because of political expediency, they may later try to avoid its application or dispute their interpretation. As they do not tolerate manifestations of individual freedom on the part of their citizens but prescribe their thinking and acting in accordance with strict over-all plans, so also do they wish to impose their politico-economic philosophy upon those nations that do not recognize the validity of their ideology. Since they cannot in the majority of cases succeed in doing that, their main objectives are the creation of confusion and stalemate and the use of the international forum as a propaganda platform. They are not willing to relinquish one iota of their sovereign prerogatives; for them, giving up these rights would imply giving up their aspirations for the imposition of an ideological sovereignty of their own making.

Such a dim outlook for effective international co-operation must affect the thinking of democratic policy makers as it will influence the development of the United Nations. It will postpone indefinitely the ideal of world government that envisages the abolition of sovereignty by national application of international law. Correspondingly it seems to limit to like-minded nations the field of international co-operation and development.

When the Covenant of the League of Nations was submitted to the scrutiny of the sponsoring statesmen, little time was available for a thorough study of the draft and its implications. Moreover, the negotiations remained steeped in traditional diplomacy. The statesmen were not equipped, on short notice, to grasp the concept of international co-operation through organization. In contrast, the establishment of the United Nations was carefully prepared over a period of years. The Atlantic Charter was signed on August 14, 1941 and, on its basis, the Declaration of the United Nations proclaimed on January 1, 1942. Consequently, for almost two years, preparations for a United Nations organization were made in the United States. Official notice was taken of these preparations at the Moscow Conference of October, 1943. The Teheran Conference of December, 1943, made further mention of the United Nations when the three leaders of the United States, Great Britain, and the Soviet Union stated that they would seek the "cooperation and active participation of all nations, large and small, whose peoples in heart and mind are dedicated, as are our own peoples, to the elimination of tyranny and slavery, oppression and intolerance . . ." and they would welcome these peoples "into a world of democratic nations." [8]

The meeting at Dumbarton Oaks, August to October, 1944, painstakingly prepared for, led to the production of the Dumbarton Oaks Proposals, which not only stated the purposes of a United Nations organization but also recommended the responsibilities and obligations of the members and the organizational framework within which the UN would work. The proposals left unsolved the question of voting procedure, and it was only at the Yalta Conference in February, 1945, that a formula was agreed upon by the leaders of the "Big Three," which became an addendum of the Dumbarton Oaks Proposals (as Section C, Chapter VI). After intensive deliberations of various plans by the constituent governments, a conference was convened at San Francisco on April 25, 1945, which through many weeks of difficult negotiations finally succeeded in creating a Charter. Almost four years after the United Nations was conceived, it was born and accepted by the member governments.

Ruling out world government at the outset, and thereby following the League conceptions, the United Nations Charter is "not a constituent act of the peoples of the United Nations, but rather an agreement freely entered into between governments." [9] In this contract between governments, the "principle of the

[8] *Department of State Bulletin*, IX, p. 409.
[9] L. M. Goodrich and E. Hambro, *The Charter of the United Nations, Commentary and Documents*, World Peace Foundation, Boston, 1946, p. 19.

sovereign equality" is recognized as a fundamental approach (Art. 2). Like the Covenant of the League, the United Nations Charter stresses voluntary co-operation among the nations and makes it clear that this co-operation concerns "common objectives" whose basis is, of course, "international peace and security." (Art. 1).

In Article 2, paragraph 7, there is the very important statement that "nothing contained in the present Charter shall authorize the United Nations to intervene in matters which are essentially within the domestic jurisdiction of any state and shall require the Members to submit such matters to settlement under the present Charter . . ." If, however, such matters seem to be characterized as threats or breaches of peace or aggression, the Article adds, not quite consistently, that the principle involved "shall not prejudice the application of enforcement measures under Chapter VII." Chapter VII, of course, contains provisions for the creation of an international armed force which is to cope with an aggressor at the discretion of the Security Council.

It is true that the provisions of Chapter VII, at least in theory, signify a long step toward concessions on sovereignty. So does the creation of an International Court of Justice and, to a degree, some of the provisions of the Trusteeship Council. Yet all these organizations and their policies are based "on the principle of the sovereign equality of all its Members." This combination of sovereignty and equality is somewhat of a redundancy, for only sovereign states are legally equals in the sense of the Charter. On the other hand, such states are not necessarily political equals as they vary in size and economic power. As a result, members do not need to be absolutely equal but they must be absolutely sovereign.

Goodrich and Hambro quote the interpretation of "sovereign equality" by an UNCIO (United Nations Committee on International Organization) Committee, according to which

sovereign equality includes the following elements:
(1) that states are juridically equal;
(2) that each state enjoys the right inherent in full sovereignty;
(3) that the personality of the state is respected, as well as its territorial integrity and political independence;

(4) that the state should, under international order, comply faithfully with its international duties and obligations.[10]

It seems, then, that the age of national sovereignty is still in full swing and that the threat of an ideological sovereignty [11] stiffens rather than relaxes national sovereignty. Yet sovereignty, whether absolute or relative, is as unadaptable to international organization as oil is to water. International co-operation is bound to remain superficial so long as international law does not supersede national law. No wonder policy makers find themselves in a precarious position when they try to formulate foreign policies for national security without being able to consider collective security.

The organization to provide such collective security is the UN but this very organization, through Soviet-United States disagreements and the ensuing paralysis of the Security Council, has not succeeded in ensuring universal confidence in the possibility of maintaining world peace. The raising of the standards of living of afflicted or destitute peoples throughout the world is seriously retarded as a result of the ideological disputes that have weakened the effectiveness of the United Nations since its inception.

Nontotalitarian statesmen must cope with such policy problems as: the unrestrained use of the veto on the part of the USSR; the fact that the completion of the United Nations machinery proceeds exceedingly slowly and that the work of the established agencies of the UN does not seem to enjoy prestige; the fact that one of the most important provisions of the Charter, military and economic organization for sanctions against breakers of the peace, has not as yet been carried out; the fact that the USSR has failed to collaborate in most of the economic, social, and educational organizations of the UN; the fact that no agreement has as yet been reached in the UN with the USSR on an effective control of atomic energy. Moreover, there has been little if any progress toward international limitation of armament and the manufactur-

[10] *Ibid.*, p. 66.
[11] Cf. *supra*, p. 230.

ing of all such modern technical devices as may be used for purposes of warfare.

As a result, nontotalitarian policy makers are confronted with a dilemma. They must take into account, in their political planning, the existence of the United Nations organization, but, on the other hand, they realize that not only is this machinery as such imperfect but that the spirit that moves some of the most important member nations in their attitudes and decisions is far removed from global harmony. It has become very clear that the totalitarian members, that is, the Soviet Union and its satellites, are not prepared to make permanent concessions toward governments whose political philosophy they hate and tend to destroy.

Now it is probably too much to expect that every government, in the era of sovereignty and nationalism, should exercise the democratic virtue of being a good loser if important resolutions or decisions are not unanimous. Certainly the United Nations has not yet succeeded in reeducating its totalitarian or ultranationalistic members to accept defeat graciously. The Soviets and their satellites seem unready to consider any view not entirely consistent with their own, and the behavior of the Arab states after the decision of the General Assembly to partition Palestine does not demonstrate a high degree of international responsibility on their part. The democratic maxim of majority rule and minority rights has not been too popular with some members of the UN who choose either to disregard or to boycott majority decisions in all those bodies of UN where they were in the minority and yet could veto them. For example, the creation of a permanent "Little Assembly" to be continuously in session, though voted by the General Assembly, was boycotted by the Soviets and their orbit governments; so too, was the establishment of a Balkan commission for the investigation of the Yugoslav-Bulgarian-Greek border incidents, which constitute a definite threat to the peace.

Under such adverse circumstances, the most staggering of all political problems—that of maintaining a workable and profitable balance between national interest and international co-operation—has become even more difficult, and the injection of ideological attempts at world sovereignty seems for the time being to have ruled out any compromise solution. Yet in both formulation and execution of foreign policy, it is no longer possible or desirable to ignore international organization.

Such is the plight of midcentury postwar nontotalitarian statesmen. The totalitarians have a much easier stand; all they need do is insist upon a negative policy and attempt to sabotage or discourage the return of peaceful and constructive normality. For they know that the success of their policy depends on the extent of the turmoil and the destitution. Their participation in international organization continues to serve them as a propaganda device mainly, inasmuch as it provides them with a gratuitous international sounding board.

Nor are these problems limited to relations between members of UN and their governments. For there are a number of international agencies whose objectives are of considerable concern for domestic politics. They are related to social, economic, and cultural matters; and decisions reached in the respective organizations have of necessity a bearing on any nation's internal conditions and attitudes. For example, there are, under the general coordination of the Economic and Social Council of UN, a number of "specialized agencies" (Art. 57, par. 2), such as:

social: World Health Organization (WHO)
         International Refugee Organization (IRO)
         International Labor Organization (ILO)
economic: International Bank for Reconstruction and Development
         International Monetary Fund
         International Trade Organization (ITO)
         International Civil Aviation Organization (ICAO)
cultural: United Nations Educational, Scientific and Cultural Organization (UNESCO)

Under the wings of the Economic and Social Council (Art. 63), these organizations are to carry out the social, economic, and cultural objectives of the Charter and work for the removal of the socioeconomic and intellectual causes of war. In establishing them, the UN has without doubt progressed farther than the League of Nations, which did not have such a broad conception of, or program for, approaching the basic problems of international conflicts. If the Social and Economic Council should succeed in creating a spirit of readiness for co-operation in its fields, the cause of peace would indeed be greatly furthered. But the social, economic and cultural problems for which agreement is sought must of necessity challenge domestic politics in individual nations, not to mention the ideological commitments of totalitarian countries. If individual governments reject the challenge and turn down the recommendations of the majority in the respective UN organizations, insisting upon their sovereign rights, to prevent interference in their own affairs, they may be legally correct but guilty of having impeded the cause of international co-operation in the search for national security.

Such impediments, growing out of domestic opposition in the free countries or of ideological disagreement on the part of the totalitarian regimes, will increase the policy maker's vicissitudes, in addition to the general global problems and difficulties. To illustrate the complexity of this problem, let us look at a few of the specialized agencies under the Economic and Social Council. Take, for example, the International Trade Organization (ITO), which was created for the purpose of expanding world trade and employment by reducing trade barriers, curbing cartel and monopolistic restrictions, and guiding international commodity arrangements. Some recommendations made for the implementation of these principles are bound to be unwelcome to either the business interests of free trade or to Soviet Marxist economies. In other words, some government is almost certain to resent ITO actions as infringing upon its economic sovereignty or perhaps its social concepts to some degree. Instead, agreements may be reached between like-minded nations.

Divergences are also bound to occur, as they already have, in such organizations as the International Labor Organization (ILO). In the democracies, labor unions are bodies fighting mainly for economic objectives but yet have their say in their country's political development. On the other hand, the trade unions in the USSR or the Soviet satellite nations are politically powerless, economically regimented, rigidly thought-controlled, and a constant target of co-ordinated political indoctrination. Obviously, such differences are detrimental for the creation of a global, unified labor program.

UNESCO is a third sample of potential disagreements along ideological lines. If its thesis of ending war where it begins, "in the minds of man," should be universally accepted, it could not help but interfere with a sovereign nation's educational philosophy by seeking a new approach to interpretation of national and universal history and civics. Such a revision may well radically change previous historic conceptions particularly if it would give priority to world peace rather than to nationalism and its creed, sovereignty. Theoretically, the nations are all for such a course, but on the basis of reciprocity only. But in order for UNESCO to succeed in making education for international peace mandatory by international law, it would first be necessary to bridge the ideological cleavage and national prejudices that keep the nations apart and suspicious of each other. Until this has been accomplished, a government that would permit such a new trend without having the absolute assurance that the other nations do the same would commit national suicide by weakening the morale of its citizens in the face of possible ideological or imperialistic aggression.

These are some of the tremendous difficulties that confront a policy maker from without and within, when he tries to adjust his country's foreign relations to United Nations requirements. They clearly show that, barring miracles, it will take considerable time before the United Nations can really become a going concern: probably as long as its members cling to national or ideological sovereignty. The realistic observer of international organization (and international law) cannot help coming to the conclusion that some form of world government—free from ideological compulsion—may be the only way to guarantee international co-operation for the maintenance of lasting peace. In spite of increasing pressures and dangers, there is little hope that such a goal can be reached in the foreseeable future. However, it is increasingly realized that an organization like UN is a useful if not indispensable premise for the ultimate establishment of world unity. No statesman responsible for the formulation and execution of foreign policy can escape this recognition and each must act accordingly, in the interest of his country's well-being and security.

CHAPTER NINE

Organization of National Foreign Policy for the United Nations

ADMINISTRATION

THE United Nations is an organization established to make possible international co-operation. This means that the member governments, in addition to their individual diplomatic activities in foreign countries, are enabled to tackle certain aspects of their relations with other countries by means of this association, so as to maintain the peace by collective action. Administratively, such an enterprise falls in the category of foreign affairs, which, of course, are handled by all sovereign and semi-independent nations through their foreign offices. In other words, foreign offices are charged with the supervision and guidance of national policy in connection with the United Nations, subject to (a) the same constitutional or political checks that shape the formulation of individual national policies and (b) the obligations agreed upon by member governments when they signed and ratified the Charter.

Presumably all sovereign nations, certainly all the members of UN, have set up special offices exclusively concerned with UN affairs. The development of these bureaus is as yet in its infancy and little has been published, so far, about their administrative aspects. However, an attempt can be made to present a brief sketch of such offices in the United States, Great Britain, and France. So far as the USSR is concerned, only deductions and speculations can be offered.

The Bureau of United Nations Affairs, U.S. Department of

State, handles UN affairs for American foreign policy; the United Nations Department for the British Foreign Office; the Secretariat of Conferences in the secretary general's office for the French Ministry of Foreign Affairs. All three offices seem to have found their basic form and, while modifications may be expected in the future, their present status demonstrates the significance of their approach.

The Bureau of United Nations Affairs, U.S. Department of State. Although the United States has never before participated in an international organization for the maintenance of peace, it has from the outset made considerable efforts to contribute its share to the organization of UN. Soon after the creation of the UN Charter and the end of World War II, the United States government established, within the Department of State, an Office of Special Political Affairs, which developed an organization for the co-ordination of United States policies and actions regarding the UN. With the rising tension between the western powers and the Soviet bloc, the role of the UN became increasingly important, and it was felt that a more broadly planned bureau should be established.

Therefore, in 1948 the SPA was reorganized into an Office of United Nations Affairs which became a Bureau in 1950. It is charged with the most effective use of the machinery of international organizations and is responsible for United States relations with international organizations provided that there are no other diplomatic channels available. It formulates the United States positions on a "constructive development of the world community and the development of the United Nations and its charter"; it deals with political and security problems of an international scale and with such problems as displaced persons, human rights, freedom of information, and dependent areas. It co-ordinates United States interests with that of international organizations and determines the extent and character of American participation in official and private international organizations, conferences, and congresses.[12]

[12] This and the following description takes into account the organization manuals of 1948 and 1950.

It is the purpose of the bureau to ensure the most effective use of the machinery of international organizations in the conduct of United States foreign affairs. It is expected to stimulate and co-ordinate the development and presentation of constructive policies and programs for the participation of the United States in UN and affiliated international organizations. In doing this, it will collaborate with the appropriate departmental offices as well as with other federal agencies that may have a legitimate interest in UN affairs.

The bureau thus serves as a focal point in the Department of State for co-ordination of policies and the application of such policies concerning United States participation in UN. It therefore prepares instructions for United States representatives to the UN and its related agencies and disseminates information about the status of United States participation in the UN to the department, which in turn, through the Office of Public Affairs, will make much of this information available to the general public.

The bureau will keep track of the development and execution of United States foreign policy from the multilateral aspects of an international community; it will recommend measures for the development of the UN after having appraised its progress; it will review the problems of international law connected with the UN in general and United States constitutional law in particular; it will interpret for the department and other federal agencies the provisions of the Charter, prepare reports to the United States Congress, and analyze controversies for which it may recommend solutions—or at least try to find solutions.

To the office of the Assistant Secretary of State for United Nations Affairs, there are attached three working groups. One consists of an Executive Staff whose primary responsibility is the supervision of the organizational apparatus of the bureau, its planning and carrying out operational programs and the general co-ordination of administrative services. The second is an Information Staff for the dissemination of policy decisions within the departmental units at home and abroad and for advising the Department's domestic and foreign information services as to the utilization of these policies. The third, the Refugees and Displaced Persons Staff, is concerned with United States interest in refugees and displaced persons, particularly in connection with problems which arise in the UN, in the International Refugee Organization, or in occupied areas.

The *Office of International Administration and Conferences* has the important responsibility of studying and co-ordinating United States policy concerning administrative and budgetary problems of the United Nations and other organizations; since it prepares requests and justifications for United States contributions to such agencies, its work is of great importance for the United Nations organization's very existence. The office is also interested in the extent and character of American participation, governmental and private, in international conferences, congresses, and fairs and, in particular, is responsible for the conduct of international meetings within the United States.

To implement the tasks set for the office, two divisions are organized to deal with international administration and international conferences.

The Division of International Administration works chiefly on the financial aspects of United States participation in UN. It formulates United States policy in budgetary matters and prepares requests for appropriations of American contributions to international organizations on such diplomatic matters as the privileges and immunities of international organizations and their personnel. Such problems may arise—in fact, have already arisen —from the position of the United States as host to the United Nations.

The Division of International Conferences, as the name indicates, is responsible for the organizational and administrative aspects of international conferences in which the United States participates. In co-operation with other bureaus of the Department, it will nominate delegates and prepare instructions for them; it will make arrangements for their activities and serve as liaison agency with the permanent United States representatives at UN.

The *Office of United Nations Economic and Social Affairs* concentrates its efforts on the most effective use of international organization relative to such aspects of United States foreign affairs as pertain to economic, social, and humanitarian programs. In this connection, one of the major functions of the office is the co-ordination of United States participation in the Economic and Social Council and its subsidiary bodies. It not only co-ordinates the council's functions with the policy-making bureaus of the State Department but also with other federal agencies that have a legitimate interest in economic and social matters. It not only initiates and co-ordinates policy in matters of organization and constitution of the Economic and Social Council and its attached organs but it also prepares for United States participation in the General Assembly on matters that concern economic, social, and humanitarian activities. Specifically, it is concerned with human rights, social, health and freedom of information problems and, in this connection, with the relationships of non-governmental international organizations to those specialized agencies of UN which are concerned with such matters.

The *Office of Dependent Area Affairs* deals with problems that may arise from United States participation in the UN with respect to nonself-governing territories. It has to make certain, with the concurrence of other appropriate departmental offices, that the interests of the United States in such territories are consistent with the UN Charter and the agreed terms of trusteeship.

The office prepares studies and proposals regarding United States participation in the UN or other international organizations as they affect nonself-governing territories and does the same for regional advisory commissions dealing with trust territories. It stimulates the preparation of such functions as the formulation of proposals for the furtherance of United States interests in the advancement and well-being of nonself-governing peoples (in so far as these fall within the competence of the UN) and arranges meetings for the Trusteeship Council or the Security Council so that matters concerning such areas, whether they be strategic or nonstrategic, can be discussed.

Paying close attention to the activities of both these bodies, it appraises its activities as they affect the interests of the United States and is responsible for the preparation of reports on such

nonself-governing territories as are under United States administration. It especially assists the Carribean Commission and the
South Pacific Commission with work facilities and serves as a
channel of communication between these commissions and appropriate federal agencies.

The *Office of United Nations Political and Security Affairs*
deals with political problems that may arise through United
States participation in any of the international organizations. It
is to ensure the full utilization of the appropriate organs of the
United Nations in the presentation and implementation of United
States policies. In view of the fact that UN has become a forum
of the world in which the powers air their grievances, this responsibility of the office is of paramount importance.

The office's field covers a wide range of matters concerning the
Security Council, the Military Staff Committee, the General
Assembly and the subsidiary bodies of these basic organs of the
UN. In particular, it is charged with the development of such
United States policies and programs as are concerned with the
peaceful settlement on international disputes. This means co-
ordination with appropriate agencies—such as the International
Court of Justice—for arbitration and nonmilitary measures of
enforcement and supervision.

It furthermore formulates and co-ordinates United States policies and programs in the field of international military security;
one of its foremost tasks is to ensure the full utilization of those
UN organs responsible for the maintenance of peace. The office
also initiates policy and action with respect to the system of
international regulations of armaments and international traffic
in arms. It is, from a policy-making point of view, easily the
most important unit in the Bureau of United Nations Affairs because it works out ways and means for "peaceful settlements of
international disputes and for non-military measures of enforcement and supervision.

Altogether the Bureau shows a tendency to comprehensive
coverage of all aspects of foreign policy that pertain to the United
Nations and clearly aims to cope with problems of international
organization in a thorough and understanding manner.

The United Nations Departments, British Foreign Office.
There are three departments, responsible for political, economic-social and refugee problems. The UN Political Department also deals with the Council of Europe. Although the departments have chiefly a co-ordinating role, they will handle specific UN issues such as:

> Any questions of *general policy* regarding the United Nations, including procedure, administration, secretariat, time-table of meetings, interpretation of the Charter (in conjunction with the Legal Adviser) etc.;
>
> Political questions arising out of the work of the *Security Council*, including questions concerning the Military Staff Committee, the international regulation of armaments and the international control of traffic in arms . . .;
>
> All questions concerning the international control and development of *Atomic energy*, and especially the work of the Atomic Energy Commission; and all other matters relating to atomic energy; The elaboration of the *Trusteeship* system (in conjunction with Colonial Office) though in certain cases, e.g., Palestine, the geographical departments concerned are primarily responsible; Social questions of the Economic and Social Council, e.g., Human Rights, Freedom of Information, Status of Women, etc.;
>
> Activities in the fields of *Labour and Health* and the related Specialized Agencies—the International Labour Office, World Health Organization (for which outside the Office the Ministries of Labour and Health respectively are primarily responsible); International Court of Justice in cooperation with the Legal Adviser.[13]

It is emphasized, moreover, that the "co-ordinating role of the United Nations Department is of the greatest importance to ensure that His Majesty's Government's policy in relation to the various organs of the United Nations and the Specialized Agencies is consistent and also that the work of these organs and the Specialized Agencies does not overlap, so leading to waste of effort." [14]

As elsewhere, specialized questions will be handled by the responsible geographical or functional divisions. In other words, problems pertaining to a particular country or area will be dealt

[13] "Foreign Office Guide," Second Edition, April 1947, p. 22-23.
[14] *Ibid.*

with by the appropriate political or functional desks in conjunction with the United Nations Departments that would co-ordinate
such specialized issues and represent the British views vis-à-vis
the United Nations.

The co-ordinating role of the departments is not limited to
purely political problems. It is the link between the British Foreign Office and the British delegations at UN and is primarily
responsible for the composition of the delegations. They furthermore co-ordinate not only Foreign Office business for the UN but
also the work of various other governmental departments that
may have to deal with the United Nations or are interested in
aspects of international organization. In fact, the United Nations
Departments represent the Foreign Office's views on a number of
"interdepartmental panels dealing with particular aspects of the
work of the United Nations or the specialized agencies." [15]

The competence of the departments is rather extensive, particularly when the above-mentioned specific issues are considered.
This implies clearly that the British government, as well as the
Foreign Office, attributes great importance to United Nations
activities, somewhat more in fact than does the French government, whose administrative set-up concerning the UN seems by
no means equally well organized and detailed.

*The Secretariat of Conferences, Secretariat General, French
Foreign Office.* More or less, the office handling UN affairs at the
Quay d'Orsay is organized along lines similar to the British
United Nations Departments, though its tasks seem to be somewhat more general, implying very inclusive co-operation of the
political and functional divisions. As its name indicates, it is not
a UN division only; it also takes care of international conferences
outside the United Nations. It provides general documentation
and special studies concerning treaty preparations and international problems.

It handles liaison between the French government and the
United Nations with all its bodies and special commissions. It
studies, in conjunction with the interested divisions, such problems

[15] *Ibid.*

of international agreements as are discussed in the UN organizations. It does preparatory work for these meetings, organizes the French delegations, and services them. It also deals with cultural questions such as international intellectual co-operation and UNESCO.

Unlike the American and British foreign office UN bureaus, it also has the job of liaison between the French government and UN concerning war crimes. But like the Washington and London UN bureaus, the French bureau relies heavily upon its specialized desks, and acts as a co-ordinating rather than policy-making or policy-executing organ.

The UN and the Minindel. Although information about a UN bureau within the Minindel is not available, some rather evident conclusions may be drawn as to Soviet administrative handling of UN affairs. It may be presumed that the existence of a UN division in the Minindel would serve about the same purposes as do the political divisions and that all decisions concerning USSR policies at UN will be made by the Politbureau. The Foreign Minister and his chief deputy are important factors but not necessarily the ones who tip the scales of policy. The chief Soviet delegate to UN, who is the USSR representative on the Security Council, is probably under the direct orders of the Kremlin policy makers and not under the authority of Minindel. In view of the Soviet outlook upon world politics, the Politbureau's great interest in the UN is not strictly consistent with that expressed in the Charter, but resides rather in the possible influence the USSR may exert, politically and ideologically, through the use of an international sounding board. In fact, all international meetings and conferences, the Council of the Foreign Ministers included, are used in this way by Soviet politicians.

REPRESENTATION

In signing the Charter, the member nations bound themselves to be properly represented at the UN. Specially appointed emissaries, envoys of a kind, were sent to serve the interests of their respective countries. As a rule, they do not need to be confirmed by their parliamentary bodies but are nominated and chosen by their heads of state and/or foreign ministers. Nor does the United Nations have to give them an *agrément*. Possible consultations with the UN secretariat concerning the appointee are entirely at the discretion of the appointing power.

Although designated to co-ordinate their country's interests with those of the international organization, they are first and foremost agents of their own government and strictly accountable to it. They remain, more or less, representatives of their foreign offices, under whose jurisdiction UN affairs are. Indeed, no important decisions can be made by the delegates without consultation with their governments. This is particularly evident in sessions of the Security Council and the General Assembly, which deal with essential matters of foreign policy or international relations. Only in exceptional cases, if a delegate of the Security Council or a delegation leader in the General Assembly happens to be the chief of his own government, for example a prime minister, does he make his own decision, perfectly aware however, that he will have to defend his action before his cabinet and parliament at home.

Whether or not delegates to the United Nations are to be regarded as having diplomatic status and enjoy all those prerogatives which international law has accorded to regular diplomats has not been stated in an unequivocal manner. In defining the status of delegates and officers of the League of Nations, its Covenant was more articulate than is the Charter of the United Nations. Article VII, paragraph 4, of the Covenant held that "Representatives of the Members of the League and officials of the League when engaged on the business of the League shall enjoy diplomatic privileges and immunities." The Swiss Government concurred and helped to make this provision a reality.

In contrast, Article 105, paragraph 2, of the Charter of the United Nations provides that representatives of the members are granted "such privileges and immunities as are necessary for the independent exercise of their functions in connection with the organization" and leaves it up to the General Assembly to determine "the details of the application . . . of this article" or to "propose conventions to the members of the United Nations for this purpose." Paragraph 1 of the same Article determines that the "Organization shall enjoy in the territory of each of its Members such privileges and immunities as are necessary for the fulfillment of its purposes." This no doubt is not a very generous allowance of diplomatic privileges when compared with those of the League. Yet there can be little doubt that the United States, elected host to the United Nations, would have accepted a broader interpretation of the status of delegates and officers of the UN just as Switzerland, once host to the League of Nations, recognized the agents of the League "as having first class diplomatic status." [16]

It is possible that the chief delegates have been given high diplomatic titles to compensate them for their equivocal diplomatic status. Naturally, every sending government is concerned that its representative be accorded the honors every envoy expects, not so much for himself but rather for the government he symbolizes. Many large as well as small states have made their leading representatives ambassadors, possibly assuming that such rank carries with it privileges, granted not by the Charter but by international courtesy.

Just as a delegate's liaison agency with his government is his foreign office, so is the secretariat his liaison agency with the United Nations. It should be mentioned that the personnel of the secretariat consists of international civil servants and is pledged to loyalty to the UN rather than to their own country. While their status, as already mentioned, does not quite measure up to the peculiarities of their position, there is at least one indication that they are held to be "above" the nations, namely, their exemption from taxes. Usually only regular diplomats are given such privileges. However, there is no provision in the Charter to make international civil servants extraterritorial. (It is interesting to

[16] P. B. Potter, *Permanent Delegations to the League of Nations*, Geneva Special Studies of the League of Nations Association of the U.S., Geneva, November 1930, Vol. I, No. 8, p. 5.

note that "efficiency, competence and integrity" are not the sole factors to be considered for the selection of the staff of the secretariat. Article 101 determines that "due regard shall be paid to the importance of recruiting the staff on as wide a geographical basis as possible.")

A few words about the activities of the permanent delegates at UN. The members of the Security Council, many of whom possess ambassadorial rank, are exponents of their respective governments' foreign policy as it tends to contribute to and take advantage of global security under the principles of the Charter of the UN. Each of the five permanent members is represented by one delegate; so are the six nonpermanent members, who are elected in the General Assembly to serve a term of two years (Art. 23). While there is only one representative for each member state that serves at the Council, a delegate may transfer his responsibilities temporarily to an alternate of his government's choice. The advisory staff to the members of the Security Council, which is not limited in numbers by the Charter, has no special standing in the organization.

To repeat, the delegates at the Security Council are strictly executing their national foreign policies. They are not policy makers and their authority is smaller than that of a chief of a diplomatic mission.

Similarly, the representatives of all members of the UN at the General Assembly are emissaries of their respective governments. The maximum representation of each member is five delegates. However, more generous than the League Covenant, the Charter does not forbid the use of alternates, political and technical advisors, and experts on special problems. In view of the extensive work on many committees of the Assembly, where national representatives must be delegated by their chiefs, the delegations are rather substantial bodies, reflecting individual national policies in the political, economic, social, and cultural fields. While it is obvious that these delegates will have to try to co-ordinate and correlate their government's policies with the overriding requirements of global harmony, they still remain the mouthpieces of their prescribed national policies. They will have to implement these policies but cannot make them. The same is true of the Trusteeship Council or the Atomic Energy Commission, whose members are obviously bound by the decisions of their governments. This procedure is somewhat less stringent in the case of the Economic and Social Council or, in certain instances, of the General Assembly, if the resolutions adopted are advisory rather than legislative.

The increasing importance national governments attach to the United Nations is further indicated by the fact that most members have found it necessary to appoint delegates other than their regular diplomatic representatives. At the beginning of UN meetings, ambassadors and ministers were designated to represent their countries at UN functions. Very soon, the pressure of business made this double assignment impossible. In a number of cases, diplomatic personnel was retained for UN activities exclusively and replaced by new staff members at the regular missions. For example, Russia's Ambassador Gromyko, who became the first Soviet chief delegate at the Security Council, was assigned to this post on a full-time basis and replaced in Washington by a new Soviet ambassador. The same happened with Polish Ambassador Lange. However, a number of smaller states, mainly for reasons of economy, have assigned their envoys to represent them at UN. Yet while such envoys make the opening speeches, the actual work, as it progresses in the various agencies and committees, is then left to specialized personnel, delegated by the envoys.

Membership at the various organizations of UN, including the commissions, committees, and subcommittees, is determined by the respective countries and not by UN. Generally, it will be up to the chief delegates to see to it that their governments are properly represented. Frequently, governments have outstanding citizens or specialists appointed for particular jobs.

For the Secretariat of the United Nations, the delegations constitute a liaison center linking it with the nation the delegation represents. Vice versa, member governments use their delegations as liaison between themselves and the United Nations.

Since there is no *corps diplomatique* at UN and delegations have no necessary contact with each other, except that of working together in the UN, the Secretariat is the center where international information converges, and where universal trends and tendencies are most noticeable. Being a "neutral" meeting ground, it is conceivably the main source of UN "intelligence"—if this term can be applied at all.

Conclusions

World politics consists of a multitude of national policies, each of which contributes to the nature of global relations. Every single policy may become decisively important for the state of world affairs, whether it be developed by large or small nations. The formulation and implementation of such policy, as we have seen, is the result of a wide variety of facts and attitudes or circumstances and is subject to ideological interpretation of the respective constitutional laws. The very process of developing policies is, therefore, bound to influence the nature of those policies profoundly.

The understanding of national foreign policies as either isolated or world political phenomena must consequently be linked with the knowledge of the mechanics of their making, the ideological handicaps policy makers have to cope with, and the technological developments that deeply affect the relations between governments and peoples.

To summarize, let us briefly review the most pertinent points of policy making that must be kept in mind when trying to evaluate foreign policy at home or abroad.

1. Foreign policy is inextricably tied with domestic issues and ideological trends. It is not only a political problem but economic, social, and psychological as well. It is not only related to the internal conditions of the country that creates it but also influenced by currents and pressures from within other countries, whose foreign policy is, in turn, influenced by their own domestic conditions. The myth that international relations can be maintained without interest in/or interference with other countries' home affairs has at last been exploded. There can no longer be sharp differentia-

tions between foreign affairs and national affairs, for each is a part of the other.

2. Foreign policy will inevitably reflect the economic ideals of the creator nations. It will be shaped in accordance with the economic status of the issuing governments, that is, their own material and potential wealth and their relative economic solvency. The economic conditions in a country's general area and the political and economic pressures brought to bear upon it by powerful neighbors are also points to be considered. However strong such considerations may be, the economic part of a foreign policy will inevitably be ideologically and politically conditioned. It would be wrong to attribute primary importance to economic influences upon foreign policy. This is no longer so much the case as it used to be a generation or two ago. Finance, commerce, international trade, or currency questions may contribute to definite formulations of policies but are not the sole motive power behind ultimate policy objectives.

3. Foreign policy is as strong as the relative defensive or offensive potential it has at its disposal (which consideration includes the factor of the speed with which this potential can be mobilized). The degree of effectiveness of co-operation between policy and strategy profoundly influences the character of political aims and the feasibility of the enforcement of such aims. Administrative dovetailing of political and military organization and collaboration between political and military planners is a premise for successful policy formulation and implementation, at least for powerful nations—somewhat less perhaps for small countries. (The latter will have to resort to consultations with their greater neighbors if they feel that they cannot neutralize themselves in a given area.) Lack of co-ordination between political, economic, and defense agencies or failure of unity of purpose among the three inevitably leads to national disaster.

4. Foreign policy is as good as the information it uses for the basis of its approach. There can be no question that the quality and practicability of a policy is closely related to the veracity of the intelligence material, the lucidity of its analysis, and the experience and erudition—not to mention the intuitive talent—of

its evaluation. One may state as a maxim of universal validity that the best foreign policy will be created by a government that has spared no effort or expense to secure the objectively best intelligence, the finest analysts and researchers, and the ablest interpreters of informative material, all of whom should be free to express their opinion and be afforded the chance to be heard—and heeded.

5. Foreign policy is as applicable as its implementation or enforcement is able to make it. In other words, its principles must first of all cope with the two new developments that make the contemporary world so different from past eras: the ideological and technological problems. It must adopt its ways of reasoning to ideational as well as material issues. It must, in both formulation and execution, consider the scientific advancement of the twentieth century, which has created revolutionary new aspects of civilization: promising, and mortally dangerous, at the same time. This implies that foreign policy will have to develop adequate techniques in all branches of its endeavors; that it will have to be able to work or change quickly when necessary; that it will have to be versatile to the utmost in order to meet new problems with alternative policies or a choice of tactical methods of application. Since there is little doubt that the fate of the nations and of the world depends largely upon the principles which underlie the relations between them, there can be just as little doubt that the machinery of foreign policy is, in the last analysis, the crux of world politics.

By its very nature, foreign-policy making is complex and extremely delicate. Its formulation involves questions concerning almost every problem of the lives of nations and citizens. Its creation demands more from experts and statesmen than does any other task in government. Its processes require close co-operation between heterogeneous elements.

Policy cannot be formulated by one man alone without endangering a nation's security, as Hitler's example vividly demonstrated. It cannot be decreed by a few who rule without the benefit of popular representation and scorn the counsel of forthright experts, as the case of Japan has shown, lest a nation's principles of relations with other countries lose contact with its people, ignore its natural aspirations, and drift toward chaos.

There can be no quick decisions of foreign policy other than tactical or temporary ones. Basic policies can only hope to become successful if they can be developed slowly and deliberately, with the co-operation of the nation's best minds, the concurrence of the parliamentary bodies and the support of the people as a whole. Fast-moving events can be met with swift provisional counter-moves; they may even necessitate a revision of fundamental principles. But only in the long run can a nation's aspiration develop according to plan.

That country whose citizenry is best educated in international affairs, whose parliament provides the means for a first-class foreign relations organism, and whose statesmen are most able to take a reasonably long-range view—that country will indeed be able to provide the best machinery of foreign policy and thereby the best plans for its future development.

Selected Bibliography

As pointed out in the Foreword, there are no co-ordinated studies available which present an integrated picture of the machinery of foreign policy. Hence the following recommendations for supplementary reading either pertain to certain aspects of policy formulation and execution or refer to general background studies.

While only works of individual merit have been selected in this short bibliography, the writer wishes to emphasize that he by no means identifies himself with the point of view of every book he recommends. Rather, his principle of selection was utilitarian. Those works have been preferred which seemed most suitable for either supplementing or illustrating this study or which seemed to contribute most to the reader's background information on matters of the conduct of foreign affairs.

Fundamentals of International Relations

Sharp, W. R., and Kirk, G., *Contemporary International Politics*, Rinehart & Co., New York, 1946.

Simonds, F. H., and Emeny, B., *The Great Powers in World Politics*, American Book Company, New York, 1935.

Smith, R. A., *Your Foreign Policy: How, What and Why*, The Viking Press, New York, 1941.

Sprout H. and M., eds., *Foundations of National Power*, Princeton University Press, Princeton, N. J., 1945.

Geopolitics and Global Strategy

Baldwin, H. W., *The Price of Power*, The Council on Foreign Relations, New York, 1948.

Borden, W. L., *There will be No Time; the Revolution in Strategy*, The Macmillan Company, New York, 1946.

Beukema, H., *Strategic and Critical Raw Materials*, Government Printing Office, Washington, D.C., 1942.

Fairfield, R. H., and Pearcy, G. E., *Geopolitics in Principle and Practice*, Gin & Co., New York, 1944.

Fairgrieve, J., *Geography and World Power*, 8th rev. ed., E. P. Dutton & Co., Inc., New York, 1941.

Spykman, N. J., *The Geography of Peace*, Harcourt, Brace & Co., New York, 1944.

U.S. War Department Library, *National Planning and Strategy*, a working bibliography for the educational system of officers of the Army, Washington, D.C., 1946.

Weigert, H. W., and Stefansson, V., eds., *Compass of the World, a Symposium on Political Geography*, The Macmillan Company, New York, 1944.

Government and Ideology

Buck, P. W., and Masland, J. W., *The Governments of Foreign Powers*, Henry Holt & Co., New York, 1947.

Communism in Action, a documented study and analysis of communism in operation in the Soviet Union, Library of Congress, Washington, D.C., 1946.

Fascism in Action, a documented study and analysis of Fascism in Europe, Library of Congress, Washington D.C., 1947.

Gross, F., ed., *European Ideologies*, with introduction by R. M. MacIver, Philosophical Library, New York, 1948.

London, K., *Backgrounds of Conflict: ideas and form of world politics*, The Macmillan Company, New York, 1945.

Ogg, F. A., *European Governments and Politics*, The Macmillan Company, New York, 1947.

Commercial Policy and International Trade

DeMille, J. B., *Strategic Minerals: a summary of uses, world output, stockpiles, procurement*; McGraw-Hill Book Co., New York, 1947.

Hansen, A. H., *America's Role in World Economy*, Penguin Books, New York, 1946.

Heilperin, M. H., *The Trade of Nations*, A. A. Knopf, New York, 1947.

Lasswell, H. D., *World Politics Faces Economics*, McGraw-Hill Book Co., New York, 1945.

Sikes, E. R., *Contemporary Economic Systems*, Henry Holt & Co., New York, 1940.

Towle, L. W., *International Trade and Commercial Policy*, Harper & Brothers, New York, 1947.

Public Opinion and Foreign Policy

Bailey, T. A., *The Man in the Street: The Impact of American Public Opinion on Foreign Policy*, The Macmillan Co., New York, 1948.

Lasswell, H. D., *World Politics and Personal Insecurity*, McGraw-Hill Book Co., New York, 1935.

Price, J., *Foreign Affairs and the Public*, Royal Institute of International Affairs, London, 1946.

Smith, B. L., Lasswell, H. D., and Casey, R. D., *Propaganda, Communication and Public Opinion*, Princeton University Press, Princeton, N. J., 1946.

Intelligence and Espionage

Boucard, R., *The Secret Services of Europe*, S. Paul & Co., Ltd., London, 1940.

Espionage and Counter-Espionage, a bibliography compiled by Ruth Sloan for the Office of Strategic Services, Washington, D.C., 1943.

Pettee, G. S., *The Future of American Secret Intelligence*, The Infantry Journal Press, Washington, D.C., 1946.

Yardley, H. O., *The American Black Chamber*, The Bobbs Merrill Company, Indianapolis, 1931.

Foreign Office Organization

Bolles, B., *Who Makes Our Foreign Policy*, Foreign Policy Association Headline Series, No. 62, New York, March-April, 1947.

Henderson, L. W., *Foreign Policies: Their Formulation and Enforcement*, Dept. of State Publication 2651, U.S. Government Printing Office, Washington, D.C., 1946.

Hulen, B. D., *Inside the Department of State*, McGraw-Hill Book Co., New York, 1939.

Norton, H. K., *Foreign Office Organization*, The Annals of the American Academy of Political and Social Science, Supplement to Vol. CXLIII, May, 1929, Philadelphia (partially outdated).

Tilley, Sir J., and Gaselee, S., *The Foreign Office*, G. P. Putnam's Sons, London, 1933.

Foreign Policies of the Great Nations

UNITED STATES

Brookings Institution, *Major Problems of U.S. Foreign Policy*, Washington, D.C., 1947.

Lippmann, W., *U.S. Foreign Policy: Shield of the Republic*, Little, Brown & Co., Boston, 1943.

Peffer, N., *America's Place in the World*, The Viking Press, New York, 1945.

Shotwell, J. T., *The Great Decision*, The Macmillan Company, New York, 1944.

Spykman, N. J., *America's Strategy in World Politics*, Harcourt, Brace & Co., New York, 1942.

Welles, S., *The Time for Decision*, Harper & Brothers, New York, 1944.

Wright, Q., ed., *A Foreign Policy for the United States*, a symposium, University of Chicago Press, Chicago, 1947.

GREAT BRITAIN

Frost, R., *The British Commonwealth and World Society*, London, 1947.

Grigg, Sir Edward, *British Foreign Policy*, Hutchinson & Co. Ltd., London, 1944.

Langford, R. V., *British Foreign Policy, its formulation in recent years*, American Council on Public Affairs, Washington, D.C., 1942.

Medlicott, W. N., *British Foreign Policy since Versailles*, Methuen & Co., Ltd., London, 1940.

FRANCE

Encyclopédie de la France et du Monde: Politique Extérieure de la France et des Grandes Nations, Editions de l'Encyclopédie de l'Empire Français, (vol. II) Paris, 1948.

Thomson, D., *French Foreign Policy*, Oxford University Press, London, 1944.

USSR

Beloff, M., *Soviet Foreign Policy 1929-1936*, Royal Institute of International Affairs, London, 1947.

Dallin, D. J., *Soviet Russia's Foreign Policy 1939-1942*, Yale University Press, New Haven, Conn., 1942.

Dallin, D. J., *Soviet Russia and the Far East*, Yale University Press, New Haven, Conn., 1948.

Dean, V. M., *United States and Russia*, Harvard University Press, Cambridge, Mass., 1947.

Fisher, L., *The Soviets in World Affairs*, two vols., J. Cape, London, 1930.

Laserson, M. M., *Russia and the Western World*, The Macmillan Company, New York, 1945.

Laserson, M. M., *The Development of Soviet Foreign Policy in Europe 1917-1942*, Carnegie Endowment for International Peace, New York, 1943.

Schuman, F. L., *Soviet Politics at Home and Abroad*, A. A. Knopf, New York, 1946.

Towster, J., *Political Power in the USSR 1917-1947*, Oxford University Press, New York, 1948.

Diplomacy

Gibson, H., *The Road to Foreign Policy*, Doubleday, Doran & Co., New York, 1939.

Hankey, Lord M. P. A., *Diplomacy by Conference*, E. Benn Ltd., London, 1946.

Nicolson, H., *Diplomacy*, Harcourt, Brace & Co., New York, 1939.

Satow, Sir E., *A Guide to Diplomatic Practice*, Longmans, Green & Co., revised ed., New York, 1932.

Stuart, G. H., *American Diplomatic and Consular Practice*, Appleton Century Co., New York, 1936.

von Redlich, M. D., *International Law as Substitute for Diplomacy*, Independent Publishing Co., Chicago, 1928.

Propaganda

Carr, E. H., *Propaganda in International Relations*, The Clarendon Press, Oxford, 1939.

Carroll, W., *Persuade or Perish,* Houghton, Mifflin Co., Boston, 1948.

Childs, H. L., and Whitton, J. B., *Propaganda by Shortwave,* Princeton University Press, Princeton, N. J., 1943.

Doob, L., *Public Opinion and Propaganda,* Henry Holt & Co., New York, 1948.

Kris, E., and Speier, H., *German Psychological Warfare,* Oxford University Press, New York, 1944.

Linebarger, P. M. A., *Psychological Warfare,* The Infantry Journal Press, Washington, D.C., 1948.

McMurray, R., and Lee, M., *The Cultural Approach: Another way in international relations,* University of North Carolina Press, Chapel Hill, 1947.

International Law and Organization

Galt, T. F., *How the United Nations Works,* Thomas Y. Crowell Co., New York, 1947.

Goodrich, L. M., and Hambro, E., *Charter of the United Nations, commentary and documents,* World Peace Foundation, Boston, 1946.

Harley, J. E., *Documentary Textbook on the United Nations; humanity's march toward the peace,* Center for International Understanding, Los Angeles, 1947.

Hershey, A. S., *The Essentials of International Public Law and Organization,* rev. ed., The Macmillan Company, New York, 1927.

Jessup, P. C., *A Modern Law of Nations,* The Macmillan Company, New York, 1948.

Krout, J. A., ed., *World Organization,* Academy of Political Science, Columbia University Press, New York, 1945.

von Redlich, M. D., *The Law of Nations,* World League for Permanent Peace, New York, 1937.

Winfield, P. H., *The Foundations and the Future of International Law,* University Press, Cambridge, 1941.

Index